Biofuels, Food Security, and Developing Economies

The last decade has witnessed major crises in both food and energy security across the world. One response to the challenges of climate change and energy supply has been the development of crops to be used for biofuels. But, as this book shows, this can divert agricultural land from food production to energy crops, thus affecting food security, particularly in less developed countries.

The author analyses the extent to which biofuels feedstocks fit within the national food security strategy, agro-export orientation, and rural development plans and policies of developing economies. Two case studies, from Tanzania in East Africa and Borneo in Malaysia, are considered in detail, using the non-edible crop of jatropha as an example of how compromises can be reached to balance food and energy goals as well as export markets. The author develops a novel integrated approach, the Institutional Feasibility Study, as the basis of her analysis.

She addresses key issues such as: how do global initiatives for green growth, energy security, and sustainable development incorporate biofuels industry development? Does global biofuels trade present meaningful foreign and local investment opportunities for developing countries? To what extent does biofuels feedstock production help with poverty reduction and agricultural sector modernization? What role do the EU and the US commitments to biofuels blending targets play in the rapid industry development in developing countries? How does the biofuels industry fit within existing formal and informal institutional frameworks? Who are the winners and losers in the biofuels global value chain?

Nazia Mintz-Habib is Lecturer in Public Policy at the University of Cambridge, UK. She was a Post-Doctoral Research Fellow in the Kennedy School of Government, Harvard University, USA, and also a Research Fellow in Development Studies at the University of Cambridge, UK.

'Nazia Mintz-Habib's fascinating study explores how, and in what circumstances, biofuel crops contribute to either perpetuating or alleviating poverty and food insecurity by considering the complex interactions among agricultural commodity and energy markets, climate change mitigation finance, and farming communities.'
Jomo Kwame Sundaram, Coordinator for Economic and Social Development, Food and Agriculture Organization of the United Nations

'This book provides a highly original application of the Institutional Feasibility framework to the analysis of developing countries' roles within global value chains in primary commodities. It makes a valuable contribution to public policy and development studies.'
Peter Nolan, Chong Hua Professor and Director, Centre of Development Studies, University of Cambridge, UK

Biofuels, Food Security, and Developing Economies

Nazia Mintz-Habib

Routledge
Taylor & Francis Group

LONDON AND NEW YORK

First published 2016
by Routledge

2 Park Square, Milton Park, Abingdon, Oxfordshire OX14 4RN
711 Third Avenue, New York, NY 10017

Routledge is an imprint of the Taylor & Francis Group, an informa business

First issued in paperback 2018

British Library Cataloguing-in-Publication Data
A catalogue record for this book is available from the British Library

Library of Congress Cataloging in Publication Data
Mintz-Habib, Nazia.
Biofuels, food security and developing economies / Nazia
Mintz-Habib.
pages cm
Includes bibliographical references and index.
1. Biomass energy industries--Developing countries. 2. Food
security--Developing countries. 3. Economic development--
Developing countries. I. Title.
HD9502.5.B543D4464 2015
333.95'39091724--dc23
2015017030

ISBN: 978-0-415-72970-3 (hbk)
ISBN: 978-1-138-58891-2 (pbk)

Typeset in Sabon
by Saxon Graphics Ltd, Derby

Contents

Figures

Tables

Preface

In the midst of the storm are the poor, trapped by food shortages, speculation in commodity markets, dietary demand changes, water scarcity, land-use change, insufficient energy resources, threats of climate change, and rising oil prices. Higher food prices impose a greater burden on the household budgets of poor households than on those of their affluent counterparts. Poorer households in developing countries, in particular, suffer more because they tend to spend a greater proportion of their budget on food with no social safety net to mitigate the growing cost of food. *The Atlas of World Hunger* (Bassett and Winter-Nelson 2010) estimates that doubling food prices would increase food expenses of the poor households in developing countries by the same proportion, whereas the shock is far less on the poor households in rich countries with access to social safety nets. So, for example, a poor household living on $1.25 per day may spend 75 per cent of their income on food, and will suffer twice as much from the doubling of food prices, requiring them to spend a total of 150 per cent of their income on food. In other words, when global food prices rise, the threat of food insecurity intensifies a great deal more in developing countries. After ensuring food availability, food access, and food use for the family, a poor household is left with next to nothing. A direct relationship exists between food consumption levels and poverty. It is a complex topic, standing in the intersection of many disciplines. Hence, this topic requires a multidisciplinary approach to understand its complexity. To this end, the proposed book is an ambitious effort.

Have we not learned anything from rapidly expanding global food insecurity and the agricultural market meltdown in 2008? Most studies estimate the impact of rising food prices based on macroeconometric simulation models, secondary literature, blamed biofuels, and growing natural disasters while failing to connect with the process of price and policy transmission (Soetaert and Vandamme 2009; Chakravorty 2012; Hester and Harrison 2012; Pimentel 2012). Price and policies are created by formal institutions like markets and states, but informal institutions' norms and values connect the global value chain with poor farm households at one end and global consumers at the other. Even the International Food Policy

Research Institute (IFPRI) states that 'these simulations often generated unconvincing results, and most were limited by the absence of general equilibrium effects, country-specific price changes, and other relevant shocks, such as rising fuel prices' (Headey and Fan 2010).

Policies informed by miscalculations and incomplete information can lead to negative outcomes, such as the rapid loss of the ability to access adequate resources and nutrition to maintain an active and healthy lifestyle. Food security is not only a measure of ensured access to essential nutrition, but also an assessment of human well-being and a measure of the institutions created as safety nets for societies and human beings to cope with insecurities and uncertainties. From global to local level, institutional safety nets have failed to prevent people from slipping into food insecurity and becoming victims of the 'perfect storm' that we knew was coming. By extension, we academics have failed to rewrite the history.

Objectives

In this book, I explore one of the main drivers of recent global food insecurity – biofuels – and explore why developing countries continued to strive to join the global value chain at the peak of the debate in 2008. Biofuels technology is not new; in fact, Rudolf Diesel ran an engine on peanut oil at the World's Fair in Paris in 1900. For most of the twentieth century, interest in biofuels was confined to specialty projects and laboratories. Toward the end of the century, biofuels caught public attention. In the last decade, with a growing energy crisis and threats of climate change raising the call to action, a number of European countries introduced biofuels blending policies in the energy economies, which then rapidly went global (Durham *et al.* 2012). The two main biofuels are biodiesel, made from the blending of oil crops like soybeans, rapeseeds and palm oil with diesel; and bioethanol, made from the blending of starchy crops like corn, wheat, and so on, with petrol. Two distinct markets developed for the European transportation sector which demands biodiesel and the United States' transportation sector, which demands bioethanol.

Edible crops are the main basis for the first generation biofuels. The impacts of growing demand for biofuels both in the United States (US) and the European Union (EU), therefore, have considerable effects on crop production systems and the food value chain. Government policies like the Blair House Accord introduced incentives for Western consumers to replace fossil fuels with more sustainable, secure, and green biofuels; agricultural-based developing countries, on the other hand, pursued by the global trade regime to modernize and commercialize in order to benefit from globalization, introduced biofuels feedstock production in the food value chain. To provide much needed investment in the agricultural sector, diversify income sources, and pursue poverty eradication strategies and global market access for the stagnant agro-business sector, agricultural countries rushed to biofuels feedstock production. Unfortunately, little is understood about how price and policy information cascade down directly and indirectly into the local agricultural market causing land-use change, altering production priorities and influencing biofuels feedstock production decisions (Erb *et al.* 2012).

It is true enough that the agricultural sector suffers from high quality data limitations. Unfortunately, ill-defined policies are one of the major outcomes of data scarcity. The majority of analyses done in recent agricultural sectors, including nascent sectors like biofuels are carried out based on secondary data or on industry-provided estimates and published as edited books (Soetaert and Vandamme 2011; Hester and Harrison 2012; Pimentel 2012). Although these studies offer useful insights, they suffer from data collection irregularities, unobserved heterogeneity in the *longitudinal studies,* selection biases, and a coherent narrative that reveals disconnections between markets and society (Mundlak *et al.* 2012). In 2011, a joint report produced by the Commission on the Measurement of Economic Performance and Social Progress attributed the global economic crisis to a lack of integrated research approaches (Stiglitz *et al.* 2009). The following year, 2012, the National Academy of Science held a two-day workshop and identified that human endeavours to reduce poverty and sustainable food security are being challenged because of knowledge gaps and methodological weaknesses in improving our holistic understanding of the dimensions (quantitative, qualitative, and geographical) of the issues (National Academy of Science 2012). The objective of this book is to offer an integrated analytical approach to overcoming part of the challenge and show how price and policy information flow through the nodes of the global value chain.

Acknowledgements

A list of people whose help I need to acknowledge would be too long. So, in order not to forget anyone, I would like to thank my family, teachers, mentors, friends, and grantors who made this research possible. I would also like to thank my research associates, interviewees, and editorial team for helping me through the process with patience and inspiration.

Also, the book is written in a way so that readers can skip any chapters and yet be informed about the contextual analysis.

Acronyms and Abbreviations

9MP	Ninth Malaysia Plan
AOA	Agreement on Agriculture
ASDP	Agricultural Sector Development Programme
AWSB	Alam Widuri Sdn Bhd
BATC	Bionas Agropolitan Technology Corridor
BEFS	Bioenergy and Food Security
CAPRI	Common Agricultural Policy Regionalized Impact
CDM	clean development mechanism
CEO	Chief Executive Officer
CGE	compugeneral equilibrium
CIF	Cost, insurance and freight
COP	Conference of Parties
CSR	corporate social responsibility
DOE	Department of Energy
EABD	East Africa Biodiesel
EBB	European Biodiesel Board
EPA	Environmental Protection Agency
EU	European Union
EUR	Euro
FAO	Food and Agriculture Organization
FDI	foreign direct investment
FELDA	Federal Land Development Authority
G-20	Group of Twenty
GATT	General Agreement on Tariffs and Trade
GCC	global commodity chain
GDP	gross domestic product
GHG	greenhouse gas
GNI	gross national income
GTAP	Global Trade Analysis Project
GTZ	German Technical Cooperation
GVC	global value chain
HDI	human development index
IEA	International Energy Agency

IFPRI	International Food Policy Research Institute
IFS	Institutional Feasibility Study
IMF	International Monetary Fund
IPCC	Intergovernmental Panel on Climate Change
IPO	Initial Public Offering
LCA	life cycle assessment
MARDI	Malaysian Agricultural Research and Development Institute
MDG	Millennium Development Goal
MKUKUTA	National Strategy for Growth and Reduction of Poverty
MP	Malaysia Plan
MPOB	Malaysian Palm Oil Board
MYR	Malaysian Ringgit
NCR	native customary rights
NEP	New Economic Policy
NIE	New Institutional Economics
PE	partial equilibrium
RA	Reinvestment Allowance
RC	Regional Commissioner
RSB	Roundon Sustainable Biofuels
SALCRA	Sarawak Land Consolidation and Rehabilitation Authority
SCORE	Sarawak Corridor of Renewable Energy
SGR	strategic grain reserve
SIDA	Swedish International Development Cooperation Agency
TIC	Tanzania Investment Centre
TZS	Tanzanian Shilling
UK	United Kingdom
UN	United Nations
UNCCD	United Nations Convention to Combat Desertification
UNDP	United Nations Development Programme
UNDSD	United Nations Division of Sustainable Development
UNEP	United Nations Environment Programme
UNIMAS	Universiti Malaysia Sarawak
US	United States
USD	United States Dollar
USDA	United States Department of Agriculture
WFP	World Food Programme
WGI	World Governance Indicators
WTO	World Trade Organization
WWF	World Wildlife Foundation
WWI	World War I
WWII	World War II

1 Introduction

The one duty we owe to history is to rewrite it.

Oscar Wilde

The year 2008 was marked by commodity price volatility, for example, crude oil price changes and simultaneous food price increases which led to food riots in developing countries. Looming threats from climate change, food insecurity and growing poverty pose challenges for supporting the world's growing population. Sustainable economic progression cannot follow traditional industrial means. Such contemporary uncertainty spurs the pursuit of a different way of life. The demand is high to rewrite the history of human development if we are to sustain ourselves. This book presents a historical, political, economic assessment of the food versus fuel debate. The reassessment of the relationship, as has been played out since the middle of 2000, is accomplished by presenting an innovative theoretical framework that aims to improve understanding about complex and multifaceted commodities such as biofuels that connect the energy market with the agricultural market through the threads of the global value chain.

Biofuel is one such idea that has gained attention from engineers, scientists, social scientists, and development practitioners. Biofuels are based on renewable biological feedstocks converted mechanically and chemically to produce bioethanol, compatible with gasoline, and biodiesel, compatible with diesel. Commercial biofuel applications in the transportation sector have expanded very rapidly recently from high income countries to developing countries. Several themes underpin biofuels' commercial and political attractiveness – the global energy crisis, climate change and growing rural poverty.

The energy sector has a history of crisis and mythology over the existence of proven oil reserves capable of supporting the human race or bringing about economic catastrophe. For example, in the 1970s based on Hubbert's seminal work which predicted, many believed that the world would exhaust its oil supplies within 30 years, as it had 30 years of proven reserves (Hubbert 1956). Today, 40 years later, there is still debate over proven oil reserves, while over-pumping of oil and shale oil from the western hemisphere has suddenly dropped the price to below USD 60 per barrel. Speculation over reduced oil demand, improved oil substitution technologies continues to cause sudden price fluctuations, disrupting the flow of the global economy. For example, in December 2014;, the Russian economy rapidly lost its currency value due to a record low oil price. In contrast, in 2008, price spikes to above USD 147 per barrel pleasantly surprised the Russian economy while shocking the global energy authorities like the International Energy Agency (IEA) and the United States (US) Department of Energy (DOE) who were operating on the 2004 projection of low oil prices (~USD 25 per barrel) (Wirl 2008). The global oil market is an unresolved mystery, mainly because of information asymmetry over production, diplomatically taut relationships, and pricing insecurity between producer and consumer countries.[1] This has exacerbated oil insecurity fears in the US[2] and EU[3] countries, bringing oil security to the forefront of national agendas. Moreover, rapid growth in the emerging economies combined with growing demand for already declining fossil fuel reserves contributes to global energy insecurity concerns. Biofuels gained attention as an energy independence solution following the experience of Brazil, which began investing in and using biofuels for transportation after the oil crisis of the 1970s. Today, more than 80 per cent of the Brazilian transportation sector is run by domestically produced biofuels (EIA 2007; Europa 2006).[4]

Biofuels gained further prominence due to increasing concerns over global climate change, which could cost at least 5 per cent to 20 per cent of gross domestic product (GDP) annually by 2030 if left unaddressed, depending on the risks and impacts considered (Stern 2006). The Intergovernmental Panel on Climate Change (IPCC) establishes transportation emissions as a major anthropogenic factor for global warming (IPCC 2007). The report shows how rising sea levels and increased incidences of natural disasters in the tropics increase vulnerability, hitting the agricultural sector the hardest, and directly linking developing countries populations' livelihoods with the consequences of climate change. To mitigate climate change, biofuels are proposed as a substitute for transportation fuel with lower carbon emissions until better technological solutions arrive, simultaneously providing higher income opportunities for poor farmers whose income from agriculture is insecure due to climate change.

So at the time of the rush to expand the biofuels value chain in the remotest parts of developing countries, it was widely anticipated that the global first generation biofuels, already occupying a million hectares, would grow tenfold by 2015, while attracting about one billion dollars in investment annually, despite intense scientific scrutiny.[5] In less than ten years, that estimate was downgraded by scientists and the enthusiasm for investments in this sector was reduced (Fritz *et al.* 2013). By now it is known that the biofuels industry stretches from developing countries' farmland to developed countries' transportation sectors, integrating energy and agricultural markets (Demirbas 2009). A wide range of studies came out between 2007 and 2010 analysing the relationship between global food price hikes and biofuels feedstock demand conflicting with food supplies. This point is further elaborated in the next chapter.

Effects of the price hikes include world agricultural trade dropping for the first time since 1982 and global agricultural unemployment, projected to reach 7.4 per cent as government food budgets run dry[6] (ILO 2009). There are negative aspects to biofuels industry expansion, such as dramatic food price increases of 130 per cent for wheat, 74 per cent for rice, and 87 per cent for soya in 2008, which sparked food riots in 40 countries in a single year (Patel and Gimenez-Holt 2010). The effects of climate change on agriculture have a multiplier effect on the overall economy. This compounds existing problems for agrarian populations, which occupy marginal lands, suffer incomplete land rights, lack access to credit markets, depend heavily on rain fed production systems, and are exposed to natural calamities and price fluctuations.

Achieving food security is a political and economic goal. Biofuels market expansion in developing countries is considered an essential marker of success by both national governments and the international community. A world of plentiful food where a billion people suffer from hunger, more than 70 per cent chronically, makes humanity wonder if something has fundamentally gone wrong with economic development (Patel and Gimenez-Holt 2010). The inclination is to try to fix it by expanding the global value chain into the remoter parts of the world, and bringing unutilized resources like land, labour, and capital into play. While there is no simple prescription to achieve that, enthusiasm for poverty reduction, propelled by global motivation to make Millennium Development Goals a success, caused biofuels to be seen as a magic bullet. Biofuels connect the underperforming agricultural sectors of developing countries with an efficiently performing energy market, and this raised the expectations of developing countries' governments who are struggling with long-standing poverty and food insecurity.

Understanding food insecurity requires critical analysis of the fundamentals of poverty, human empowerment, and the institutional development process that protects human rights. It is widely acknowledged that since the 1970s, when food insecurity calculation really started, as the world population grew, the size of the food-insecure population also grew. So, the total number for the last three decades has remained at around one billion and continued to challenge any claims of food insecurity reduction.[7] Food security is defined as a 'situation [...] when all people, at all times, have physical, social and economic access to sufficient, safe, and nutritious food that meets their dietary needs and food preferences for an active and healthy life' (FAO 2002). Notably, the 12th Human Rights Council of the United Nations (UN), 2009 called for a global moratorium on biofuels expansion:

[T]he international community should work towards achieving a consensus on international guidelines guiding the production and consumption of agrofuels.[8] Such guidelines should include environmental standards, since the expansion of the production and consumption of agrofuels results in direct and indirect shifts in land use and often has negative environmental impact, taking into account the full life cycle of the product. They should also incorporate the requirements of human rights standards, particularly as regards the rights to adequate food, to adequate housing, the rights of workers, indigenous peoples, and women's rights.

(de Schutter 2009: 5)

And yet the rush to join the global biofuels market remained strong in developing countries. The plea to the UN Human Rights Council indicates major gaps in biofuels policy and underlines predicaments for globalization. A broad body of research studying the phenomenon of globalization found that the ability of nation states to effectively control many dimensions of social, political, and economic life within their borders is increasingly limited (Held 1995; Keohane and Nye 2000; Scholte 2000). The global financial crisis has had a dramatic effect on the global economic environment very recently, which illustrates how globalization and humanity stand at a crossroads (Nolan 2009). Capitalist globalization has certainly benefited humanity immensely, by freeing people from natural domination, reducing production costs, lifting a large number of people out of poverty, and giving a technological boost to human creativity, but 'it has a Faustian duality to its nature, producing profound threats to sustainable development in relation to inequality, ecology, and financial stability' (Nolan 2009: 255). Developing countries are subject to the duality and are pondering at the same crossroads with growing unemployment, poverty, threats of climate change, and the quandary of how to pass through the 'Lewis phase'[9] of development which has just begun for many countries in the past couple of decades.

Notwithstanding this unresolved debate, high income countries' demand for biofuels continues to rise, while global initiatives put forth green funds, renewable energy funds, carbon trading platforms and promises to reduce subsidies for fossil fuels, and agricultural practices continue to support the low-carbon economy. This warrants a careful assessment of the industries that promise a low-carbon economy. The biofuels industry, being one of them, which depends on outsourced feedstocks from developing countries, needs further scrutiny and consideration of various questions: do biofuels present meaningful foreign and local investment opportunities for developing countries? To what extent does biofuels feedstock production in developing countries help with poverty reduction and agricultural sector modernization? Who are the winners and losers in the biofuels industry development in developing countries and how does it fit within the existing formal and informal institutional frameworks?

Since the beginning of modern industrialization, there have been efforts to find cheaper and more reliable sources of energy for transportation. Since the ascendance of the automobile industry and related transportation systems, links between transportation infrastructure development and economic development have been studied intensively (Craig *et al.* 1998; Fogel 1964; Hawke 1970). Efficient and effective transportation is essential for globalization (Hart 1993; Krugman 1995: 328). Securing fossil fuel supply sources to run transportation systems is a global priority, more so than infrastructure development or technological innovation. About 77 per cent of global energy consumption is derived from fossil fuel sources like oil, natural gas, and coal (Goldemberg and Johansson 2004; Koh and Ghazoul 2008). Of this, 80 per cent is used by transportation and this is projected to increase due to growing transport demands in developing countries (EIA 2007). At this rate, global demand is expected to climb from 85 million barrels a day in 2008 to 105 million barrels a day by 2030 (IEA 2009).

Finding oil alternatives has become a critical world policy agenda since dramatic oil price volatility in the 1970s, as seen in Figure 1.1, bringing alternative energy sources for transportation like biofuels to prominence (Hazell and Pachauri 2006). It is not a surprise that biofuels prices follow oil prices very closely (Searchinger 2009). The transportation sector can use up to 5 per cent biofuel blended with fossil fuels without any engine modifications.[10]

There are three phases of biofuels technological development – first, second, and third generation. While the first generation biofuels are mainly derived from food (maize, sugarcane) and oil crops (soybeans, rapeseeds, *Jatropha curcas*), second generation biofuels come from non-edible sources such as fast growing trees (willow), grasses (elephant grass), and carbon-rich waste materials, and third generation biofuels are produced from laboratory experiments on biological autotrophic organisms and are not yet commercially viable. This leaves first generation biofuels as the best alternative for present-day decisions and, consequently, is the focus of this research.[11]

Global agricultural sector investment in developing countries lagged for 20 years, but demand for biofuels feedstock brings interest in revitalizing the global agricultural management system (World Bank 2008a). The World Energy Outlook's baseline scenario projects that biofuels' use in transportation will grow 437 per cent between 2005 and 2030: up to 4.3 per cent of total energy consumption (IEA 2007). EU member countries are making significant political, societal, and commercial commitments to develop sustainable, low-carbon energy sources. These countries are the largest consumers of first generation biofuels. They also promise to contribute to sustainable economic, rural development, and food security agendas of feedstock producing countries (UNCTAD 2009). The EU consumed 63 per cent of global biofuels in 2007, mostly in the form of biodiesel, and is forecast to demand more, especially from non-edible feedstocks for their perceived characteristic of not conflicting with food

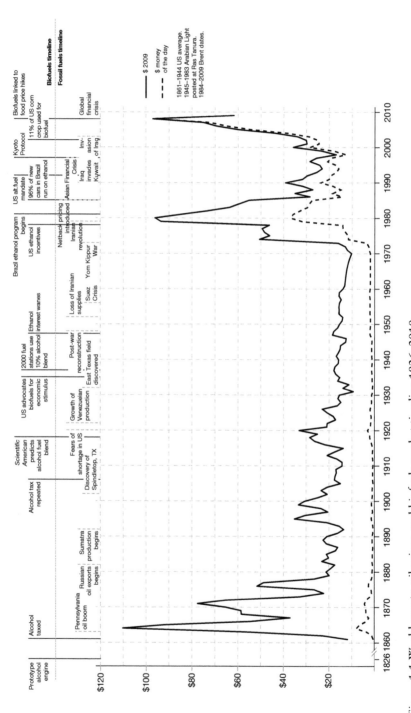

Figure 1.1 World events, oil prices, and biofuels market timeline 1826–2010
Source: Author created based on BP 2010 and Wirl 2008.

crops. As a consequence of EU consumers' preference, the book has narrowed its focus to biodiesel and, specifically, the newest version of non-edible biofuels feedstock, *Jatropha curcas*.

The recent *Biodiesel 2020* publication, which tracks global markets for biodiesel growth and details major feedstock trends, validates this research focus as it states that:

> [T]he global markets for biodiesel are entering a period of rapid, transitional growth, creating both uncertainty and opportunity. The first generation biodiesel markets in Europe and the US have reached impressive biodiesel production capacity levels, but remain constrained by feedstock availability. In the BRIC nations of Brazil, India and China, key government initiatives are spawning hundreds of new opportunities for feedstock development, biodiesel production, and export.
>
> (Thurmond 2008)

Given the intensity of the food versus fuel debate, this research focuses on the non-edible feedstock crop *Jatropha curcas,* hereafter jatropha, and to examine to what extent the widely argued position held on jatropha, that it has a lower propensity to conflict with food crop cultivation, is valid. Moreover, in emerging countries, both in Asia and in Europe the majority of vehicles are powered by diesel engines, which translates into a potential growing domestic demand for biodiesel (FuelsEurope.eu 2014). This also creates a tremendous opportunity for developing countries to revitalize their stagnant agricultural sectors and create employment through biofuels feedstock cultivation (Masangi and Ewing 2009).

While the proponents argue for jatropha's relatively high oil content, productivity on degraded and saline soil, low water needs, direct substitution for diesel, and non-edible properties, plant scientists have highlighted the crop's poisonous characteristics that can be harmful to humans and animals. Further on, in Table 3.5, more light is shed on this from evidence found in the scientific literature. Similarly, private sectors seeking to invest in biofuels production argue that, along with agricultural employment creation, by-products such as soaps, biofuels-pellets, and fertilizers can offer opportunities for local small enterprises to be developed. In general biofuel sector development offers great potential for pro-poor development programmes. Furthermore, it is believed that jatropha will put less pressure on the demand for land and food production, and eventually reduce food prices because of the crop's adaptability to marginal lands (UNCTAD 2009). However, others claim that this is rarely true if a high yield is to be achieved. Leading countries like China and India are racing into the biodiesel feedstock market, while prompting other developing countries to join the race by creating hybrid and improved jatropha seeds, markets, and relevant regulations.

South–South and North–South competition has led to increased agricultural innovation and productivity, but also increased pressure for return on investment. In developing countries, poor farmers make up a significant share of the production chain and they are the focus in this research. Poor farmers as economic agents can obtain an assured income from jatropha and would convert arable land to jatropha unless otherwise legally mandated or socially institutionalized. The guarantees of income in most countries are driven by contract farming schemes. Unfortunately, in most countries biofuels policy is unclear on how to define biofuels contract prices, as they are tied to the conventional fossil fuel market. Jatropha contract farming, unlike other cash crops, appears to have an unclear legal domain with limited institutional capacity to monitor or assess implications on farmers. This research delves into two different competing developing countries' jatropha-based biodiesel industry development experiences and provides an IFS to contextualize the impacts.

1.1 Adequacies of policy informing frameworks used to promote the global biofuels market

While some biofuels case studies look at economic returns, a major portion of biofuels related analytical work is carried out based on scientific and product engineering methodology to measure the environmental footprint of biofuels. All of these studies are useful in their own right, as they provide more insight to this young industry. However, the major weakness of these studies is that they often try to provide a generalized view of the crop, technology, industry, or utility.

Generalization is problematic for biofuels because it is not only geographically connected; various policies of economies and segments of sciences like agro economics and agro science have come together under the embeddedness of socio-political–economic and climatic conditions. Three main kinds of analytical frameworks are summarized here along with their weaknesses: first, life cycle assessment (LCA) which examines the carbon footprint of the biofuels production pathway; second, cost–benefit analysis; and third, macroeconomic sector modelling which evaluates impacts on the overall economy. All of these studies are quantitative in nature and provide scientific and business assessments of the biofuels industry.

1.1.1 LCA

Biofuels gained global attention due to their climate friendly, carbon advantageous characteristics as a substitution for fossil fuels in the transportation sector. However, serious doubts have been raised by scholars, mostly scientists, about biofuels' carbon friendliness (Pimentel *et al.* 2002; Pimentel and Patzek 2005). LCA models produce an aggregated estimation of the energy flow embodied in each of the productive resources like land, water, technology, and energy consumed in the supply chain of a particular biofuel. This is an environmental engineering model which, in theory, permits a 'one for one' comparison of variously sourced and processed final products and co-products (Kammen *et al.* 2007). Most LCA studies conceptually set out to capture the overall impacts of energy inflow and outflow in inputs associated with a particular output at every stage of the life cycle which is linked through the value addition process of product development.[12]

LCA-based studies estimating the environmental impacts of biofuels production chains on the environment produced diverse estimations. These are mainly used by the consumer countries to determine the environmental impacts of their consumed biofuels in order to fulfil their carbon emission reduction targets. This analysis serves a special policy purpose, and is used in the creation of global regulatory environment categories. How can they then regulate industry standards and certification processes to protect the environment, mitigate climate change, and reduce poverty all at the same time? Moreover, there is no consensus on methodology as, while the Environmental Protection Agency (EPA) applies consequential LCA[13], The UK Renewable Fuels Association and The European Commissions do not use consequential LCA, hence producing widely different policy standards (Delucchi 2004; Europa 2006). LCA is therefore not appropriate to create meaningful comparative analyses and forecasts to promote or deny access to the global biofuels supply chain for developing countries.

In addition, LCA measurement is inadequate for calculating direct GHG emissions along different production chains such as the use of electricity, the use of hand pressed motors, and the indirect emissions caused by the other inputs in the supply chain – like forest clearing to develop biofuels crop lands, pumping underground water for irrigation, and transporting intermediary goods for value addition. For example, the PEAT-CO_2 project attempts to assess the amount of emissions released from deforestation in South East Asian peatlands in order to plant palm trees to meet the growing demand for biodiesel. The report estimates that from both drained decomposition (~632 million tons per year) and deforestation (~1400 million tons per yr) the total CO_2 of 2000 Mt/yr equals almost 8 per cent of global emissions from fossil fuel burning (Rieley *et al.* 2008; Wang *et al.* 2011). The weakness occurs because not all LCAs treat emissions, such as gases like NO_x, VOCs, SO_x, CH_4,, NH_3, and black carbon, the same which creates almost order of magnitude differences in ranking fossil fuels substitutions (Delucchi 2006; Kammen *et al.* 2007). There is also little environmental and social intuition in LCA calculations, which undermines realistic impacts (Hooijer *et al.* 2006).

1.1.2 *Cost accounting modelling*

Cost accounting models are based on accounting principles, not on economic principles (Rajagopal and Zilberman 2007). Depreciation and amortization of costs of investment helps with the product market feasibility studies. The purpose of such modelling is to estimate the profitability of an activity for a single-price taking agent such as a farmer or processor. Cost accounting models are primarily used to identify cost and revenue structures of the investment on given parameters like a specific crop, cost of seeds, available land size and land preparation costs, labour costs, transportation costs, and potential sale prices. The production function is considered static and follows a constant growth rate, along with cost of production, yield, output price, and demand.

Other studies found that financial performance of representative biofuels crop processing depends on feedstock prices, oil prices, biofuels prices, co-product prices, natural gas prices, and interest rates. Financial performance is also influenced by subsidies and alternative crop usage (like sugar used for food versus ethanol) (Gnansounou *et al.* 2005; Tiffany and Eidman 2003; Tyner and Taheripour 2007). It was also found that tax credits for bioethanol production may increase relative miles travelled by vehicles and may delay the adoption of more fuel efficient automobiles (Bento and Jacobsen 2007). As a result, on the one hand, the ambition to reduce GHG emissions from the transportation sector may not be fulfilled, and on the other hand the tax and subsidies related to blending mandates will impose additional costs on the economy to promote biofuels.

Moreover, this kind of model is static in nature as it does not consider dynamic changes in production related to crops, biotechnology, market dynamism, and change in harvesting periods. To see differences between costs and benefits, different sets of accounting-based studies need to be based on crop variety (e.g., perennials or intercropped species), production period, harvesting procedure, conversion technology, fixed cost structures, and government taxes or subsidies (Rajagopal and Zilberman 2007). For example, monocropped sorghum shows the lowest cost per ton of biomass compared to monocropped perennials and intercropped species, but most developing countries' smallholder farmers are not monocropping sorghum. Such itemized analysis can only serve a limited purpose for a specific region, and should not be generalized. Furthermore, even market feasibility studies based on cost accounting models cannot provide adequate information on how cost and revenue structures, that are often unstructured in developing countries, react to long-term monetary valuation changes due to exchange rates, interest rates, and land and production costs. The resulting loss of marginal return of investments does not feature in the analysis, until reality hits and investors abandon their biofuels investment in developing countries as it is no longer an unknown. In sum, reality is much more dynamic than accounting principle models assume and this book tries to shed more light on this using a more innovative and complementary thinking approach.

1.1.3 *Macroeconomic sector modelling*

To capture nuanced and dynamic changes in the biofuels economy, some economists undertook macroeconomic sector modelling. Partial equilibrium and general equilibrium models are designed to see how biofuel mandates increase marginal returns in the agricultural market, along with mandate adjustment in the fossil fuel or energy markets. The modelling exercise also looks at the effects of biofuels on other policies in relevant markets. Subsidized biofuels processing may reduce transport fuel prices and hence stimulate demands for energy, whereas mandatory directives could increase fuel prices and depress demand due to price pressure. This affects the rest of the economy as the energy policy domain influences the path of modernization. This is why computable general equilibrium (CGE) and agricultural partial equilibrium (PE) are mainly used, depending on the nature of the research. Each model benefits from the specialized nature of the theory and perspective it follows. While CGE is based on aggregate economic analysis, PE offers more detail regarding spatial, environmental, and commodity disaggregation, and considers domestic agricultural policies.

Table 1.1 reviews major biofuels literature that influenced global policy thinking during 2006–2008, utilizing CGE or PE. If we consider the current outcome, as we know it from the shift in the biofuels market and the reduction in the fuel price, the static nature of the models is a major source of misunderstanding about the past, present, and future. The static nature of the model assumes baseline scenarios – for example, the terms of technology, feedstock mix, and input qualities (seeds, meal, and first press) are all considered quality neutral and price unchanged since the base year – and then draws a forecasting model for the next five to ten years (see for example FAPRI 2009; Link *et al.* 2009; Msangi and Ewing 2009; Rosegrant *et al.* 2008). Such models, as presented below, created anticipation for demand and supply constraints, pushing up the expected price for biofuels in the future. This has led to the rush, that we now know has a probable relationship with global food price rises, and food insecurity interactions between agricultural markets and relevant factor markets that influence the quality of agricultural productivity (e.g., seed yield and oil yield). Biofuels market prices are influenced by changes in energy and transportation markets.

Most biofuels models reviewed do not include oil prices, instead focusing on mandates, which leads to a misguided market outcome. The general equilibrium model-based literatures, though they consider the energy market in the calculations, do not take into account the market power differences of the relevant sectors. For example, the energy market has much greater power than the biofuels market in national economies. Finally, such models cannot consider multiple policy alternatives which could achieve the single stated goal of reducing carbon emissions – for example, climate change policies, alternative energy policies, and renewable technology policies. Therefore, combining these limitations in PE models, researchers argue that the inherent flaws in these models make them risk adverse; models such as GTAP or CAPRI can be reality void (for example, concerning farmers' production choices between crops) and overstate output levels with unestablished price forecasts, and so policy insights based on the simulations

Table 1.1 PE model based literature review

Study	Data focus level	Findings	Methodology
International Model for Policy Analysis of Agricultural Commodity and Trade developed by IFPRI (Msangi and Ewing 2009)	Global level supply and demand of agricultural commodities, with no change in yield.	Aggressive increase in future demand will drastically reduce food availability for humans and increase child malnutrition levels in developing countries.	PE model
AGLINK-COSIMO developed by FAO and OECD (OECD 2008)	Global agricultural product markets, commodity supply, demand, prices, trade and policy effects, and changes based on alternative settings against baseline projections benchmarks.	Predicts that crop prices in 2014 may increase by 2 per cent while oilseeds and sugar rise by 60 per cent.	PE model for global agriculture
Common Agricultural Policy Regionalized Impact (CAPRI) analysis, developed by the University of Bonn, with EU funding (Adenäuer 2008)	Global impact analysis of exogenous demand for agricultural products from the biofuels industry, with special attention to the EU market.	The overall prices on food crops will rise. The emphasis is on biodiesel as the EU anticipates more demand for biodiesel than bioethanol.	Multi-feedstock based PE model
Center of Agriculture and Rural Development of Iowa State University (Tokgoz et al. 2007)	National level. Projections of US ethanol production and its impacts on planted acreage, crop prices, livestock production and prices, trade, and retail food costs are presented under the assumption that current tax credits and trade policies are maintained.	Expanded US ethanol production will cause long-run crop prices to increase. Cellulosic ethanol from switchgrass and biodiesel from soybeans do not become economically viable in the Corn Belt under any of the scenarios.	A multi-product, multi-country deterministic PE model

Study	Data focus level	Findings	Methodology
Food and Agricultural Policy Research and Institute Oilseed Model (FAPRI 2009)	National focus. Considers prices of corns, bioethanol and by-products (soaps, fertilizers, etc.) with production, processing capacity, land and tax policy. Quality and yield neutral.	Building additional ethanol production capacity will increase corn prices, but reduce prices of bioethanol and by-products. Livestock and poultry will be affected relatively less than other models predict.	A non-spatial, PE, econometric world model
The Forest and Agriculture Sector Optimization Model (Link *et al.* 2009)	The EU and US forest and agricultural sector specific research based on loss of welfare and market conflict between food versus fuels, loss of welfare and promotion for carbon sequestration.	Model attempts to maximize the net present value of the sum of consumers' and producers' surpluses at baseline carbon prices. At a carbon price equal to USD 40, there is no role for corn ethanol to restore carbon emissions, but for above USD 70, ethanol can help with mitigation.	A multi-product, multi-country deterministic PE model
Global Trade Analysis Project (GTAP) (Hertel *et al.* 2010)	The global competition in feedstock is mainly driven by the EU and US blending targets. Price changes and land-use changes at the global level are assessed for between 2001 and 2006, and forecast for 2015.	By 2015 if the US and EU mandates are indeed fulfilled the impact on global land use could be substantial, with potentially significant implications for greenhouse gas emissions.	CGE models

Source: Author.

become weak (Searchinger 2009; Taheripour *et al.* 2010). By ignoring heterogeneity in the biofuels production factor market, conditions such as land rights and land fertility, together with the foreign investment environment, the policy for biofuels becomes very complex and inadequate to save either the environment or livelihoods (Clancy 2013). At the time of this research the information on some of the latest models is unavailable so it is difficult to identify the quality of the work. However, it is important to note that any projection-based model projects that use predefined qualifiers and conditions, are often limited in representing the reality of the situation. In addition, when such information is proprietary, costly, time consuming, and unavailable, validation of the models and accurate estimation by the local governments, especially by developing countries' governments and researchers, is limited. In such cases, project models almost become a source of faith or belief. Evidence-based policy making should not be a practice based on faith or unrealistic models.

1.2   The need for reassessment

Given the challenges and weaknesses of the existing analytical models, this book lays out a set of reasons for why there is a need for a new framework to analyse biofuels and any such complex commodities that cross over multiple global markets, such as agriculture and energy markets. There are global agriculture markets for commodities like wheat and maize that with the emergence of biofuels technology, became commodities for the energy market.

First, there is a wide consensus among development scholars that global poverty will intensify along with food insecurity. There are several reasons behind the expectations, such as the recent financial crisis coupled with volatile commodity markets and growing threats from climate change, which have a multiplier effect on poverty and food insecurity (Godfray *et al.* 2010). Furthermore, factor market imperfections affect individual agents' investment decisions, which in turn affect their families' future occupations, assets, and livelihoods. In addition, recent studies suggest that the world will need 70 to 100 per cent more food by 2050 (Royal Society 2009; World Bank 2008a). This is significant for the one billion people living in poverty, 80 per cent of whom derive their livelihoods from agriculture in developing countries (World Bank 2008b).

Second, neoclassical quantitative welfare measures offer empirical precision but often fail to provide information on the structure of the economic processes that generate the observed outcomes. Political institutions, social norms, and exogenous influences like the trade environment can be constructed into a descriptive analysis of what the economic agents really care about, the nature of their preference, and community objectives. Since the 1970s, when development economics began addressing issues of rural development, many insights have been generated on land and credit markets, building roads, introducing new commodities, and bringing in new investors. These are all fundamental to growth, but how well this fits with the local community, natural environment, economic behaviour, and pre-existing relationships is missing (Mookherjee 2005). Over time, linkages missing between underlying behaviour and structural relationships helped development scholars to rethink the reasons behind policy failure, market failure, and development failure in developing countries.

Moreover, the very nature of randomized experiments is limited to short-term effects, side effects, or a narrow range of policy interventions. As a result, it is difficult to rely on quantitative assessments derived from biofuels studies to design efficient and effective policies. Before undertaking, commissioning, or allowing extensive investment plans or experiments with new agro-commodities like biofuels feedstocks, developing countries need a wider assessment of the nature of payoffs, compatibility, costs, and alternative factor usage. This requires better knowledge of the underlying behaviour and structural relationships between agents in the biofuels value chain, agents within their social and natural environment, and calibrations of existing product markets with policies, political apparatuses, and legal frameworks.

Human society embedded in its own agency is far more complex than assumed in neoclassical economics. While neoclassical economics acknowledges that institutions matter, less importance is given to integrating institutions analysis into econometric analysis, leaving room for theoretical development (Williamson 2000). Before designing a quantitative model to promote a new industry like biofuels, a qualitative picture is needed covering the new market order, regulatory structure, and change in institutional structure. The need for institutional analysis is far greater in developing countries, where the cost of failure often outweighs any benefits as the former is largely borne by the poor while the latter is mostly realized by the rich.

Finally, 'understanding the structure of economic relationships is an objective of innate intrinsic importance in social science, quite apart from their usefulness in prediction and policy evaluation' (Mookherjee 2005: 13). Although many theories and methodologies are published every year, we know little about the relationship between factor market imperfections and social norms. How does this relationship evolve within changing demographics, environment, and technological circumstances? How do economic processes and communities interact? How does the tragedy of the commons persist in hierarchical society? How can we go beyond static cost-benefit analysis of markets and PE models of partial income distribution? How are economic processes marginalized for some when the state is weak, the market is distant, and the legal system is poorly enforced?

In sum, there are too many theories and too few frameworks to test the theories empirically. The biofuels industry is still in its early stages of development. Considering the substantial weaknesses in existing theories, datasets, models, and baselines, a more balanced framework is needed to temper enthusiasm to experiment more with the poor's livelihoods and aspirations to alter the conditions of their *own* poverty.[14] The IFS framework attempts to combine theoretical, contextual, and empirical understanding for better policy making which could limit negative spillover effects between commodity value chains. For this book, Tanzania and Malaysia were chosen as case study countries to utilize the IFS framework and to offer a reassessment as to how conflict between food and fuels occurred in developing countries and what lessons can be learned for the future.

It is widely understood that differences in agricultural productivity among agricultural-based economies profoundly affect income and food security. Agricultural productivity is low in tropical countries for many reasons: first, the population density reduces per unit of land used for agriculture; second, access to (credit and traders) markets reduces producers' natural propensity to produce surplus; third, a low-input agricultural system has stifled the productivity of the sector; and fourth, large areas of land available to low-density populations, as in the African context, suffer from labour inputs lower than needed for irrigation, pruning, harvesting, and so on. Also, the majority of the developing and densely populated countries are in the tropics, where poverty is high, market liberalization took place rapidly and the costs of land, labour, and inputs are much lower, thereby making agriculture an attractive sector for FDI. Interestingly, the jatropha belt also lies in the tropical zone as indicated in Figure 1.2. Notice that not only is it the global agricultural belt, but it also represents the area of greatest food insecurity (GEXSI 2008; Raswant 2009).

In Tanzania, in particular, agriculture supports almost 90 per cent of the poor population. More than in any other sector, it is agreed that rural agricultural improvement is critical to poverty reduction. As a case in point, Malaysia reduced poverty rates from 50 per cent in the 1970s to its current 3 per cent mainly by improving the agricultural performance throughout the peninsular by introducing a major cash-crop scheme: palm oil estates. While Tanzania has a long-standing history of food insecurity, poverty, and low human development, Malaysia has a rather successful trajectory in all of these areas.

Both Tanzania and Malaysia entered the global biodiesel feedstock market *circa* 2007 and began formulation of the institutional arrangements – formal and informal governance systems to shape the incentives and constraints of agricultural sector development to facilitate biodiesel feedstock production. The case studies are developed from this starting point and investigate the relationship between jatropha producing companies' supply chains and decision-making processes of rural smallholder producers in these countries. The comparative case study analysis between Tanzania and Malaysia will illuminate empirical evidence on the role of global governance in the biofuels value chain, national government responses to high food prices, and local decision-making processes of smallholder farmers. Comparing the transformation of Tanzanian and Malaysian historical agro-economic regulatory frameworks, this study attempts to understand to what extent poverty and food insecurity issues are addressed in the context of biofuels industry development.

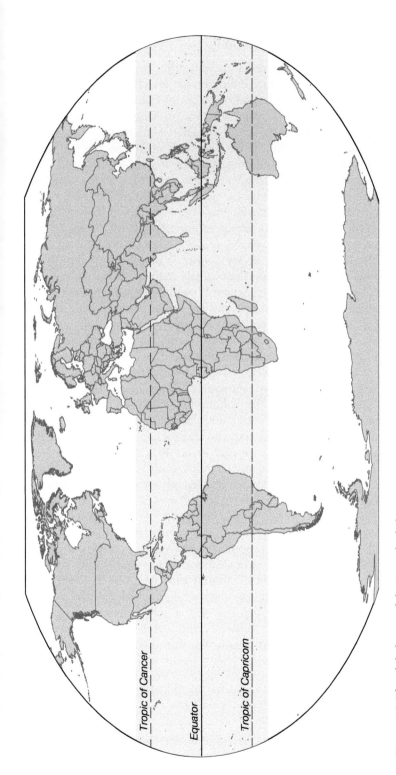

Figure 1.2 The global map of the jatropha belt
Source: Author created using data from FAO and Naturalearthdata.com. Scale 1:10 m.

1.3   Major contributions of this book

To substantiate the broader research aim, this book investigates the economic process and governance conditions in which the first generation biofuels industry development has taken place in Tanzania and Malaysia to export to the European market from 2008 to 2010. During these three years 'the end of wild capitalism and the future of humanity' met at the crossroads.[15] Below are the four contributions that the book makes on the subject of biofuels, food security, and developing economies.

The first major objective of this book is to contextualize the food and biofuels debate by offering readers a clearer and simpler picture of the biofuels sector development in developing countries. Much biofuel-related analytical work is based on a product engineering premise that measures the environmental footprint of biofuels. Moreover, the methodologies are often too complex for policy makers or lay people to assess the quality of the analysis. This is not only because the biofuels industry is young, but also because the agricultural sector, primarily within developing countries, suffers from high quality data limitations. Published biofuels literature and policy reports are mainly based on secondary literature or collected commentaries. Therefore, little knowledge has actually been created on the complexities such as the internalization process of people from developing countries who are choosing between survival options: food security through subsistence farming or a secure income source by becoming contract farmers for biofuels companies. Given the volume of crop-based feedstocks that are converted annually, any decisions made regarding biofuels production will have implications for food markets and social decisions to arrange resources, such as customary lands (Erb *et al.* 2012). There is very little literature on resource allocation in the value chain available. Therefore, more analytical studies are needed to understand the extent to which biofuels feedstocks fit within the national food security strategy, agro-export orientation, and rural development plans and policies, especially for developing countries.

The second contribution of this book is to challenge the deep rooted faith in quantitative analysis and growing affinity among sustainability scholars for the quantitative approach. Understanding the roles of biofuels and food security are critical to understanding sustainability, which is often reduced to predictions and predictive analysis of the future based on specific scenarios. Sustainability is a time sensitive issue, and there is a finite number of choices that science, society, and markets can make to address sustainability. 'Researchers should not only concentrate on the question of whether a theory yields coherent and accurate predictions, but also ask whether it works: do the theoretical concepts and principles inform practices in productive ways?' (Van den Akker 1999: 10) A couple of edited books have made an effort to show there is a need for both quantitative and qualitative understanding of biofuels sector development, but they rely heavily on secondary data and do not connect science, society, and sociology as they influence markets and policies (Gasparatos and Stromberg 2012). The concentration here is on analysing relevant institutions, policies, industry projects, and agricultural growth trajectories, in order to ascertain a nuanced analysis on how the global value chain of biofuels influences the food security situation in a given location.

The third theme of this book is to highlight the forgotten story of globalization and decentralization. How do developing countries actually gain or lose from rapid expansion into the globalized feedstock markets? Decentralized governance and market systems, introduced in developing countries throughout the twentieth century promised agricultural growth. While agricultural growth is necessary, it has not been sufficient for sustained hunger and poverty reduction. Such historical, political, and economic issues are also important in understanding why modern agricultural growth, instead of involving smallholders, especially women, who are most effective in reducing extreme poverty and hunger, have focused on commercial farmers who have large landholdings. For any action, whether introducing a new policy, promoting a technology, commodity, or behavioural change, it is important to understand how an economic development trajectory has fed itself over time and influenced formal and informal institutional arrangements. Limited understanding prevails on how institutional vulnerabilities reinforce each other in liberalized and decentralized governance systems (Morton 2007; World Bank 2008a).

Finally, as this research is hardly the last word on the subject, this book aims to provide an alternative perspective on the food security analysis based on case studies using a novel integrated analytical approach – the Institutional Feasibility Study (IFS). Two very interesting case studies, using the IFS framework, from Borneo, in Malaysia, and Tanzania are presented here. These countries were chosen because the growing biodiesel feedstocks industry was accused of generating harmful impacts in these localities, ranging from the near extinction of the orang-utan in Borneo to pushing the poorest even further into poverty. A comparative analysis of the curious case of jatropha sector development in Tanzania and Malaysia generates lessons for other developing countries (Habib-Mintz 2010; Mintz-Habib 2013). To consider the role of biodiesel feedstocks on food security, and to reveal how even an inedible crop can be in conflict with the local food system, jatropha was selected.

There are several reasons for selecting jatropha. First, studies suggest that biodiesel is more practical than bioethanol development. Since first generation biodiesel is more cost competitive, people can easily replace diesel with biodiesel in the engine and this will likely dominate market development as the tracking sector is on the rise globally (Eisentraut 2010). Second, biodiesel's emissions are up to 80 per cent less than those of ordinary diesel, which means a tremendous contribution toward climate change mitigation (Henry and Henry 2012). Non-edible biodiesel feedstock crops like jatropha are gaining popularity both because they are inedible and because they are suitable for arid and semi-arid land. Intuitively, jatropha production on barren land actually improves land productivity. In other words, jatropha production should not impact food security. Finally, in the US and the EU, biodiesel subsidies, which made the biofuels sector attractive, are being slashed, which means the cost of feedstock production will be higher in the US and the EU than in developing countries. This indicates greater opportunities for biodiesel crop exports, like jatropha, from developing countries.

In summary, this book aims to answer questions like: How do global initiatives for green growth, energy security, and sustainable development incorporate biofuels industry development? Does global biofuels trade present meaningful foreign and local investment opportunities for developing countries? To what extent does biofuels feedstock production in developing countries help with poverty reduction and agricultural sector modernization? What roles do the EU and the US commitments to biofuels blending targets play in the rapid industry development in developing countries? How does the biofuels industry fit within existing formal and informal institutional frameworks? Who are the winners and losers in the biofuels global value chain?

The next chapter presents an innovative framework to think more critically about the complex nature of the overarching concept of sustainable development. Sustainable development means 'meeting the needs of the present generation without compromising the needs of the future generation' (WCED 1987). In a classical definition, the path of development is sustained 'if and only if the stocks of overall capital assets remains constant or rises over time' (Pearce and Warford 1993: 2). Within the context of sustainability analysis, the equitable distribution of benefits is measured by the rise of human welfare from socio-economic and political activities. This research seeks to generate a more detailed, empirically-based understanding of the processes through which global economic governance arrangements affect the empowerment of low-income workers and producers in the developing world.

Notes

1 See for more details (IEA 2007, 2009, 2010; IEA/WBCSD 2004).
2 Net imports provide 48 per cent of US oil consumption (EIA 2007).
3 Fifty per cent of EU fossil fuels are imported and, without alternative sources, the dependency will grow to 90 per cent by 2030 (Europa 2006). The UK is in the EU energy assessment and energy saving identification scheme implemented via the ESOS Regulations 20141 and is viewed alike in this book for comparative purposes. All large UK businesses will be affected.
4 Brazil's experience has not been without criticism, particularly as environmental sustainability and human rights have gained global attention. See Hall *et al.* 2009; Kojima and Johnson 2006.

5 In the journal *Science*, two Princeton scientists argued that biofuels are 'decarbonizing' energy technology. Another view is that biofuels are carbon-neutral because CO_2 released during combustion is offset by carbon fixation during plant growth (Howarth and Bringezu 2009). However, an article published in *Science* argues that biofuels are worsening climate change because the total GHG emissions from biofuels development related activities (land clearing for feedstock and food due to high price) is far greater than that of burning fossil fuels (Fargione *et al.* 2008). The debate is no longer new, yet it was not considered during biofuels related policy making in developing countries.

6 The number misrepresents the real unemployment and part-time employment figures. There are two main reasons: (a) subsistence farming, home gardening, and community farming are often not accounted for in the official data; and (b) seasonality effects of the agricultural sector cause migration.

7 Since the rise of food prices in mid-2008, many scholars have noted this event marked the end of the era of low priced food. Therefore, the recent food crisis may be just a 'preview' of a world with higher food prices (Conceição and Mendoza 2009; Godfray *et al.* 2010; Hoyos and Medvedev 2009).

8 Agrofuels is an alternative term for biofuels, as defined earlier. This book uses the term biofuels, rather than agrofuels.

9 Agriculture is the basis of industrialization as set out in the Lewis model. The ample availability of food is also important as a crucial pre-condition for industrial development, providing a healthy labour force and inputs for processing, and also ensuring cheap and plentiful food to feed the growing urban population to keep the economic cycle moving. This was the primary blueprint for industrialization for developing countries in the 1950s and 1960s (Lewis 1954).

10 Bioethanol blended with petrol in proportions up to 5 per cent is known as E5, and the same ratio of blending of biodiesel is known as B5.

11 For more information see Brittaine and Lutaladio (2010), available online from FAO at www.fao.org/docrep/012/i1219e/i1219e.pdf. See especially Figure 1 (p. 4), which illustrates the process of first generation biofuels production from primary agricultural commodities.

12 For more information see Kammen *et al.* 2007, available online from OECD at www.oecd-ilibrary.org/transport/energy-and-greenhouse-impacts-of-biofuels_235683015007. See especially Figure 3 for a simplified life cycle analysis of fuels.

13 There are other models like the Forestry and Agricultural Sector Optimization Model known as FASOM, developed at the Texas A&M University for US domestic agriculture and forestry and the Food and Agricultural Policy Research Institute model (FAPRI) which is being used at Iowa State University to simulate international agriculture effects of US biofuel production.

14 For more discussion on the limitations of empirical evidence, internalization processes of the poor, persistent vulnerability, and insecurity, see Sen and Dreze 1989; Appaduri 2004.

15 For an excellent reference to this theme see Nolan 2009.

2 An innovative framework

Many variables have been studied that offer potential explanations for differences in economic performance patterns and livelihoods around the globe. These variables include global trade policies, macroeconomic stability, investment shares of companies, openness to trade, rule of law, religion, geographical position, environment, and infrastructure such as roads and telecommunications (see, for example, Romer 1994; Eicher and Leukert 2009; Sala-i-Martin 1997; Tamura 2006). Almost all of these factors are variables that are influenced by human beings over time, primarily through institutions. Institutions influence the way decisions are made, actions take place, and changes happen. Institutions are in turn affected by their historical origin, the actors' cultural values, the flow of information, and perceptions about the future (Acemoglu *et al.* 2001, 2008; Nunn 2009).

An understanding of how institutional factors determine economic gains is, therefore, important for evaluating their potential impacts on economic outcomes. Technology adoption has various degrees of impact on producers' vulnerabilities, employment, food security, and poverty. Eradicating poverty and hunger requires a comprehensive political–economic understanding of the ways global markets and local government create livelihood opportunities (Gereffi *et al.* 2011). There is then the need to formulate policies, particularly in developing countries, aimed at improving competitiveness and entrepreneurship, including those that address institutional competencies, such as workforce capacity, especially among women and youths, and access to opportunities moving up the global value chain (GVC).

To better understand the relationship between technology adoption and use within the GVC, it is also critical to identify policies and economic incentives that will facilitate adaptation to new technologies, and gain an understanding of information flows to/from producers within local, national, and global level organizations (Lall 2013; Altenburg and Christian 2006).

> The evolution of global-scale industrial organization affects not only the fortunes of firms and the structure of industries, but also how and why countries advance – or fail to advance – in the global economy. Global value chain research and policy work examine the different ways

in which global production and distribution systems are integrated, and the possibilities for firms in developing countries to enhance their position in global markets.

(Gereffi *et al.* 2005)

Information flow creates the incentive structure affecting technology adoption rates and strategies. Very little is understood about how information flows through the GVC affect the incentive structure for the way agents select actions, or choose in other instances a set of actions (e.g., through the utility function) such that it affects economic performance (Schwartz 1999). Whereas North (1990) studied the 'rules of the game' governing interactions among individuals, this book studies the building blocks of those rules. These are the underlying factors affecting the decisions of the individuals themselves, decisions which later shape the interactions and rules of a collective sum, who are engaged and operating within a GVC.

To examine the role of information and knowledge flows as determinants of technology adoption impacts in both a national and global context, a novel conceptual framework is used here, the IFS framework. The IFS framework integrates the properties of different economic structures, characteristics of actors, governance structures, innovation types, and environments and displays their relevance to the specific value chain in focus and the effects of value chain structures on economic outcomes. However, a formal application of the conceptual framework will require additional fieldwork to gather more data than we have collected to develop a proof of concept.

Very little is understood about how various types of information flow through the GVC and how they affect the incentive structure for the way agents select actions to establish or sustain backward and forward linkages, and how these affect economic performance among the weakest links of the chain, namely the smallholders, poor labourers, and local buyer agents. The changes within the political, economic, and environmental context influence each of the agents' attitudes and strategies within the value chain affecting each other's transaction costs. Transaction costs in governing, collaborating, and exchanging information (price, power of law) and resources (products, services) can be understood as magnets in the market that have both positive and negative power to attract institutions both from formal and informal sectors to cooperate, collaborate, and govern the state and the market.

Efforts to reduce transaction costs offer opportunities to innovate institutions and institutional innovations are needed both at the market and state level to create and offer shared prosperity from trades and exchanges. This is a report based on a rapid scoping analysis to develop a broader research agenda, in an effort to help develop a research approach to support the Second Economy Initiative to link maize producing smallholder sectors with the existing maize value chain. This study offers a preliminary analysis of what makes particular South African smallholdings in various settings unique and successful and what factors complicate their success.

2.1 The IFS framework

According to Ostrom (2011: 7):

> Frameworks are the most general forms of theoretical analysis.
> Frameworks identify the elements and general relationships among
> these elements that one needs to consider for institutional analysis and
> they organize diagnostic and prescriptive inquiry. They provide a
> general set of variables that can be used to analyze all types of
> institutional arrangements. Frameworks provide a meta-theoretical
> language that can be used to compare theories.

The conceptual framework introduced here, the IFS, brings together two
distinct approaches, the GVC framework and an institutional analysis and
development framework for sustainable development, into a single
framework for evaluating GVCs.

The IFS incorporates the major types of institutional structural variables
– formal and informal – at the global, national, and regional levels. In a
horizontal analysis and at each level, there are a number of relationship
types between institutions and individuals that influence economic
performance. For example, the global trade policy of a commodity will
influence the investment decision of a system integrator (market leader) in
the value chain. To some extent, such conditional behaviour is generalized
to come up with a meta-theoretical language than can compare alternative
theories about a phenomenon at hand.

After the horizontal analysis, a vertical analysis is conducted by identifying
governance polycentricity. Polycentricity refers to a system of governance in
which authorities from overlapping jurisdictions (or centres of authority)
interact to determine the conditions under which these authorities, as well
as the respective groups within the system, will function. The multi-tier
conceptual map of IFS helps researchers to use the meta-theoretical language
approach to analyse local to global level economic performance. The
analysis is done considering actors – which can be public, private,
community-based, or a hybrid organization – performing functions within a
specialized GVC. Actors in this approach could include those that perform
research and development, distribution, production, consumption, and
transportation in the value chain. As can be seen in Figure 2.1, the analytic
framework, therefore, has three levels. Each level has two dimensions,
vertical and horizontal, which are used to investigate and compare relevant
theories and models.

Figure 2.2 is a stylistic representation of how the world economy is
connected with various economies through the commodity value chains.
These commodity value chains connect people who are embedded in their
socio-economic, political, and geographical context.

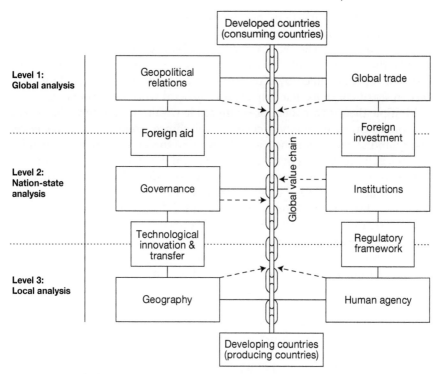

Figure 2.1 Underlying concepts affecting the GVC
Source: Author.

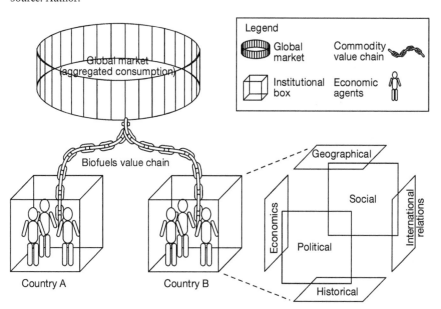

Figure 2.2 Stylistic view of how the GVC connects producers with global markets
Source: Author.

The IFS framework does not select among competing or alternative theories, but provides guidelines for selecting theories relevant to the posed research questions. The IFS framework enables researchers to identify and specify their own set of theories, depending on the research topic. The research topic is guided by a portfolio of underlying theories, following a certain set of concepts that help create a general working hypothesis.

Multiple theories are therefore compatible within this framework, such as economic, game, transaction costs, social choice, common pool resource, and symbolic interaction theories. The types of theories selected help identify the concepts and models that will be used to validate the working hypothesis. Concepts are ways of summing up a set of specific behaviours or qualities observed in a generalized context, while trying to put them into a higher level of abstraction. Models use variables (concept abstraction), and parameters that explain relationships between concepts, to validate a theory and derive precise predictions. Game theory models, agent-based models, experimentation models, and other means are used to explore systematically the relationships between consequences of assumptions on a limited set of outcomes. Multiple types of models can be attuned with most theories (Ostrom 2011).

The IFS framework focuses on how issues related to different governance systems and information flows within the value chain influence selection of technologies, develop value propositions and derive benefits that allow countries to catch up to or fall within the value chain. The IFS framework helps researchers organize multidisciplinary data information, conduct diagnosis on each node of the GVC, and identify capabilities that can be prescriptive to decision-making on issues such as those related to whether to carry on with business as usual or not. The IFS aids in synthesizing knowledge from the empirical study of institutions and analysing the efforts made in the past that influence current decision-making processes. Market and governance hierarchies are often analysed in isolation of each other, whereas in reality there is a symbiotic working relationship between each segment of the market and the governance hierarchies that transact information, including price information, up and down the value chain.

2.2 Understanding concepts used in the IFS framework

The IFS framework can help categorize the influential factors present in the decision-making process and relevant value chain analysis. Horizontal analysis will consider global level interactions that influence the institutional decision-making process, which, in turn, impacts on consumers' decisions. Vertical analysis is a top-down assessment, from global to local actors. The top-down assessment helps identify transaction and opportunity costs that flow down to the bottom of the supply chain.

2.2.1 Level 1: at the global level – the GVC and global trade

'Value Chain' is a generic term for an input–output structure of value adding activities which start with commodity production (e.g., land preparation, crop harvesting) and end with activities such as processing, marketing, and distribution of final products to the buyers. The concept is founded on the work of Gereffi and Korzeniewicz (Gereffi and Korzeniewicz 1994; Gereffi *et al.* 2005). The term GVC emphasizes the geo-political boundaries crossed during the value adding process. A similar concept, the Domestic Value Chain (DVC), then emphasizes the value adding steps conducted within a single country. Figure 2.3 depicts a simple version of a generic GVC and DVC. A common pattern in today's globalized economy is for the initial DVC of primary commodities to occur, often in developing countries, while product consumption can take place in developed countries. This chapter treats the terms value chain, commodity chain, and production chain synonymously.

A convenient device for understanding a particular domain of economic activity through easily identifiable local institutions and networks, as well as those directly connected to global markets, is the drawing of a boundary around industrial clusters and associated global production chains. This approach permits a broader view of cross-sectoral and industry relationships than would be possible using traditional definitions of industries or sectors as it shows the linkages between all components of the GVC. In addition, this approach facilitates a more focused consideration of localized institutions, policies, and relationships, particularly those involving the poor directly, than standard value chain analysis while providing a clear framework for elucidating micro to global relationships and dependencies.

An important objective of the GVC conceptual framework is to attempt to understand how the 'controls' within the production possibility function, which in turn is a product of localized resources, policies, and the trade environment (Wallerstein 1974; Raikes *et al.* 2000; Gibbon 2001). In practice, a GVC is made up of a series of firms, companies, or farms linking producers and consumers across socio-political borders and economic settings. Each of the firms, companies, or farms has specific processes, divisions of labour, and market boundaries (e.g., oil-seed market), denoted

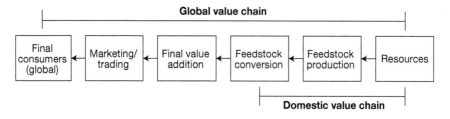

Figure 2.3 Basic linkages in the GVC
Source: Adapted from Habib-Mintz 2009b.

as 'nodes' in the value chain. A commodity chain can be described as 'a set of inter-organisational networks clustered around one commodity or product, in which networks are situational specific, socially constructed and locally integrated' (Gereffi 1994: 2). The GVC is then a tool, rather than a theory, and is aimed at helping policymakers conceptualize and contextualize how resources are redistributed through the nodes of production in a supply chain as it transcends geo-political borders in a modern world.

GVC analysis focuses mainly on input–output structures and geographical coverage. GVCs can be either buyer-driven (e.g., chocolate, coffee, footwear), or producer-driven (e.g., automobiles, medicine). To help understand the GVC it is useful to differentiate between two configurations known in the literature as 'governance' and 'upgrading'. *Governance* applies to vertical coordination of economic activities through inter-firm linkages and financial, material, and human resource allocations. The notion of inter-firm linkages indicates barriers to entry and a degree of coordination within the GVC. At the heart of the governance discussion, there lies a debate, that is yet to be reconciled, on how to incorporate developing countries' producers into the GVC and provide opportunities to improve their livelihoods and social conditions within the conditions of global trade. Nevertheless, primary commodities, such as agriculture, fishing, and forestry are considered part of buyer-driven value chains, since buyers largely control their governance.

The concept of *'upgrading'* is relatively new – focusing on learning that takes place between producers and suppliers. Upgrading is based on the interlinked information relationships, as well as sharing and coordination between components (Gereffi 1999). Although most GVC studies have focused on technological and high-end manufacturing industries (e.g., automobiles), the upgrading concept is observed as a socio-economic mechanism, known as *social capital*, in developing countries. In one study, suppliers leveraged social capital to position themselves as the preferred supplier of low-technology components and, over time, improve their economic and social condition (Dolan *et al.* 1999). Others found that such advantages are contingent on chain membership and the acceptance level imposed by the 'lead firm'.[1] There are exclusions and deprivations if memberships or contracts are not adhered to in practice, an example being labour rights abuse in developing countries. The pressure to cut costs cascades down the supply chain from lead firms, or 'producers without factories'[2] and hurts the poor producers the most (Raikes *et al.* 2000; Nolan *et al.* 2007).

Researchers using the GVC framework have underlined the power of key agents and their capacity to incorporate or exclude less powerful actors. Many of the power-based hypotheses studies in practice view firms as *vertically and horizontally integrated* into the market. The *vertical integration* is the connectivity of productive agencies that add value to the commodities by improving the productive functions of inputs (e.g., technology, design). *Horizontal integration* refers to the inter-linkage between socio-political and economic institutions of the country, where the production or value adding activities are taking place. During the mid- to late-1990s, value chain analysis expanded from the apparel and footwear industries to study low- to mid-level technology-based and manufacturing industries, such as automobiles and auto parts. In the early 2000s, the focus of GVC research shifted to the agricultural sector, particularly export-oriented produce like fresh fruits and vegetables, coffee, cocoa, and so on (Gereffi 1994, 1999; Barnes and Kaplinsky 1999; Schmitz 1999; Fold 2001; Barnes *et al.* 2003; Humphrey 2003; Kaplinsky *et al.* 2010). It became apparent from reviewing voluminous research on the GVC that despite the contribution made to understanding production to consumption pathways in globalized markets, much of the research, in fact, looked only at the top-down value creation process within a supply chain.

For example, Fold (2000), among others, emphasized that a common feature of early discussions on buyer-driven commodity chain analysis of the agro-industrial sector in developing countries, lacked an ability to detect or determine the importance or impact of state regulation and national industrial policies on value chain development. Based on an examination of the necessary policy reforms and the importance of state-governed institutional arrangements within the oil-seed chains in Malaysia and Brazil, Fold showed that the state regulations, especially the use of differential export taxes in both countries, played a pivotal role in balancing the unequal treatments between rich versus poor producers, agents, buyers, and consumers involved in the global trade environment (2000). More research like this will not only highlight the analytical problems using only GVCs as a framework, but also provide policy insight on what works and why.

One of Fold's findings, which is similar to that of many such studies, is that the aggressive nature of modern supply chains has reduced any buffers or tolerance for mistakes. This exacerbates the insecurity and vulnerability of poor producers (Martha and Subbakrishna 2002; Chopra and Sodhi 2004; Lee 2004; Hendricks and Singhal 2005). The developing countries' firms 'face immense difficulties in catching up with the powerful firms that now dominate almost every segment of the supply chain, the invisible part of the "iceberg" that lies hidden from view beneath the water' (Nolan *et al.* 2007: 136). The market liberalization argument against state-led industrial policy does not seem to support the historical evidence of industrialization in current high income and newly developed economies like Japan and Korea (Nolan *et al.* 2007).

Since the end of the 1980s, the world economic system has changed and a new discourse has emerged for globalization, decentralization, and democratization of the marketplace. Many developing countries have liberalized and decentralized their national governance system too quickly. As rightly put by Dicken:

'Openness', then, is the name of the game .... Simply opening up a developing economy on its own will almost certainly lead to further disaster. There is the danger of local businesses being wiped out by more efficient foreign competition before they can get a toehold in the wider world.

(Dicken 2003: 575)

Comparing or replicating the experiences and pathways of one industry with those of other industries, or other countries, despite having similar global market opportunities and conditions is not easy. Furthermore, decision-makers need to obtain a clear understanding of market conditions and the context in which all agents operate in order to define an appropriate policy with which to proceed with market liberalization policies especially in those situations where there is a working market structure which may be led or guided through policies by the state. Why? This is actually part of the cautionary note that indeed once a state-led strategy is eroded it is not easy to recover. Thus, caution is indeed prudent when introducing a market liberalization policy in a country where the market/private sector may not be ready to take on the task of making markets work. This was probably the case in the cotton and coffee sectors in countries in Africa and Latin America where the World Bank introduced market liberalization based on some of the benefits observed from simple value chain analysis observing vertical integration hypotheses. The state-owned and/or parastatal enterprises were demolished, subsidies were cut, and the market was liberalized. In an ideal world one should strive to liberalize markets and have a fluid coordination between public and private sectors, but we do not live in an ideal world or in a perfect market economy. With a clear understanding of a desired state of the world, the lesson learned is that it is important to study the origin, strengths, and weaknesses of the existing national institutional system before undertaking market liberalization policies and running the risk of promising benefits from any changes which may not happen, whether they are market- or state-driven.

GVC analysis is a good starting point and a useful analytical tool for understanding supply-chain operations. Subsequently, though, other conceptual tools are needed to analyse the preconditions, political economy, and governance mechanisms of the national system (centralized or decentralized government) within which certain commodities become attractive and productive prior to their mass introduction to food-insecure, poor farmers in developing countries.

2.2.2   Level 2: at the national level – institutional analysis and embedded political economy

Institutional analysis and development is another overarching framework for de-layering the processes of institutional interactions within a given political economy. It is not the intention here to cover the variety of thoughts or debates, but to focus on some seminal findings and raise issues that are particularly useful for a comparative understanding of information flow and decision-making processes. To achieve this goal, the perspective provided below, based on the notion that *'institutions matter over anything'*, is a 'boiling cauldron of ideas', with more room for theoretical development and conceptual enrichment (Williamson 2000: 610; Rodrik *et al.* 2004).

'Institutions', as Douglass North describes, 'define the rules of the game' of economic life (1990). As such, institutions provide the underpinning standards of a market economy by establishing rules of laws, property rights, enforceable contract laws, information coordination, knowledge management, balancing the demands and power of different social groups, and ensuring opportunities for broader populations by controlling unhealthy and anti-market competitive behaviours (North 1990; Rodrik *et al.* 2004; Acemoglu *et al.* 2006). Along with national institutions, international institutions have significant influence on overall formal institutional standards, legal proceedings, and policies. Such standards are also constructed by informal institutions, such as legitimacy and socially and economically accepted behaviours related to the exchange of productive factors (e.g., land, labour, capital, and technology) and the nature of competition. Behaviours may include peer pressure, social capital allocation, favouritism, and nepotistic and aggressive behaviours.

A national level of analysis has several levels of operations. First, researchers need to draw national schematic representations of the commercial and social environment within which the concerned nation's formal and informal institutions and political economies are 'embedded'[3] before attempting estimation of the effects of policy changes and providing policy advice. The essence of embeddedness, however, remains the same. This involves a change in the way we think about geography and the experience of localness. Despite the overall theoretical criticisms of the embeddedness concept made by Granovetter (1985), Markusen (1999), and Hodgson (1995, 1997) these researchers made an important point; that is, that socio-political embeddedness is fundamental to the modern economic epistemology and policy making. Although this is a slightly different approach to that presented in the mainstream New Institutional Economics (NIE) literature, GVC operations are an integral part of developing countries' economies and, therefore, a framework needs to be able to capture those elements of institutional embeddedness critical for the analysis, especially for understanding institutional arrangements at the national level. The development of efficient institutional arrangements is necessary to prevent factor market failures, which negatively affect the success rates, sustainability conditions, and the extent of welfare distributions from GVC integration among the poor in developing countries (Poulton *et al.* 2004).

Second, national level assessments require a clear understanding of the origins of formal institutions and the capacity and capability of the regulatory frameworks that guide them. To illustrate the analytical observation further, looking at African agricultural market liberalizations, undertaken as a response to structural adjustment programmes in the 1980s, may have raised the availability of intermediary factors, i.e., fertilizer, machinery; however, this came at the cost of widespread currency devaluation and the elimination of subsidies. This resulted in higher prices for inputs and probably contributed to decreased input consumption in agriculture, since three out of four developing countries do not have subsidy structures in place (World Bank 2008a, 2008b). Observing this relational outcome, some argued that this may have led to lower crop quality and yields while the cotton sector could have endured disproportionately high taxation, causing persistent poverty (Dorward *et al.* 1998; Friss-Gensen 2000; Rashid *et al.* 2008). The key feature is not so much *price*, but the observed persistent level of poverty and lack of institutional structure to protect land rights, provide marketing channels and social products like education, health services, and energy sources (Rodrik *et al.* 2004; Bardhan 2006).

Third, attention should be paid to the sources of governance power of regulatory institutions over national natural resources, physical resources, and outputs. Some authors found that the legacy of colonial institutions remains very much active in the bureaucratic system in many of the post-colonial developing countries in Asia, Africa, and Latin America (Acemoglu *et al.* 2001; Engerman and Sokoloff 2002).[4] Along with this, natural resources continue to play an important role as they are only decreasing in quantity, quality, and accessibility due to climate change and other anthropogenic reasons (IPCC 2011, 2012). When considering the productive usage of the natural resources, such as the availability of water, in economic activities, there is no doubt the production capacity will be different and what used to be a comparative advantage perhaps is no longer a valid one. So, in other words, when land availability and the map of rivers flowing through the heart of Bangladesh are looked at, specialization in the agricultural sector appears to be the best decision. However, the nature of specializations changed over time with the emergence of the garment industry. Similarly, desertification and water scarcity affect farming conditions in Tanzania and other sub-Saharan countries (Fischer *et al.* 2007; Howden *et al.* 2007; IPCC 2007). Instead of focusing on agriculture, attention should be moved to other sectors to identify new niches and comparative advantages. However, looking at the post-colonial land maps, colonial land rights policy and nineties market liberalization policies lock decision-makers' views and weaken institutional capacity to break the mould.

Fourth, within the present global context and the diversity of insecurities, it is important to acknowledge the importance of infrastructure status (e.g., the best road conditions, vehicle quality, mobility) and to assess the impact of infrastructure status on productive economic activities (e.g., industry, pottery, farming) and natural resources (e.g., forests, land, air). Any quantitative assessment of the environmental resource impact requires infrastructural analysis to help identify the horizontal connections between each node and, therefore, access to natural and wealth-creating resources.

An example of a context-specific observation of the connection between economic activity, infrastructural connectivity, and natural resources comes from India. In this country, particularly in regions where property rights are insecure, roads are underdeveloped, or there are areas with a lower natural resource base, a relatively lower investment in human capital is made through education and health and, to a lesser degree, agricultural development (Banerjee and Iyer 2005). The lesson learned from these experiences is to examine and define feasible and proper institutional contexts and structures, which in turn define policy and infrastructure modifications, as opposed to 'quick-fixing' a problem with ill-defined policy interventions.

Fifth, institutional analysis on a national scale should consider the role of informal institutions. The ability of informal institutions to act effectively as a collective force in an independent community and to demand improvements in human productivity, rights, economic activities, security, and other fields may be directly or indirectly a response to control and unfair treatment by formal institutions in the country. The literature on this topic is vast, but the general argument has been that informal institutions play an important role in developing countries, especially in the small–medium enterprises. They are often unregistered, operated by family and friends and distributed through local networks of agents and buyers. Much of the operations are performed outside of the structural support and punitive protections generally offered by the regulatory framework of the formal institutions in a country. Moreover, from the informal sectors' perspective, the formal institutional structure can be considered weak and biased toward large enterprise. Low productivity is associated with high chances of corruption or anti-social behaviours. Given this environment, people may opt to engage in negative forms of informal institutions (e.g., gangs) (Olson 1965, 1982; Rapaczynski 1987; North 1990). Furthermore, the consumers are also not too far from the producers, who, producing at a smaller scale, often have limited interest or need for value addition. Lack of need, or opportunity, to add value is connected with low innovation and technology adoption. The producers and consumers connected with the informal economy are often known as the shadow economy, based out of peri-urban and rural areas. This potentially means a weaker institutional environment that could suffer leakage of economic gains and growth potential, and perpetuate continuous and ever-growing inequality among rural or peri-urban producers. Those are the people who are at the bottom of the supply chain for many primary commodities stemming from developing countries and entering the GVC. However, in the absence of formal protections, and if the cycle is not broken, informal institutions continue to protect human rights, improve labour productivity conditions (e.g., easy knowledge transfer), have a fair income distribution system, and be better able to protect their environment (Hall and Jones 1999; Dietz *et al.* 2008).[5]

In sum, what influences interdependent and interconnected institutions at the national and local levels is a critical question that does not have any clear path or development strategy solution. Therefore, any industry-specific questions, regarding the extent to which a specific type of technology adoption will affect food security and poverty, will likely require context-specific baseline knowledge on institutional embeddedness. This, in turn, entails incorporating the national and natural, geographical, and regulatory frameworks of both formal and informal institutions and their members. In this context, clearly defining what kinds of information and content of communication influence people's choices is critical to understanding how to improve the GVC.

The IFS is not complete without a thorough understanding of the localized decision-making processes of its members.

2.2.3 Level 3: at the local level – firms, resources, and power

This subsection discusses possible linkages between three existing themes explored in the literature. These include examining decision-making for firms and whether it is resource-based or power oriented in practice. Examining these three themes will help better understand how decision-making takes place within an asymmetric information environment, which may be a common situation in developing countries.

A decision-maker, whether a human or a firm, has a complex set of goals that are related to many facets of the respective life cycle. Sometimes, decision-makers are not aware or are unable to evaluate a full set of goals, given an asymmetric information environment. Decision-makers, therefore, often depend on heuristics or observed trends to minimize the risk arising from bad decisions. To better define decision-making, knowledge about the decision-makers is therefore critical. The decision-maker's position in society, the economy, and the policy making environment may conflict with their personal gain and security. This, in turn, may reduce the effectiveness of any effort by either the state or the market to improve the outcomes arising from this group's decisions. So far, the application of localized knowledge to decision-making processes has received insufficient attention from researchers, and has been largely overlooked by policy makers. Options are proposed to overcome these limitations in the social sciences field.

First, understanding *firms' positions in the market* is critical. Firms, as the first factor-level of analysis, are a function of resources, namely, human, land, capital, and technology. Resources in the firm need to be managed properly in order to improve internal organizational strength to maintain competitive advantage, seek opportunities, identify threats, and manage knowledge. A firm, as a collective decision-maker, not only provides an efficient governance structure for GVC management by reducing transaction costs, but also for the institutionalization of knowledge that is either created, learned, or otherwise obtained (Madhok 2002). Transaction costs are a function of all activities involved in organizing production and exchange operations, and managing opportunities and threats, as informed by price and other information (Coase 1937).

Second, it is important to identify *the sources of influence* within the value chain. Firms are represented by private companies at all levels of the value chain. Firms engage in value creation activities and can transfer costs and information that may influence other firms' decision-making processes. The GVC literature identifies different types of firms including large firms that can alter their means of resource coordination to act as system integrators. Large firms, due to their size, become a source of hierarchical authority and affect prices and resource allocation in markets and, thus, substantially influence the outcomes for people operating at the end of the supply chain. For example, a large food firm such as Tesco can dictate healthy food standards through private contracts along the value chain, which can influence the decision-making of agricultural suppliers, and hence farmers, with regard to the use of inputs such as seeds.

Third, it is important to critically examine *the levels of success achieved by decision-makers with respect to competitiveness and value creation*, given the heterogeneity of decision-makers' resources and the mobility of those resources. For example, some resources such as land are not time-specific, but are institutional structure-specific. Land is needed, not only during the planting season, and land rights are determined by the land regulating institutions. Resource-base analysis is useful for this level of assessment[6] which is primarily a business tool to identify the accessibility of strategic resources that a firm needs to be competitive. To maintain competitiveness, heterogeneous resource accessibility provides the best result (Kogut and Zander 1992; Ghoshal and Moran 1996). A firm or a human being, as a social, political, and economic decision-making agent, needs to have both capacity and capability to access and appropriate heterogeneous resources.

Fourth, accessibility and capability to appropriate various resources are important concepts needed to understand how the decision-making process takes place within a given context. Schumpeter, a major figure of this perspective, shared the same viewpoint in 1954 in the *History of Economic Analysis*:

> [e]conomic analysis deals with the questions how people behave at any time and what the economic effects are they produce by so behaving; economic sociology deals with the question how they came to behave as they do. If we define human behavior widely enough so that it includes not only actions and motives and propensities but also the social institutions that are relevant to economic behavior such as government, property inheritance, contract, and so on, that phrase really tells us all we need.
>
> (Schumpeter 1954)

Finally, *political power* is another factor that influences the individual decision-making process. Political power usually implies taking advantage of *information asymmetry*, which forces humans to make choices constantly or to be faced with alternative choices to solve problems (Simon and Newell 1972; Mantzavinos 2001).[7] Political power strives to increase an agent's utility by delving into a problem-solving mental map. This process differs from orthodox rational choice theory, where the decision is based on 'the terms of payoffs, the expected payoff, the subjective expected payoff, or some such criterion' (Carruthers 2002). Payoffs are also factors in structural theory, which refers to the powers of significance, legitimization, and domination within the domain of political, legal, and economic institutions of the society that constitute the social value of modernization (Giddens 1984, 1990; Arts and Tatenhove 2004).

A thorough understanding of the critical dynamism of behaviour is important for understanding the logic of surplus production and the redistribution of income, as well as other social maladies within the value chain such as corruption and nepotism (Putterman 1995; Murphy 2002; Kadigi *et al.* 2007). The exertion of power occurs through the mediation of social interests and interactions, which in turn are based on individual and common choice aspects (Khan 2005). *Social networks* and social capital, although their definitions are still undergoing refinements, are particularly useful to follow how the notion of 'power' can explain the social inclusion and exclusion of individuals and groups taking advantage of, for example, expansion in a specific market.[8] As Arts and Tatenhove said, 'Power is always constituted and exerted in social relationships' (2004). Therefore, research in this area must consider the peculiar mixture of informal values and behaviours within formal institutions (i.e., the governments), in the value chain.

Within the decision-making perspective, decision-makers, or their followers, are seen as dynamic agents of choice. These agents may have dual utilities: first, a sense of self-interest and, second, a common pursuit of benefits. This is a paradox for economists because, although self-interest relates to utilitarian concepts, common pursuits rely on *moral* economics, where people might prefer to cooperate at levels beyond their own self-interest (Sen 1977). In the context of power analysis, it is also important to assess *how* power can be challenged (Sen 2005). In developing countries, it is often done through collective protest, but the process of achieving a collective consensus can be very slow. The results of a slow consensus development process may be the deterioration of public goods and human welfare. The nature of informalization and the relative power practice observed in agricultural sectors in developing countries are different to that explained by conventional power theory.[9]

2.3　Limitations of the IFS framework

The IFS framework is methodologically flexible and open to alternative approaches. It allows researchers to formulate an integrated approach, which can be suitably applied to the unique constraints found in different countries of study. Yet, due to these same characteristics, the IFS framework can be a challenge during data analysis if the researcher is not aware of existing analytical limitations. Five of these limitations are now described.

Individual people can become invisible. The framework dissects the GVC and identifies clusters of people operating within the segments of activities. The danger is that the IFS analysis can be a mechanical and quantitative cataloguing exercise. Quantification certainly feeds into the current vogue for data-driven, evidence-based research.

'Context specificity' is core to the analysis. Determining relevancy/irrelevancy in a particular context can be very subjective. It may seem superficially straightforward but, during application, the researcher must be mindful about the scope of the context. For example, there are differences between owning land and renting land for cultivation. There are theories and models to predict how ownership influences the production behaviour of farmers. To generalize land ownership patterns in a farming community that is taking part in the GVC, the researcher would need to draw a boundary based on certain predefined conditions stemming from the broad research question, although it may violate the principle of avoiding 'sampling bias' in quantitative work.

Related to this point, 'self-selection bias' can also be an issue. Group research depends on a survey-based approach, which observes open participant practice. In this case, participants' decisions to take part may be correlated with traits that affect the study, making the participants a non-representative sample. For example, questions about assets like land, which may seem straightforward, could have tax implications for participants if they are avoiding tax or government reporting. It would not be surprising, in that case, if the participants were to withhold information about the area of land owned and, thereby, cause underestimation. Depending on the research question, this data may mean a lot or nothing to the outcome of the research. An extensive data triangulation method needs to be in place to overcome such sampling bias.

'Power' is a highly debated topic in social science disciplines. The balance of power between parties can have psychological, sociological, political, and/or economic outcomes. Yet, power is very hard to detect and measure. There are many research tools available to study power. For example, net-mapping could be used to reveal the node of a 'power-house' within a defined structure, but it is very hard to measure the density of power or multiple access points to that power. Also, the flow of power and its internalization depend on the individual's power within the network.

While there is an attempt within the IFS framework to assess vulnerability through the assessment of shocks and trends, the possibility exists of having a great deal of unpredictability around these estimates as well as uncertainty, especially at the macro-scale. This has become all too clear following the food price hike of 2008/2009 and its global ramifications. Such shocks have had massive impacts at the household level, including abandonment of land

and migration, political unrest, and riots, but have been impossible to predict, except on relatively short timescales. As a result of the above-mentioned limitations, the IFS study can be complex and time consuming if researchers do not pay attention to the underlying theories and research methodologies of the framework.

2.4   Operationalization of the IFS and the analytic process

There is no framework that is without limitations. It is prudent for any researcher to know the limitations first before diving in. The purpose of the IFS is not to claim it as a panacea, but to utilize the strengths as complimentary support to compensate for the weaknesses of policy informing frameworks such as LCA. Research on the governance of technology implementations intends to answer concerns related to a specific context; however, given the key research question, there are limits to the investigation of the case study that follows. For policy designers, certain policies are assumed as given and the focus is, instead, more on policy redesign at the national level than adoption at the local level. For policy implementers, the regional and local levels are most relevant to categorize as key influencers. For areas of agricultural farming practice, the choices of local producers are crucial to identify the role of the exogenous factors over the decision-making process. Three exogenous factors influence every decision-making process within a context: (a) the biophysical and geographical conditions; (b) human agency, which is influenced by education, social status, and cultural values; and (c) the political economy and legacy that characterize governance structures and give legitimacy and, hence, efficacy to its rules.

2.4.1   Context specification and case study justification

The selection of an appropriate case study is critical to operationalize the research framework. The case under study needs to be justified as generalizable to the wider context of the global economy. The selection of the case considered in this study was driven by a set of core specifications: a globally traded commodity, operating in a set of producing countries, competing in the same market, and in the presence of a systems integrator or lead firm. The steps taken to ensure that the case study fits the IFS specification criteria are listed below.

Step 1: identify the core research questions driving the case study country selection process

Some examples of questions:

- What are the key innovations, regulatory and institutional policies, and market failures that promoted the biofuels?

- Why have science, technology, and innovation not contributed more to economic development in the specific country and/or region in Africa?
- What is the impact of government regulatory and innovation policies on agricultural productivity for different types of crop value chains (e.g., insect resistant versus conventional cotton) on smallholders?
- What is the impact of different levels of integration for the palm oil value chain? Is regulatory rationalization necessary and sufficient to promote innovation?
- What are the market failures and bottlenecks; in particular, what and how does information and knowledge flow to and from producers across the value chain and across the different cotton value chain components?
- What alternatives or barriers can be identified so that cotton markets can become more accessible to the poor?

Step 2: global context clarification

Some developing countries, driven by growing global demand for biofuels and the desire to improve producer income and livelihoods, have actively pursued the cultivation of feedstocks of biofuels. The commercialization of biofuels feedstock has required sustained investment as well as an enabled economic environment conducive to innovation and technology deployment. Under such conditions, countries like Brazil, India, and China have embraced biofuels crops and have a large share of smallholder producers. These three countries have successfully captured a large portion of the global biofuels feedstock market.

Step 3: global commodity selection justification

Insect resistant (Bt) cotton is gaining popularity among cotton producers, including smallholders, due to two potentially beneficial impacts. First, Bt cotton may reduce yield damage caused by specific insects as it incorporates a protein toxic to targeted insects and, thus, increases production. Second, Bt cotton technology can reduce the number of pesticide applications necessary to control target pests and, thus, lower production costs. The benefits for farmers of using Bt cotton technology may include a higher net income and improved purchasing power (Elbehri and Macdonald 2004; Tschirley *et al.* 2009; ISAAA 2011; Kathagel and Qaim 2014).

Step 4: country context specification

The successful adoption of Bt cotton in developing countries is linked to the institutional framework where adoption occurs. Institutional factors such as access to credit and complementary inputs, technical information, regulatory and seed system policies that foster innovation, and knowledge flows, have all been listed in the literature as important determinants of cotton farmers' abilities to capture benefit from adopting Bt cotton in developing countries (Falck-Zepeda *et al.* 2009; Fischer *et al.* 2015). Gaining an understanding of how institutional factors determine economic gains is, thus, important for evaluating their impact on potential adoption outcomes. Technology adoption may have an impact on producers' vulnerabilities, employment, food security, and poverty. Eradicating poverty and hunger requires a comprehensive political–economic understanding of the ways global markets and local governments create livelihood opportunities (Gereffi *et al.* 2011). A study examining insect resistant (Bt) cotton adoption would need to address institutional competencies, workforce capacity – especially among women and youth, competitiveness, entrepreneurship, and accessibility to economic opportunities from the GVC.

2.4.2   *Value chain and institutional arrangement mapping*

To conduct a multidisciplinary analysis based on IFS, the GVC can be broken into four segments (labelled A, B, C, and D). Figure 2.4 derives the nodes of the GVC and then splices them, based on vertical and horizontal integration. While on the vertical alignment producers and intermediary agencies to consumers are included, on the horizontal axis lies the institutional apparatus from all levels influencing agents' decision-making processes. It is important to note that the companies studied engage in intermediary actions, with smallholders as their business models. Producers and intermediary agents (A and B) are considered to be on the *supply side,* whereas consumers are on the *demand side.* A questionnaire and other methodological tools can be developed based on the positioning of the nodes.

Interview guides specific to each segment and cluster analysis can be applied for comparative assessments. Interviews can be targeted to selected groups within each node for each country engaged in exporting, processing, or distribution of a *commodity* by a company or agent. Companies or agents can be selected on the basis of their market status (e.g., net investment, net worth), competitive strategies (e.g., business models, middle-tier operations), claimed benefits, and ability to foster relationships with the input suppliers. The latter may be identified in preliminary literature and news media research. Gains and losses can be identified in order to capture the vertical and horizontal circumstances of agents involved in the commodity supply chain (such as contract farmers or labourers on estate farms). Companies or agents selected at each level of the value chain depended on the analyst's decision and resource availability. Measures used include the opportunity costs of giving up land, labour, and other resources (e.g., government-discounted fertilizers) for commodity production versus continuing with pre-existing cash and food crop production.

To internalize their situation and decision-making process, attention is given to the local geography, access to productive factors like land, irrigation, fertilizers, and extended services, and the level of food security among a selected population.

To examine the income potential of *primary commodity* cultivation, the nature of competition and off-farm income opportunities need to be studied. The producer selection criteria are based on two hypotheses: (a) in an extremely impoverished agricultural economy (both at the local and national level) there is a high degree of desperation to receive outside involvement and (b) higher competition among farmers can contribute to faster integration with the emerging supply chain. Variations in these dimensions between countries would be particularly useful to contextualize differences in market emergence rates. The above discussion can be expressed in Figure 2.4, which shows the linkages (darker arrows) and the clusters of groups that can be analysed in each case study to conceptualize IFS. There are four clusters: (a) smallholders, (b) national companies, (c) global commodity traders (e.g., shipping and processing) and consumers, and (d) global-to-local-level institutional systems, which influence the behaviour of each of the clusters.

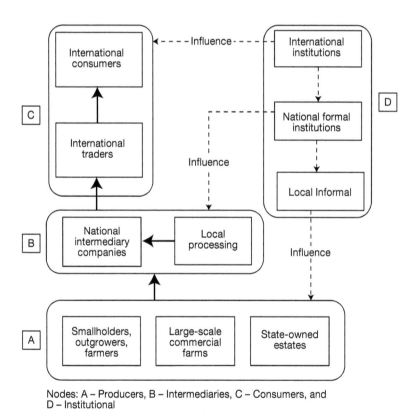

Nodes: A – Producers, B – Intermediaries, C – Consumers, and D – Institutional

Figure 2.4 Major nodes followed during fieldwork
Source: Author.

Finally, the most important factor in the research planning is contextualizing the type, characteristics, and governance of poverty within the agricultural system under threat of global economic system collapse in 2008. Vertical supply-chain developments are analysed within institutional units, which are, as Dietz *et al.* made the case for, 'complex, redundant, and layered institutions', with a mix of institutional types to facilitate communication, experimentation, and the adaptation of conservation or conversion of natural resources like land, forests, and water for economic development (Dietz *et al.* 2008). Different economic groups face different levels of accessibility and dependency on natural resources. For example, it may be comparatively easy for close, neat, small, territorially attached, and relatively homogeneous subsistence farmer communities to form a collective decision about consumption and the conservation of available natural resources. However, they may find it difficult to resist external threats or persuasions when the community as a whole is deeply economically impoverished, environmentally vulnerable, politically underrepresented, and subjected to long-standing urban migration. Hence, to follow up Dietz *et al.*'s struggles of the commons, the IFS framework is used to dissect the layers of institution embeddedness.

2.4.3   *Methods of data collection and categorization*

Decision-making processes and the flow of information about value, price, and practice, can both increase or decrease organizational adaptability. The adoption of technology depends on actor choices, especially in three interrelated decision areas, where polycentric governance overlaps the jurisdictions in a given context. More precisely, an analysis of governance requires data at three levels of operation:

- *At the local level:* why farmers decide to adopt a particular technology or practice.
- *At the national level:* what the policy makers are responsible for during implementation and monitoring of adopters' compliance within a restriction or incentive structure.
- *At the global level:* how the global policy makers define concrete restrictions and communicate to influence investment and value, and send market signals to countries participating in the value chain.

In terms of data collection the primary objective is to help with the decision-making processes. This involves data mining at these three levels which are further influenced by three exogenous factors: the biophysical condition, human agency, and the political economy and legacy that characterize the effectiveness of the governance structure.

Data inquiry guideline

Given the challenges of measuring these complex factors to operationalize IFS, the following research domain and questions are provided as a guideline to come up with more context-specific questionnaires.

The value chain specific questions driving the case studies fall into two main categories: demand side and supply side.

- Demand side:
  - What are the main reasons for growth in the specific commodity or technology demand in developed countries?
  - What are the main functions of the relevant and respective emerging markets and who are the most important actors?
  - To what extent have developing countries entered the global commodity market?
  - Do producing countries give differential preferences to buyer countries?
  - As a buyers' market, what is the nature of contracts between large buyers or agents?
  - What is the extent and nature of public infrastructure (e.g., roads, gas pumps)?
  - What is the extent and nature of supply coordination?
  - How much room is there for geopolitics to influence supplier linkages?
  - What are the relationships between the investor countries and their investors operating in developing countries to fulfil their output targets?
- Supply side:
  - To what extent can different developing countries' consumers contribute to total demand for specific commodities and to the technologies utilization market?
  - On what basis do countries choose to enter into relevant and respective markets as suppliers?
  - What is the extent of interlinked contracts between companies and producers at the bottom of the supply chain?
  - What are the access patterns for the utilization of agricultural extension services for food crop and cash crop production?
  - What are the access patterns for the utilization of agricultural factors of production, like land, labour, and fertilizer?
  - What kinds of farmer organizations or unions exist to balance power between farmers and intermediary agents?
  - To what extent is the production function influenced by pre-existing sluggish local agricultural conditions?
  - What are the trade-offs between non-food crops and food stocks?

Table 2.1 Research domain, guiding questions, and data sources

Research domain and guiding questions	Type of questions	Data sources
Theoretical and practical basis		
How was the programme planned and developed to institutionalize a global policy plan and apply it in the national apparatus?	Documenting	Open-ended interviews, programme planning documents, meeting minutes, legislative materials, public interest and advocacy group reports.
Which goals is the programme designed to meet? Are they feasible?	Documenting and assessing	
Who are the stakeholders involved in the programme design, implementation, and assessment phases?	Documenting and assessing	
How are the programme's prescribed policies, procedures, activities, and services designed to advance the general and specific goals?	Documenting and assessing	
What is the design for a targeted population and administrative system? Is it feasible?	Documenting and assessing	
What are the theoretical foundations and practical bases connecting the programme to its goals? Are they sound? If not, how and why? How many programme designs have been improved to help achieve the goal?	Explaining	

Resource requirements and capacity

What types of resources are required (human, capital, natural), and who sets their benchmarks?	Documenting	Open-ended interview and focus group with state and local-level administration, other agency-relevant staff, management reports, and structured observations.
What are the origins of the programme resources?	Documenting	
Given its budget and available and expected resources (skilled workforce), are the programme resource requirements likely to be met? If not, how and why?	Assessing and explaining	

Decision-making environment

What are the demographic, social, cultural, political, and economic environments in which production operates?	Documenting	Open-ended interview and focus group with state and local-level administration, other agency-relevant staff, management reports, structured observations, and human development indicators.
In which ways has the decision environment affected its implementation, operations, and results?	Explaining	
In which ways have variations in the programme's local environment led to variations in the programme's design and/or operations? What implications do these variations have for the programme's goals and output targets?	Documenting and explaining	

Source: Adapted from Werner 2004.

Creating a conceptual institutional framework and process map is recommended. These can be based on a literature review or a rapid assessment examining the political context within which policy formulation and execution occurs. To identify the nodes in the policy information flow, the national policy making and implementation structure is generalized and categorized. As shown in Figure 2.5, the institutional governance structure is drawn to reveal how the horizontal case study specification can be achieved. Policies may follow a similar supply-chain mechanism, although, instead of cascading costs down from the top, the supply chain of policy cascades down commands from the system integrators. This results in a movement of the global sphere to national government levels and all the way down to the village leaders. Decentralization in an institutional framework can be a significant consideration and thus will need to be assessed. As the IFS framework is laid out, the political power dynamism between the central and local government within the national institutions system influences industry development patterns and the resource access pathways of the supply-chain participating agents.

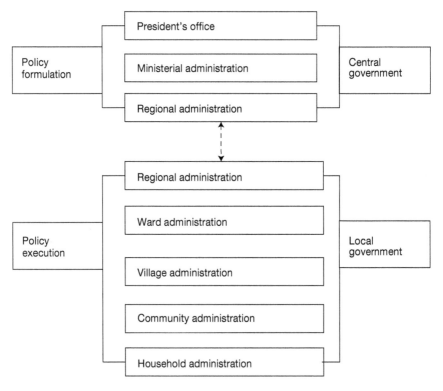

Figure 2.5 Conceptual national institutional framework (assuming decentralized government)

Source: Author.

2.4.4 *Using mixed methods for data collection*

Because scientific knowledge is cumulative, qualitative, and participatory, research that includes explanatory and descriptive studies can be as important as quantitative studies that mostly consider hypotheses-testing investigations. With its exploratory/descriptive focus, fieldwork-based qualitative and participatory research analysis is more likely to contribute to the development of scientific knowledge by discovering situations or conditions beyond the scope of a tested hypothesis. In this sense quantitative and qualitative research analyses complement each other. A combination of quantitative and qualitative fieldwork is a suitable form of research when the available information is complex, yet inadequate. The existing literature helps guide and inform the research. Furthermore, because policy implementation research is not locked only into testing a set of previously specified hypotheses, it can adjust its focus as data is gathered and grouped through carefully sequenced quantitative and qualitative research approaches.

A mixed model method enables researchers to combine qualitative/participatory and quantitative approaches, which can provide a contextual basis for analysing data and other evidence. In some cases, careful applications of qualitative and quantitative research may help widen the scope of such research and enhance the capacity of testing hypotheses on larger, and perhaps statistically representative, samples or cases. A research design applying mixed methods provides enough flexibility to allow addressing different conceptual and model paradigms without any *a priori* design limitations. The paradigm mixing flexibility further allows the implementation of a pragmatic research approach that can address the limitations of both quantitative and qualitative/participatory methods. This is important for policy analysis and policy innovation. Table 2.2 illustrates a potential portfolio of research methods that may be used in GVC research.

Although this approach adds complexity to the research design, the advantages of both the qualitative and quantitative paradigms can be used. Moreover, the overall research design perhaps best reflects the research process itself, working back and forth between inductive and deductive models of thinking (Creswell 1994).

A combination of these techniques can improve the quality of the mixed-method fieldwork research approach and outcome. Emerging fields, such as agriculture innovation governance system analysis, often suffer from a lack of data and data validation opportunities. The field research approach is useful to identify primary data sources, and interact with them to collect further data. The collected data from field research can be qualitative and quantitative. For example, to analyse institutional capacity to appropriately adopt and diffuse a modern technology like biofuels crops, the IFS required field research to gather both kinds of data.

Table 2.2 Research scales, methods, rationales, and sources

Scale of analysis	Method	Data	Rationale	Information sources
Global level	Policy review and trend analysis	Qualitative and quantitative	Aim to map rapidly to key concepts underpinning a research area and the main sources and types of evidence available. Can be undertaken as a stand-alone project, especially where an area is complex or has not been reviewed comprehensively before (Mays et al. 2001).	Literature Academic Organizational Commercial Media Major buyers' reports
National level	In-depth interviews and net-mapping	Qualitative and quantitative	In-depth qualitative interviews are flexible and exploratory interviews, in which the researcher, to seek clarity and expansion, adjusts questions later depending on how the interviewee answers previous questions. The interview style is unstructured and conversational, and the questions asked are generally open-ended and designed to elicit detailed, concrete stories about the subject's experiences.	Organizational interview Funding organizations Research and development bodies Relevant ministries Relevant departments Relevant non-governmental organizations (like seed traders)
Local level	Small group discussions, field surveys, expert consultations and net-mapping and other types of participatory fieldwork approaches	Qualitative and quantitative	A series of group discussions conducted by a variety of individuals with the aim of collecting data and recording group beliefs, reactions, and norms in respect to a particular topic or set of issues. Rather than proceeding by question-and-answer, a focus group is useful for identifying social values, norms, and capacity to change. Often, institution-building and policy research overlook social dynamics within which the institution will operate and be held accountable (Bloor and Wood 2006).	Stakeholders to comply Agricultural commodity trade associations Farmers' associations Extension officers Rural marketing boards Non-profit organizations Farming labourers

Source: Author.

Notes

1 Lead firm refers to groups who control certain functions that allow them to dictate the terms of participation of actors in other functional positions within the value chain. This term often refers to firms that enjoy the greatest market share and, hence, wield lead-firm buying power. Lead firms can also be opinion-leaders for customer groups, such as the coffee value chain experience (Ponte 2002; Nolan *et al.* 2007).

2 Those are the firms that use their brand names to subordinate producers and farmers in developing countries who earn the lowest wages in the GVC, and are the key agents controlling major production decisions on design, quality, marketing, etc.

3 Although, Polanyi's 1947 seminal work, *The Great Transformation*, established the word 'embeddedness', in economics, he actually argued the other way around; that is, when economic actions are 'disembedded', meaning not governed by social or non-economic norms, they become destructive. Polanyi viewed capitalism as anti-societal; whereby, instead of the social system, the economic system controls social relationships (1947). While some have regarded this as a complete theory, others see it as a starting point. This theory has been further developed by the works of later scholars of New Institutional Economics (NIE) North and Thomas (1973) and Granovetter (1985). In sum, Polanyi concludes, the economy needs to be 're-embedded' and socio-political control over the economy should be re-established for progress. For a review of this concept see Hess 2004 and for critical reviews of this theory see Granovetter 1985; Markusen 1999.

4 The institutional role in economic development is a hugely debated topic. For more details see Rodrik *et al.* 2004. Although these studies have significantly influenced the discourse, there is considerable uncertainty about the quality of data analysed in their quantitative research. This suggests that there might be some limitations to consider when using these studies for ultimate correlation. For a more detailed discussion, see Rodrik 2004; Bardhan 2005a, 2005b.

5 Dietz *et al.* (2008) found that informal institutions that have, for centuries, protected local environments are now facing grave challenges in the wake of the rapid commercialization of natural resources and cross-border pollution, tropical deforestations, desertification, and climate change over which they have negligible control.

6 Resource-based analysis techniques were extensively developed in the 1980s, but the roots of this concept can be found in the works of Coase, North, Penrose, and Williamson, who have emphasized the importance of access to resources and its implication for firms' competitiveness.

7 This view is different from rational choice theory, which underlines most mainstream business management studies done from a capitalist perspective. Gifford (2003), in the book review, highlighted the excessive affinity for the Hayekian framework, which views humans as rule-following and cognition bounded by classification systems. The simplest version of rational choice theory suggests that an economic agent makes choices or decisions under certainty; that is, an agent has all the information needed to perform a well-defined utility function and to maximize utility from all the alternatives. For criticisms on rational choice theory see Sen 1977, 1979; Mantzavinos *et al.* 2004; for a conservative criticism of the rational model see Manski 2000.

8 Habib-Mintz (2009a), based on an extensive literature review on the informal economy and the usefulness of the social capital concept to contextualize the differentiated roles of an informal economy within the broader scope of developing economies, argued that the concept still needs further development,

due to the dynamic nature of the informal economy requiring a dynamic research approach. For more detail see Habib-Mintz 2009.

9 Power, from the perspective of Western-based management studies, lies in the hands of a democratically elected government and the capitalist market that responds to consumer demand. There is a distinct difference between formal and informal rules that exert power over resources: land, labour, and capital. Moreover, and unfortunately, there are no comprehensive survey or data sources available to conduct any assessment of power observed within the agro-industrial value chain. For more, see Hurst 2007.

3   Biofuels, biodiesel, and
     regulations

This chapter presents the intersection between global biofuels initiatives as a fossil fuels substitute in the transportation sector and its relationship with agricultural sector modernization in developing countries. Subsequently, relationships are drawn between food security, the energy market, and economic development strategies. The focus therefore moves from large producers primarily selling in international markets, to medium size companies in developing countries and smallholder producers who are contracted to produce biofuels feedstock. In terms of consumption, the focus is largely on the Western consumers who buy mixed fuels from gas stations and not on the villagers who use biodiesel for small-scale energy generation. This is because the aim is to investigate to what extent the economies of scale and comparative advantages are useful notions when investigating the value proposition of biofuels feedstock production joining the GVC and earning foreign income.

Moreover, large producers invest substantial financial and political capital in agricultural technologies and supply-chain development. Such investors' biofuels supply chains may operate in a single country or may be global apparatuses. As the IFS theory suggests, it is considered that the formal economy on the one hand where government policies largely determine the destination, scope and governance structure of the supply chain and use the informal economy on the other hand, especially at the bottom of the supply chain where smallholder producers are largely outside of the regulatory framework. For example, government subsidies make biofuels feedstock production profitable for EU and US farmers up to a point, but then, to fill the tanks of a growing number of customers, the countries need to outsource biodiesel or the feedstock production. In the countries from where the feedstock is then sourced the farmers at the bottom of the supply chain do not enjoy any subsidies. As a result the economic benefits are realized vastly differently between the participants in the GVC.

Feedstock represents 70 per cent of the cost of contemporary biofuels production, which, as discussed later, is the major bottleneck of the growing biofuels sector (UNCTAD 2009; UNEP 2009b). Achieving economies of scale in feedstock production is critical for market competitiveness. The land area under biofuels feedstock cultivation has increased significantly around the world, taking over hundreds of millions of hectares of arable land for large-scale biofuels projects, thereby putting pressure on already stressed agricultural markets. To reduce pressures from arable land, companies are targeting native customary rights (NCR) lands,[1] which have limited legal protection. To make them commercially viable contract farming or outgrower schemes[2] are most often applied. Some argue that contract farming is an outcome of decentralization and market liberalization, where larger producers control the marketing, price, collection, and processing system (Arndt *et al.* 2008). Others look at outgrower scheme contributions to help smallholders configure production, marketing, and distribution networks to reach the buyers (Arndt *et al.* 2008; Ellis and Freeman 2004; ICRISAT 2007; Woods 2006). Whichever perspective is true, outgrower schemes are fundamental building blocks in agricultural GVCs. Biofuels feedstocks like maize, sugarcane, sorghums, and jatropha are emerging as dominant feedstocks to be planted worldwide via outgrower schemes, reaching the poorest communities. Outgrower scheme experience provides an interesting case study topic to understand the socio-political context of biofuels feedstock industry expansion in the poorest communities in developing countries, occupying potentially underused, commercially viable, but legally unprotected, community land.

Clear analysis is difficult because of widely differing landholding schemes in national, regional, and local policies on used, unused, and protected land. This research focuses on developing countries as non-food crop-based, first generation, biodiesel feedstock producers for the transportation biofuels market. The major rationale is the fact that food-crop-based biofuels feedstock has already received considerable global attention, which has slowed the conversion of food crops to biofuels and, instead, promotional efforts are being put in place for non-edible feedstocks like jatropha, *Moringa*, and so on, which are commercially unproven, environmentally untested crops. To understand why the food versus fuel debate emerged, it is important to consider the direct and indirect consequences of commercial, non-edible feedstock production in poor agricultural economies.

This chapter is organized as follows. First, the chapter discusses a brief history of biofuels development; the discussion then presents the current status of the biofuels market and provides forecasts for the market. These provide a useful context to rationalize why countries are interested in taking part in the biofuels GVC. The second subsection sheds light on the global biofuels value chain development, without reinventing the debate over 'food and fuel', but instead highlighting the conflicted relationship between the global system for supporting the agribusiness development and the food security situation in developing countries. Next, the chapter discusses jatropha – the non-edible feedstock which is the case study commodity for this research. Finally, this chapter concludes by highlighting building blocks useful for further analyses, the discussion of which is then taken up in the rest of the chapters.

3.1 Biofuels market development

This section reviews the market development timeline for first generation biofuels bioethanol and biodiesel.[3] Following the timeline of biofuels technology development will reveal that from the very beginning the biofuels market has had an inverse relationship with the fossil fuel market. As was shown in Figure 1.1, the early inception of biofuels started when oil was rare, but with the accessibility of cheap fossil fuel the technological innovation was phased out. In recent years, as the threats of 'peak oil' started to escalate, human civilization met globalization at the crossroads; as anthropogenic contribution to climate change became undeniable, biofuels technology came back off the shelf. Unfortunately, the technology is still at the first generation level. This research focuses on first generation biofuels and this section, specifically, provides understanding on the evolution of the first generation biofuels markets, trends, and the need for crop variety. This will help contextualize the effects of biofuels in developing countries in the following subsection and also in the case studies.

3.1.1 Historical biofuels market development

As is common in the history of industry, the biofuels industry has gone through ups and down following political–economic decisions. In the 1900 World's Fair, Rudolf Diesel showcased a peanut oil run compression engine. The first biodiesel produced was peanut based because in Europe the ingredient was supplied cheaply by the colonies in Africa (Knothe 2001). In 1908, Henry Ford commercially produced a Model T car which could run on both bioethanol and biodiesel. Income from biofuel tax played an important role in World War I (WWI) and World War II (WWII) funding schemes. During the WWI years of 1917–1919, the US produced 60 million gallons of ethanol, which increased to 600 million gallons in the WWII years[4] (Songstad *et al.* 2009). But the demand for biofuels in the automobile industry died shortly afterwards as the gasoline run engines started to dictate consumer choice, oil explorers offered lower prices per unit and eventually convinced the state to roll back biofuels industry support. Despite investor interest and scientific progression, the biofuels market opportunities in the West started to diminish. The political economy of the oil market post-WWII dictated why biofuels innovation, that had started hundreds of years previously, died prematurely in the West.

While the US and European biofuels markets declined with the emergence of cheap fossil fuels in the mid-1900s, developing countries found opportunities for biofuels in their transportation sectors. Argentina imported the first diesel engine and Gutierrez tested castor oil as an alternative source in 1916 (Shay 1993). A literature review prepared by Knothe in 2001 for the United States Department of Agriculture (USDA) National Center for Agricultural Utilization Research stated that, during WWII, Brazil had prohibited the export of cotton seed oil in order to substitute their demand for diesel oil. After importing the biodiesel engine, oil imports were reduced to improve biodiesel's commercial viability and markets. Though research materials are fragmented, Knothe suggests that China started to develop biofuels from vegetable oil during the early 1900s. India also started investigation and use of biofuels at a household level during the high oil price era of WWII. The Japanese battleship *Yamato* was noted to use soybean oil for bunker oil, as the cost of the war prohibited the Japanese government from buying expensive petroleum. Nevertheless, all the innovation and market opportunity for biofuels in developing countries declined post-WWII as it became cheaper to import petroleum oil than to convert edible crops to run transportation (Knothe 2001). With the emergence of cheap fossil fuels, the global interest shifted away from biofuels to fossil fuels. The use of fossil fuels made industrialization easier and faster than the use of biofuels promised.

3.1.2 Contemporary biofuels market development

After decades of silence, interest was renewed as a result of the periodic energy insecurities observed since the 1970s, which is noticeable in Figure 1.1, as the oil price hit a global peak. The fossil fuel global market is closely tied to the evolution of the contemporary biofuels industry development.

In addition, to contextualize the current biofuels market, it is necessary to identify the total cost factors of the product. The cost factors are made up of production costs plus opportunity costs. The production cost includes all the fixed (feedstock, machinery, factory) and variable (overheads, labour) costs necessary to produce the value-added final product and the opportunity cost includes risks factors of not doing something else instead. The market price of feedstocks, comparative crops, and substitution products (fossil fuel) affects opportunity costs, which then influence the production decisions. Most processing plants for biofuels are integrated plants. For example, in the case of ethanol plants, when the sugar price is high, the plant produces sugar, and biodiesel plants have both vegetable oil processing capacity and transesterification units. Of the biofuels production costs, 70 percent to 80 percent represents feedstock cost and 20 percent to 30 percent other production costs. Therefore, most first generation processing plants control the feedstock supply chain.

Given the growing demand for biofuels and cheap energy prices, there is a rush from developing countries to supply cheap feedstock for biofuels production. This has increased the competitiveness in the market and affected value transactions throughout the value chain, often by reducing the profit margin and labour cost.

Contract farming is a popular agro-business scheme in the biofuels industry because it reduces risks in the opportunity cost factor but, without close monitoring of the clauses of the contract, it increases the potential for manipulation and exploitation of smallholders. Most contemporary biofuels feedstock production experience case studies reviewed take contract farming at face value and do not explore the underlining factors that make a contract more socially considerate than inconsiderate. This research takes a close look into this gap in the literature and provides insights using empirical evidence.

Brazil is the leader in contemporary biofuels industry development. For 500 years the country has had sugarcane plantations and, since the 1930s, sugarcane has been used to produce ethanol. However, it was not until the global oil crises of the 1970s that Brazil pioneered large-scale production of ethanol from sugar, based on the then low price and related to the deep balance of payment constraints of the time (Cunha da Costa 2004; de Oliveira 2002). In the mid-1980s almost 100 per cent of cars produced in the country were ethanol compatible.[5] However, following the 1989 sugar crisis, the biofuels market suffered a major set-back, as producers reoriented themselves to producing sugar to cut losses from opportunity costs (de Almeida *et al.* 2007). This trend continued for a decade and, globally, ethanol industry development became sluggish once again.

However, *circa* 2000 a political decision mandated biofuels for the national transportation system and provided infant industries protection by implementing subsidies, export tariffs, or quotas to protect national security and energy independence which changed the national dynamism. While 80 per cent of bioethanol is nationally consumed, biodiesel is blended with freight and public transportation diesel fuel, Brazil exports its biofuels through the Caribbean Basin Initiative. Under this initiative Brazil exports biofuels to Central America or Caribbean countries and from there it is re-exported to the US without paying any import taxes (de Almeida *et al.* 2007). This strategy has created controversy as Brazil has developed the most intensive biofuels supply-chain management system in the world in which the domestic market is not only robustly developed, export promotion is also carefully managed, which takes advantage of import subsidies[6] (Brazil Institute 2007). Brazil has addressed environmental considerations,[7] improved human rights concerns, and sufficiently sustained the investment momentum in the country to enable a low-carbon economy by promoting various direct and indirect incentives to producers, consumers, and research and development. The trade surplus from biofuels exports, representing 3 per cent of GDP, has become a concrete example of successful biofuels sector development and a source of political legitimacy for promoting the sector.

Following economic and environmental security concerns, China, India, South Africa, and other developing countries started to support biofuels industry development and are establishing policies (Rajagopal and Zilberman 2007). From 2000 to 2007, global bioethanol production tripled from 17 billion litres to 52 billion litres (OECD 2008). In the same time frame biodiesel grew 11-fold from one billion litres to 11 billion litres, while a six-fold rate of demand-driven growth was noticed in European countries (UNEP 2009a; Wiesenthal *et al.* 2009). To put it in perspective, biofuels in transportation grew from 0.3 per cent of consumption in 2006 to 1.8 per cent in 2007. It is estimated that such rapid growth of the biofuels industry may have contributed to a 3.0 per cent reduction of carbon emissions from the transportation sector (IEA 2009; OECD/FAO 2008). As mentioned already in the Introduction, the IPCC established transportation emissions as a major anthropogenic factor for global warming and identified biofuels as a potential solution (IPCC 2007).

Unfortunately, the rapid biofuels market growth stumbled upon a critical barrier in 2007. Between February 2007 and February 2008 the global price of staple foods rose by more than 40 per cent (FAO 2009a).[8] According to the International Monetary Fund (IMF), by the middle of 2008, food prices increased 56 per cent on a year-to-year basis (Mitchell 2008). According to the World Bank, on a two-year basis, the price of wheat rose 181 per cent during 2006–2008 (World Bank 2008a). Following high food prices in 2008, many influential studies came out qualifying and quantifying the impacts of biofuels development policies on food prices. Although the extent to which biofuels production contributed to food price increases varies significantly among studies, as seen in Table 3.1, the momentum of first generation biofuels changed. Forty developing countries experienced riots in response to uncontrollable high food prices and widespread hunger (Patel and Gimenez-Holt 2010).

To understand the riots, some authors have offered explanations as to the relationships between high food prices and poverty. Based on empirical analysis using Bangladesh as a case study, Ravallion (1990, 1991) argued that, even taking into account the induced wage response to high food prices, rural poverty increased in proportion to the relative price of food staples. Similarly, using household level data, Ivanic and Martin (2008) found that high(er) food prices caused a growth in the proportion of people in poverty in eight out of nine tested countries. However, Aksoy and Isik-Dikmelik (2008) challenged the notion that higher food prices unequivocally affect poverty as most food sellers can enjoy income transfer from the richer to poorer households. Hoyos and Medvedev provide a neutral analysis by suggesting that, due to direct and indirect dependency for income or consumption on the agriculture sector by the poor, any increase in agricultural commodity price will affect the well-being of the people.

The opportunity cost of producing biofuels shot up and slowed the momentum for a couple of years. The global biofuels market was faced not only with criticism for taking away food from the poor to fuel the transportation sector of the high income countries, but the high food price also hit the bottom line of biofuels companies. Furthermore, the financial market crash of 2008 dried up investment in biofuels companies. Faced with massive losses, many applied for bailout money and others simply went bankrupt. For example, between 2008 and 2009 more than ten publicly

Table 3.1 The impact of biofuels alone on food prices

Source	Biofuels accountability for food price rises	Argument
(Mitchell 2008) World Bank	75%	Seventy to 75% of the increase in food commodity prices was due to biofuels and the related consequences of low grain stocks, large land-use shifts, speculative activity, and export bans.
(Lipsky 2008) IMF	40%	'IMF estimates suggest that increased demand for biofuels accounts for 70% of the increase in corn prices and 40% of the increase in soybean prices.'
(von Braun 2008) IFPRI	30%	'The increased biofuel demand during the period, compared with previous historical rates of growth, is estimated to have accounted for 30% of the increase in weighted average grain prices.'
(NEF 2008)	17%	Biofuels caused the biggest pressure on land for food oil production, absorbing 4.1% of available land and so driving average price increases of up to 17%.
(FAO 2008)	10%	Biofuels increase demand for food crops and contributed to 10% of global food price rise.
(USDA 2008)	3%	'The President's Council of Economic Advisors estimates that only 3% of the more than 40% increase we have seen in world food prices [in 2008] is due to the increased demand on corn for ethanol.'

Source: Author.

listed biofuels companies collapsed in Germany. These ten companies had produced 54 per cent of the EU's biofuels (Lane 2009).[9] Companies have folded 'left and right' since 2008 in the US, starting with VeraSun, the largest public biofuels company (E-EnergyMarket 2010).

3.1.3 *The future of biofuels market development*

Nevertheless, the scenario highlighted here is a short-term crisis. Major global publications, even in the midst of the global recession and the downfall of the biofuels market, projected that 9 per cent of global cereal crops and 5 per cent of the global oil-seed production would supply biofuels to meet the targets set on global biofuels usage by 2017 (see Table 3.2). Most of the increases, as noted in the table, are in the US, EU, Brazil, China, and Canada. But the table also shows the other developing countries which will catch up in biofuels usage, namely Indonesia, Mozambique, Ethiopia, and Tanzania, based on percentage change from 2005–2007 to 2017 usage (OECD/FAO 2008).

This table suggests that, aside from Brazil, the rest of the countries see huge potential for growth in biofuels demand. Until the next generation biofuels are proven to be commercially, economically and energetically viable, the first generation is the best of what is available in the mix of alternative fuel sources for the transportation sector. The future outcome of the biofuels industry expansion is almost totally unknown. At best one can look at the impacts in the countries where the first generation biofuels industry appears to have matured. Table 3.3 shows technological and commercial maturity in biofuels technology complementing the understanding that the future of the biofuels industry lies in the third generational biofuels technologies which are based on experimental biotechnology. As the technology improves, the anticipated outcomes are reduced production costs, increased energy yields and lower impacts on the food market.

Table 3.2 Increase in biofuels usage from 2005–2007 to 2008 and the projection to 2017

	2005–2007 to 2008		*2005–2007 to 2017*	
	PJ	*Percentage*	*PJ*	*Percentage*
Australia	26	323	46	582
Brazil	104	36	435	150
Canada	20	117	63	371
China	12	37	98	297
Colombia	9	156	12	206
Ethiopia	0.02	32	0.83	1,240
EU Total	135	60	520	231
India	5	30	20	137
Indonesia	3	180	71	4,522
Malaysia	2	71	5	na
Mozambique	0.05	163	0.54	1,617
Philippines	1	259	4	1,010
Tanzania	0.24	179	1.44	1,085
Thailand	2	71	26	925
Turkey	0.32	35	0.42	47
USA	361	76	759	160
World Total	679	63	2,071	193

Note: Biofuels numbers are bioethanol + biodiesel. Energy is measured in kilowatt hours (kWh) or megawatt hours (MWh) during a certain period of time, e.g., an hour or a year. 1 kWh = 3,600,000 petajoules (PJ).
Source: Adapted from UNEP 2009b.

Table 3.3 Biofuels technology matrix

Feedstock type	Biofuels type*	Major end-use	Crops in temperate climate	Crops in tropical climate	Conversion technology	Technology maturity	Commercial maturity	Source**
First generation: sugar and starch	BE	Transport	Corn, Sugar beet, wheat	Sugarcane, sorghum, cassava	Fermentation	High	High	1, 2, 3, 4, 5, 6
Oil seeds	BD	Transport	Soy, rapeseed	Palm, jatropha, castor	Transesterification	High	High	7, 8, 9, 10, 11, 12
Second generation: perennial crop, forest waste	BE, BD	Transport	Switch grass, Miscanthus	–	Biochemical Syngas-to-Fischer-Tropsch diesel, enzymatic hydrolysis ethanol	Low	Low	13, 14, 15
Third generation: algae	BE, BD	Transport	Algae	–	Chemical conversion	Very low	Very low	14, 15

Note: Compilation follows the matrix structure of Rajagopal and Zilberman 2007.
* Biofuels Type: BE = bioethanol, BD = biodiesel
** Sources:
1. Kammen et al. 2007
2. Macedo et al. 2003
3. Balat and Balat 2009
4. Jansson et al. 2009
5. Biswas et al. 2010
6. AAFC 2005
7. Sivapragasam 2008
8. Sumathi et al. 2007
9. van Eijck and Romijn 2008
10. Yee et al. 2009
11. Ericsson et al. 2006
12. Reijnders 2010
13. Hahn-Hagerdal et al. 2006
14. Naik et al. 2010
15. Sims et al. 2010.

Lastly, most studies found that the current cost of second generation biofuel is 2.1 times higher than that for the first generation biofuels (IEA 2006; Reilly and Paltsev 2007). Reilly and Paltsev (2007) estimate that second generation biofuels will be able to make a substantial contribution to energy production until 2100, while the IEA is more optimistic in suggesting 2012 to 2020 for the second generation biofuels' commercialization. But rearranging the raw data collected from OECD/FAO 2008's dataset produces rather interesting interpretations of the industry's future, as shown in Figures 3.1 and 3.2. It appears that, although over the next 18 years the actual production of biofuels will rise, the growth rate will decline over time. This could mean that the market is anticipating next generation production, or, in general, the biofuels industry will have matured and other alternative energy sources. This discussion has attempted to highlight the fact that it is difficult to project the development path of the global biofuels market.

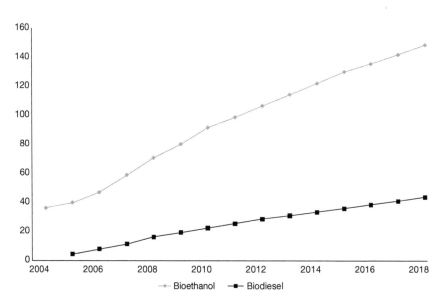

Figure 3.1 Bioethanol and biodiesel production trends 2004–2018
Note: Data after 2009 are projected.
Source: OECD/FAO 2009.

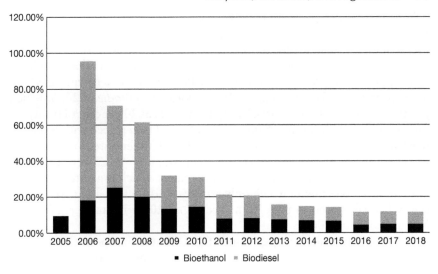

Figure 3.2 Bioethanol and biodiesel production percentage change 2004–2018
Note: Data after 2009 are projected.
Source: OECD/FAO 2009.

3.2 Biodiesel and jatropha diesel

As mentioned already this research studies biodiesel industry development by focusing on jatropha as the commodity. This section deepens the discussion started in Section 3.1 by reviewing literature that supports the proposition that biodiesel is a market opportunity with more longevity than bioethanol. This is further to assert why the biodiesel industry has been focused here and not on bioethanol. Then the discussion shifts to one specific feedstock commodity, jatropha, for the previously highlighted characteristics of the crop that outweigh other crop options.

3.2.1 The relative sustainability of the biodiesel market

Biodiesel did not make a major commercial début until the 1970s when Brazilian scientist Expedito Parente patented the first industrial process for the production of biodiesel. With this intervention, the dream of the father of the diesel engine, Rudolf Diesel, to run his engine on a variety of fuels, including vegetable oil, was realized. Diesel said, 'the use of vegetable oils for engine fuels may seem insignificant today, but such oils may become, in the course of time, as important as petroleum and the coal-tar products of the present time' (Tickell 2000: 23). This statement stands the test of time. More recently, the IEA anticipated that biodiesel would enjoy faster market growth than bioethanol (IEA 2004). Following the IEA's assessment, this subsection highlights findings from literature reviews on why biodiesel has a better long-term market potential for developing countries than bioethanol.

Results show first generation biodiesel is the most cost competitive biofuel. So, the sector will grow given a cheap source of feedstock. In this case, the cheap source is also a safe source, meaning crops which are not directly linked with edible food crops. Lamers *et al.* suggest that biodiesel consumption will grow in internal markets in the short term and medium term (post-2010) (Lamers *et al.* 2008). According to *Biodiesel 2020*, which produces market survey reports, by 2020 'as much as 20 per cent of transport fuels used in Brazil, Europe, China and India will be replaced with biodiesel from non-food feedstocks' (Thurmond 2008). Furthermore, biodiesel was found to reduce greenhouse gas (GHG) emissions by 41–75 per cent when compared to fossil-based diesel, an improvement which is greater than that of corn-based bioethanol which only reduces emissions by about 19–28 per cent when compared to petroleum (Beer *et al.* 2007; Fontaras *et al.* 2009; Murugesan *et al.* 2009).

In a recent modelling project named REFUEL, the European Commission found that increasing the use of biofuels to a 25 per cent share of transportation fuel by 2030 can be achieved using biodiesel. A market sensitivity analysis shows that, in the future, second generation biodiesel will be more cost effective than first generation biodiesel. Unfortunately, viability is a long way off and depends on continuous government investment and support (de Wit *et al.* 2010). Such support is being cut due to the current instability of the global economy and the poor financial health of Western governments, such as those of the US and EU countries, where much research and development happens. Since biofuel targets are still in place and first generation biodiesel production is currently the most viable approach, demand for oil seeds is increasing. This in turn supports higher seed prices, which brings second generation techniques closer to viability. For now, developing countries with unused, semi-arid, or arid land, such as Malaysia, Indonesia, Ghana, Kenya, Tanzania, Mozambique, Argentina, and the Dominican Republic, are becoming major players in the biodiesel market (Lamers *et al.* 2008; Mulugetta 2009; UNEP 2009a; Zhou and Thomson 2009).

Fuel type and quality requirements of existing and emerging engine technologies will also drive demand. For example, given the fuel supply chain, infrastructure set-up, and relative long lifespans of vehicle stocks, even with some policy focus alteration, projections show that, even in the 2020s, 74 per cent of US transportation will remain gasoline powered and in Europe 60 per cent will continue to be diesel powered (IEA 2010; IEA/WBCSD 2004). Regional choices of fuel types also have implications for biofuels development. The US is keen on bioethanol research and development for gasoline substitution, attracting venture capital investments along with USD 500 million in grants under the Energy Independence and Security Act of 2007 for second generation research (UNCTAD 2009). Europe is investing in biodiesel for diesel substitution. Along with the choice of type, the trend of biofuels development follows national policies on sourcing the biofuels from domestic or imported stocks.

Another observation suggested that biodiesel production would continue to enjoy favourable world prices which would drive production, whereas bioethanol prices might taper, part of which could be explained by slow growth in global prices (Matthey 2008). However, this does not hold true anymore since the price of oil started to decline in 2012. IEA reference scenarios[10] showed that biofuels for transportation would increase from 800 PJ in 2005 to 2,400 PJ in 2015 and 4.3 EJ (exajoules) in 2030 as the emerging economies grow rapidly (IEA 2009). This also does not hold true anymore as recent studies show that overall demand for fossil fuel based transportation has declined as innovation in the transport sector has boomed since 2012. Most emerging economies like India, China, Malaysia, and Russia have their own automotive industries which are moving into flex fuels technology (with the exception of Brazil which is already well ahead).

Most developing countries use diesel engines for their transportation because diesel costs less than gasoline (Demirbas 2007; Thurmond 2008). To give an example, in India, which is one of the fastest growing markets for energy and transportation, gasoline is priced at USD 5.15 per gallon whereas diesel is sold at USD 2.12 per gallon. Moreover, single cylinder engines, which are still made in India, China, and other developing countries due to the low costs, can use direct biodiesel (Brittaine and Lutaladio 2010; Demirbas 2007; Thurmond 2008). These translate into a fairly stable market opportunity for biodiesel (REN21 2009). Also, other types for heavy industrial and transportation sectors depend on diesel and changes in the mechanical features of these engines are costly and time inefficient (Britton 2010).

Second generation bioethanol can be commercially viable at production costs of USD 2 per gallon. Poet, the world's largest ethanol producer, has reduced its production costs for cellulosic ethanol from USD 4.13 to USD 2.35 per gallon over the last few years (Weitzman 2010). Expected blending targets will increase biodiesel demand to about 67.3 billion litres (17.8 billion gallons) by 2022, which will mainly be fulfilled by first generation biodiesel (UNCTAD 2009). However, given the world's installed capacity to consume biodiesel, while second generation biofuel is still unavailable, the only viable option that remains is first generation biodiesel.

In Table 3.4 it appears that palm oil has the highest productivity of any other feedstocks (eight to ten times higher). However, producing palm oil is not suitable for all countries because it requires heavy investment in land, labour, and capital. For most developing countries it will also be difficult to compete with Malaysia and Indonesia in this field. When we compare the other options, sunflower and soybean are next in line. These two crops have a high market value for their by-products. But this is not true for jatropha and castor. There is little market for the by-product, although, given its high oil productivity and utility as a drought resistant, pest resistant, low-input crop, jatropha has been globally recognized as an important feedstock.

Table 3.4 Economic characteristics of the main biodiesel feedstocks

Feedstock	Current status of availability	Status of agronomical research	Oil content percentage of dry weight	Biomass productivity (tons/ha)	Oil productivity (litres/ha)
Soybean	High	High	20	2,230	440
Tallow	High	na	–	–	–
Palm	High	High	20	20,000	4,000
Jatropha	Low	Low	30–40	na	1,892
Castor	Limited	Low	47	730	343
Cotton	High	High	15	3,000	450
Sunflower	Limited	High	40	1,500	630

Source: Adapted from Fontaras *et al.* 2009.

3.2.2 *Jatropha diesel and its market*

The feedstock focus is moving away from edible food crops to non-edible food crops, which is not possible without tremendous technological innovation and commercialization. Jatropha was proven to be significant at the International Fund for Agricultural Development (IFAD) global consultation on jatropha (IFAD 2008). Jatropha is considered as a crop suitable for clean development mechanism (CDM) programmes.[11] Private companies, like BP, D1, Shell, and other foreign companies, have made considerable investments in jatropha in developing countries. Of the 28 states in India, 16 have developed jatropha plantations on green arid and semi-arid wasteland (Pelkmans and Papageorgiou 2005). China recently set aside an area the size of England to produce jatropha and other non-food plants for biodiesel. In Brazil and Africa, there are significant programmes under way dedicated to producing the non-food crops jatropha and castor[12] for biodiesel (Brittaine and Lutaladio 2010; Thurmond 2008; Tomomatsu and Swallow 2007; van Eijck and Romijn 2008). In the past couple of years, the international aviation companies have also increased interest in jatropha oil as they have trialled flights on jatropha diesel blends. This has further strengthened the growth potential of the jatropha diesel market. Interestingly, based on a rough observation of country lists, it appears that out of the 22 heavily food-insecure countries which experienced rioting as a result of high food prices, more than 50 per cent have made some biofuels investment and, specifically, jatropha investments (FAO 2009b).

It is important to note that knowledge of agronomy and how agronomic practice improvement would contribute to yield is generally insufficient and often misguided. For example, the Global Invasive Species Programme identified jatropha as an invasive species in Jamaica, Panama, Puerto Rico, El Salvador, Honduras, and Tanzania. Yet, these countries, with the exception of Tanzania which put a moratorium on the crop due to socio-political concerns about its invasion into the rural food production system, continued with their jatropha industry establishment agenda. However, the identification caused the Indian government to re-evaluate the role of jatropha as a commercial crop and the South African government to ban jatropha in 2009. As a wild crop, the plant displays considerable genetic-environment interaction. In other words, different species and clones may perform and produce very different yields under different environmental conditions. Observing jatropha experience in India, or importing seeds from India, is by no means a guarantee of successful commercial production of jatropha in African countries. Also, data collection on jatropha is relatively recent and the earlier observations were based on independent mature plants rather than observation of a plantation system (Brittaine and Lutaladio 2010). Reported characteristics widely differ between studies, but nevertheless, Table 3.5 lists some basic characteristics of jatropha crops to provide a generalized idea for further discussion.

Table 3.5 Brief summary of jatropha characteristics

Ecological conditions	Geography: warm sub-humid tropics and tropics.
	Climate: can survive with 250 mm to 300 mm annual rainfall, but for flowering needs a minimum of 600 mm rainfall. Optimum rainfall 1,000 to 1,500 mm.
	Temperature: 20° C to 28° C. Very high temperatures can depress yields.
	Soil quality: can survive in marginal soil, saline irrigation, alkaline soil but intolerant of waterlogged conditions. Minimum pH balance 6.0 to 8.5.
Nomenclature and taxonomy	*Euphorbiaceae* family, 170 known species, only 66 identified.
	Perennial crop and takes three to five years to reach economic maturity.
	Classified as a weed.
Three major varieties	a. Nicaragua: larger but fewer fruits. b. Mexico: less- or non-toxic seeds. c. Cape Verde: widely grown, found in Asia and Africa.
	Nursery raised seedlings of wild variety plants have higher survival rates than direct sowing in the field.
Plant description	Germination: ~10 days from seeds or stem cuttings.
	Height: ~5 metres, but depends on growing conditions.
	Maturity: four to five years.
	Rooting system: main taproot, four lateral roots with secondary roots.
	Leaves: alternate on the stem, shallowly lobed and varying from 6 to 15 cm length and width, depending on variety.
	Flowering: monoecious male to female flower ratio 29:1. Needs pollination.

Table 3.5 Brief summary of jatropha characteristics *continued*

Fruit description	Vegetative growth: fruiting triggered by rainfall. One inflorescence produces ~10 fruits.
	Production phase: first and second year of growth.
	Outlook: ellipsoidal, green, fleshy, turn yellow to brown with age.
	Harvest time: around 90 days after flowering.
	Seeds: normally two to three seeds around 2 cm × 1 cm in size.
	Oil content: ranges from 18.4 to 42 per cent.[13]
Planting	Density and spacing: depends on soil quality. Density ranges from 2,500 plants per ha to 450 plants with high to low quality soil.
	Intercropping: first five years of jatropha is common practice. Groundnuts, legume and vanilla vines are commonly intercropped.
	Crop maintenance: requires irrigation, weeding and pruning for fruiting.
	Plant nutrition: fertilization to an optimum level increases yield.
	Pests and diseases: widely noted under plantation monoculture and may be of economic significance. Key pest is shield-backed or *Scutellera* bug which causes flower fall, fruit abortion and seed malformation. Other significant bugs are moths, bark-eating borers, flower beetle, cassava mosaic virus.
Harvesting and oil extraction	Seed yield: ranges from 0.4–3.0 tonnes per ha depending on various conditions.
	Harvesting: manual collection from branches. Recorded average ranged from 24 kg to 50 kg per workday in India. Synchronized fruiting would mechanize the process and be more efficient.
	Oil extraction: engine driven screw presses can extract 70 to 80 per cent of available oil. On average 1 litre of oil from 4–5 kg of dried seeds.[14]
Jatropha oil properties	Crude jatropha oil: relatively viscous, prone to oxidation in storage, low temperature fluidity, high cetane (ignition quality), less harmful sulphur dioxide and water emissions.
	Direct substitution: not more than 5 per cent possible without engine modification.

Source: Summarized from Achten *et al.* 2010; Biswas *et al.* 2010; Brittaine and Lutaladio 2010; FDA 2008; GEXSI 2008; Gubitz *et al.* 1999; IFAD 2008; Jongschaap *et al.* 2007; Sivapragasam 2008; UNCTAD 2009; van Eijck and Romijn 2008; Wiemer 1996.

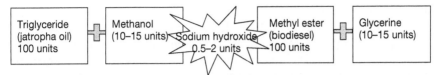

Equation 3.1 The chemical process of jatropha diesel production and typical input/
output proportions
Source: Adapted with minor changes from Brittaine and Lutaladio 2010.

The conversion of jatropha oil to biodiesel is the same as other first
generation biodiesel conversion processes, which basically involve the
conversion of vegetable oil or animal fat (tallow), consisting of long-chain
alkyl esters, by chemically reacting these lipids with an alcohol, typically
methanol. An alkali – normally sodium hydroxide – is needed to catalyse the
reaction. The sodium hydroxide reaction cuts oil molecules into pieces
enabling connection with alcohol molecules to form the jatropha methyl
ester. Methanol is normally used as the alcohol for reasons of cost and
technical efficiency. In the process glycerine (glycerol) is produced as a
by-product, which has commercial usage in the soap and biochemical
industries. For every 1 litre of biodiesel, 79 millilitres of glycerine are
produced which is about 10 per cent by weight. The raw glycerine needs
further purification to use it in cosmetic, pharmaceutical, confectionery,
plastic, and antifreeze products. The process and a typical proportional
summary is presented in Equation 3.1. For a complete understanding of the
phases of direct and indirect co-products of jatropha-based biodiesel
production refer to Tomomatsu and Swallow 2007.

Although jatropha has been identified as a pro-poor development crop, it
is the reality that the biodiesel production and quality control requires much
technological expertise, equipment, and experience in the handling of large
quantities of dangerous chemicals. For example, methanol is very toxic and
sodium hydroxide is highly corrosive, not to mention that all products of
jatropha contain toxins which are harmful to humans and animals.

3.3 Global biofuels regulatory frameworks and economic assessments

The 2009 G-20 Summit held in Pittsburgh pledged:

> To phase out and rationalize over the medium term inefficient fossil fuel
> subsidies while providing targeted support for the poorest. Inefficient
> fossil fuel subsidies encourage wasteful consumption, reduce our energy
> security, impede investment in clean energy sources and undermine
> efforts to deal with the threat of climate change.
>
> (G-20 2009: Preamble)

In response to the declaration, on 1 January 2010, the US biodiesel subsidy expired, following the EU's 2008 decision to slash biofuels subsidies for better greener options (Murphy 2010; Rosenthal 2009).[15] Unfortunately, without subsidies the US biodiesel industry cannot meet blending targets or be globally competitive.[16] Moreover, according to the National Biodiesel Board, the biofuels industry is operating at only 15 per cent capacity (Murphy 2010). Based on the widely recognized International Network for Sustainable Energy, falling subsidies in developed countries suggest greater competitiveness for biofuels export opportunities from developing countries. Also, the share of vegetable oil used for biodiesel production is expected to increase from 9 per cent in 2006–2008 to 20 per cent in 2018, which means more room for developing countries (OECD/FAO 2009). But is biofuels industry development a good idea for developing countries, particularly when the debates over the sector have not yet been resolved?

This section first discusses the layout of domestic regulation and unresolved debates then, in the second subsection, the international trade environment and related industry inconsistencies are discussed. Finally, regulatory environments are assessed for developing countries taking part in the global biofuels value chain. For reference, Appendix B describes the major biofuels blending targets and production required to meet the growing demand of biofuels globally and nationally.

3.3.1   Domestic policies buttressing biofuels industry development

A spectrum of policies exists, as seen in Table 3.6. The economic characteristics of the main biodiesel feedstocks, have influenced the development of the biofuels industry, including excise tax exemption, mandatory blending requirements, directives to improve transportation fuels standards, and other indirect policies like carbon credits, agriculture trade, and vehicle standard policies. A plethora of institutions with various capacities are engaged in biofuel producing and consuming countries to support the implementation of these policies.

It is beyond the scope of this subsection to provide a detailed assessment of any one policy;[17] instead, information is gathered here to provide a general explanation on the rationale behind such policies. Figure 3.3 gives a high-level picture of the various support policies advancing the development of the biofuels supply chain.

There are normative welfare and political–economic rationales behind biofuels policies. Primarily, the normative welfare rationales are to protect the biofuels industry from market failure, even though it is costly to the economy (Rajagopal and Zilberman 2007).[18] For example, Brazilian ethanol would not be viable without subsidies, and existing exemptions from excise duties within Brazil provide advantages over other ethanol producing countries (Wadhams 2009). The United Nations Environment Programme (UNEP) has compiled a list of 33 countries which are providing subsidies

Table 3.6 Types of policy tools with examples

Types of policy tools	Examples
Incentives – tax or subsidies	Excise tax credit for renewable energy, carbon tax, subsidies for flex-fuel vehicles, price support and deficiency payments, tariffs or subsidy payments on exports/imports
Direct control	Renewable fuel standards, mandatory blending, emission control standards, efficiency standards, acreage control, quotas on imports/exports
Enforcement of property rights and trading	Cap and trade, carbon taxing
Educational and informational programmes, Improving governance	Labelling, certification programmes, compensation for environmental services

Source: Adapted from Rajagopal and Zilberman 2007.

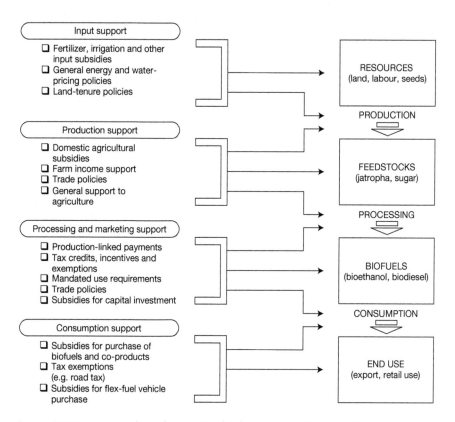

Figure 3.3 Domestic policies buttressing biofuels supply-chain development
Source: Modified from FAO 2008 (adapted from Steenblik 2007).

(supplier and consumer level) to reach their biofuels blending target for transportation fuel, sampled in Appendix A (UNEP 2009c). However, subsidies are expensive and environmentally unjustified from a climate change perspective since they do not curb carbon emitting fuel consumption. It is estimated that worldwide subsidies for energy might amount to USD 300 billion per year and simply abolishing energy subsidies and liberalizing all fossil fuel trade would cut emissions by 6 per cent annually (OECD 2000; UNEP 2008, 2009a).[19]

While some states limit intervention in their market-based economies, others provide protection from market failure to nascent industries through public research and development investment, which also creates new employment opportunities. Tax credits are often used as the main policy instrument in this case. For example, the American Jobs Creation Act of 2004 created a new income tax credit to support 100 per cent biodiesel with no fossil fuel (B100) sales and usage. Similarly, the Swedish Renewable Fuels Act (Gulbrand 2006) has directly subsidized up to 30 per cent of the total cost to promote distribution of biofuels, which has led to land acquisition in other countries and the importation of biofuels (OECD 2007). Worldwide jobs in the renewable energy supply chain had expanded to an estimated 2.4 million by 2006, including 1.1 million for first generation biofuels production (REN21 2007).[20]

Carbon tax is another important domestic policy that is favoured in EU countries to promote emissions reductions. The European biofuels market development mainly favours a carbon tax over subsidies because the former creates fair competition among producers to strive for the best technology utilization for zero-carbon emissions (Popp 2006). For developing countries, a carbon tax may reduce industrial and transportation activity, which are still fossil fuel dependent and, thereby, slow down economic development to the detriment of these countries (Gwilliam *et al.* 2001). Nevertheless, such a tax would promote a low-carbon economy with long-term payoffs. Discussions related to carbon prices for biofuels are still young and lack an overall comprehension of theory with the emerging practical experience (Neuhoff 2008).

Along with incentives and target-based policies, there are educational and promotional actions that domestic governments are engaging in to buttress the national biofuels industry development. Public–private partnership to set transportation standards and consumer warrantee support are two strategic approaches which are non-cost regulations for government. Countries in Europe are introducing vehicle standards that require compatibility with specific biofuels mixes, the products are then being labelled as 'green vehicles'. Labelling or consuming 'green' certified products, in this case vehicles, adds special socio-political status to the seller and consumer countries on the global platform. Being 'green' is a modern hallmark of the social elite. Buyers and sellers in this case participate in the premium services class, in which 'desired' social norms influence social adaptation to the new product, without any financial incentives to change behaviour. In fact, Brazil has already successfully implemented vehicle conversion requirements by mandating all gasoline to be 22 per cent to 26 per cent ethanol.[21] As a result, Brazil achieved 94 per cent flex-fuel compatibility in its transport fleet in 2009 (UNICA 2009). Countries like India, China, and Malaysia, are entering into agreements with leading vehicle manufacturers like Toyota and Nissan to extend the warranty on older model cars run with biofuels.

3.3.2 *International biofuels industry trade policies*

To assess the global market, it is important to recognize the major regulatory framework of global trade institutions, such as the WTO which governs value chain development. Importantly, the Agreement on Agriculture (AOA) covers agricultural products[22] and is based on three pillars: market access, domestic subsidies, and export subsidies. The major provision of AOA members is the ability to pay subsidies. Within AOA, bioethanol is considered an agricultural product, therefore countries which are in the bioethanol trade can promote the industry by providing various kinds of monetary incentives, as discussed already, and not jeopardize their trading position for unfair trading practices. On the other hand, biodiesel is considered an industrial good, and therefore is not subject to the AOA system. Moreover, in 2005 the World Customs Organization decided to put biodiesel in Section VI under 'products of chemical and allied industries' (HS 382490) but up until then both bioethanol and biodiesel had been treated as agricultural commodities. Bioethanol is still traded under HS 2207 in Chapter 22 under 'beverages, spirits and vinegar'. Therefore, any outcome of the Doha negotiations on agriculture and non-agricultural market access will apply to the biofuels sector, but differently. This is creating an unfair and unclear trading environment.

Sometimes unfair trade environments lead to the adoption of undesirable trade practices in order to be competitive in the wider global market. It often appears to be developed countries like the US and the EU nations which tend to take advantage of loopholes or legal weaknesses. This then leads to never-ending negotiations, disagreements, and contradictions in the dialogues between the trading partners (FAO 2008; WTO 2010). It is one of the reasons why the Doha rounds are still discussing whether to consider bioethanol and biodiesel under the single category of 'environmental goods', thus making them subject to negotiation under the Environmental Goods and Services cluster. In the crossfire of these negotiations, lie developing countries.

There are several policy mechanisms in the international trade environment that influence the biofuels industry. Import tariffs and quotas protect domestic producers and preferential tariff waivers protect special interests in select countries (Kojima and Johnson 2006; Rajagopal and Zilberman 2007). Export subsidies improve the marketability of value-added finished products, for example, the reduced export tax on Argentinean biodiesel exported to Europe and the US.[23] Pre-existing terms of trade between countries are another powerful mechanism that facilitates the international biofuels trade. For example, Brazilian ethanol exports to the US avoid US tariffs when processed in a US Central America Basin Initiative member country. Similarly, Indonesia and Malaysia export biodiesel to Europe free from import tariffs and receive a tax credit from the US of USD 0.264 per litre when it is mixed with a small amount of conventional diesel in the US, also known as 'splash and dash' (Searchinger 2009).

Integrated biofuels policies have been proposed to internalize growing externalities and remove price distortions from the biofuels production chain. Analysis on changing biofuels policy mechanisms for global trade scenarios shows that current production, future targets, and policies are intertwined with the global agricultural value chain (FAO 2008). These trade policies are the primary tools needed to attain biofuels industry development, but their effectiveness depends on pre-existing political, institutional, and economic characteristics, along with externalities like the financial crisis and global climate fund, which influence the transaction costs of cross-border biofuels trade.

However, the international trade environment is not without conflicts. Large and early adopter biofuels countries use their political power and global leadership to protect the industry at home while institutionalizing the global rules of the game. In 2008 and 2009, the European Biodiesel Board (EBB) made a complaint against the US and Argentina under anti-dumping provisions for dumping cheap biodiesel, which is related to the national subsidy policies and export incentives (Bismarck-Reppert 2009; EBB 2009; AFP 2008). But in the same year, the European Renewable Energy Directive announced new technical sustainability criteria for biofuels imports, requiring at least 35 per cent greenhouse gas savings from biofuels entering the EU market to qualify for preferential tax treatment from the WTO. According to the European Centre for International Political Economy such policies violate a number of core General Agreement on Tariffs and Trade principles (Erixon 2009) and are considered unfair trading practice.[24] This creates global trade distortion and non-tariff barriers for developing countries.

The major buyers of the biofuels market are the EU countries, which are committed to being the leaders in the low-carbon economy and cutting their emissions as dictated by the Kyoto Protocol. Major biofuels feedstock industries have evolved in the developing countries which are already known to be sellers of agricultural produce to the EU market. Conversion of land for biofuels in African countries is directly linked to EU demands for biofuels targets. While millions of hectares of land have already been converted, in 2009 the EU commission admitted that the target of 5.75 per cent biofuels on the roads by 2010 is unlikely to be achieved because of lack of supply (Biopact 2008a; Mathews 2007; Rosenthal 2009; Wiesenthal *et al.* 2009). This has increased the price of feedstock and the land conversion rate in developing countries. Along with land conversion, land grabbing and rural displacements are also being reported in the global media as the global biofuels trading environment has, since 2008, pumped up the demand for cheap feedstocks (Cotula *et al.* 2010).

Concomitantly, the major global biofuels producers are also keen on introducing various standards and certification schemes to better categorize and control the social and political implications of traded products. The major initiative in this realm is Biopact. Biopact is a major instrument which changes the global market dynamism for the biofuels market which will be dominated by EU driven demand sourced from developing countries (Biopact 2008a; Mathews 2007). Global-Bio-Pact is an EU funded project, which sees sustainable promises in biofuels demand and accordingly is working both with buyers and sellers to determine sustainable ways to produce, supply, and consume biofuels globally. Biopact elaborates recommendations on how to best integrate socio-economic sustainability criteria in European legislation and policies on biomass and other bioproducts that are produced or imported to meet the blending targets. Other certification schemes affect the global biofuels trade environment with a great variety of focus and targets (see Table 3.7). Individual countries are also forcing social funds and social standards on the traded biofuels to protect their green reputations.

Despite all efforts, the wide variety of certification schemes are becoming more confusing and creating an unfair trading environment. Hence, the rest of this chapter argues that the standardization requirements create an elusive appearance of sustainability to consumers and so does not address this topic in any detail, except where relevant to the case studies.

Policy makers and scholars are exploring alternative approaches to maximize the benefits and minimize the risks associated with biofuels in developing countries. To promote socio-economic qualifications in biofuels production mechanisms in developing countries, the Roundtable on Sustainable Biofuels (RSB) proposed definitions for direct and indirect land use to standardize the biofuels certification criteria. Britain, Germany, and Switzerland along with other EU members of the Global Bioenergy Partnership, a governmental forum, initiated policy frameworks that include blending targets, subsidies, or import policies with sustainability measures (EU 2009; Schubert and Blasch 2010; van Dam *et al.* 2008). Suggestions also include creating a unified global standard applicable to all agricultural commodities (FAO 2008), a product-specific 'risk adder' calculation applied to countries engaged in cross-border trading of biofuels (Fritsche 2008), and a global certification for all biomass product imports (Edwards *et al.* 2008).

Note that, within the global discourse of certification, the bioenergy category is inclusive of biofuels and biomass. This is because most certification schemes do not make a distinction between biofuels and biomass, as long as the feedstock is from the environment. Whereas certification schemes are supposed to reduce the negative impacts of the

Table 3.7 Certification schemes and performance standards for bioenergy production

Certification	Affiliation					Sector				Scope			Criteria		
	NGO	National government	Intergovernmental	Private	Multi-sector	Forestry	Agriculture	Biofuel	Trade	National	Regional	International	Environment	Social	Economic
Australian Forestry Standard	•	•	4	5	6	•	7	8	9	•	10	11	•	•	•
Canadian Standards Association – Sustainable Forest Management	•	12	13	14	15	•	16	17	18	•	19	20	•	•	•
Forest Stewardship Council – P&C Standard	•	21	22	23	24	•	25	26	•	27	28	•	•	•	•
Green Gold Agriculture/Forest Label (standard when no certification system is available)	•	29	30	•	31	•	•	32	33	34	35	•	•	•	•
Indonesia Eco-labelling Institute – Sustainable Forest Management	•	36	37	38	39	•	40	41	42	•	43	44	•	•	45
International Federation of Organic Agriculture Movements – IFOAM Accreditation Criteria	•	46	47	•	48	49	•	50	•	51	52	•	•	•	•
Naturland Association for Organic Agriculture – Standards	•	53	54	55	56	•	•	57	58	•	59	•	•	•	60
Rainforest Alliance – Sustainable Agriculture Network	•	61	62	63	64	65	•	66	67	68	69	•	•	•	•

Table: Performance Standards — Affiliation, Sector, Scope and Criteria

Performance Standards	Affiliation					Sector				Scope			Criteria		
	NGO	National government	Intergovernmental	Private	Multi-sector	Forestry	Agriculture	Biofuel	Trade	National	Regional	International	Environment	Social	Economic
Climate, Community & Biodiversity Alliance (CCBA) – CCB Standard	•	70	71	•	72	•	•	•	73	74	75	•	•	•	•
Fairtrade Labelling Organization – Fairtrade standards	•	76	77	78	79	80	•	81	•	82	83	•	•	•	•
International Standards Organizations (biofuels standard in development)	•	84	85	86	87	88	89	•	90	91	92	•	•	•	•
Netherlands – Agency for Energy & Environment (currently discussing certification of biofuels)		•	93	94	95	96	97	•	98	•	99	100	•	•	•
Roundtable for Biofuels Sustainability standards					•	101	102	•	103	104	105	•			
Roundtable on Responsible Soy	•	106		107	108	109	110			•	•	•	•	•	•
Roundtable on Sustainable Palm Oil	•	111			112	113	114			•	•	•			
Sustainable Forestry Initiative	•	115	116		117	•	118	119	120	•	•	121	•	•	•

Note: This table only includes some key certification and standards for bioenergy, not all are shown.
Source: Adapted from UNEP 2009a.

growing industry, the definitional ambiguity gives room for misappropriation of the certification. Moreover, because current certification schemes are voluntary and largely privately-operated, this often excludes small-scale farmers (FAO 2013). Many certification schemes are data, or information, intensive and require costs and capacities that are often out of reach for most smallholders. Similarly, the contract farmers do not see the benefits that are enjoyed by the private contracting companies that may have participated in a scheme. Certification schemes offer financial, commercial, and marketing benefits as reasons and incentives for private companies to join.

3.3.3   *Implications of biofuels policies on developing countries*

Estimates show that about 13 per cent of the USD 120 billion invested in renewable energy in 2007–2008 went to biofuels (REN21 2009). Although biofuels represents only 2 per cent of the global agricultural value chain, it has a major impact in the agricultural, trade, and investment policy environments, as well as in the lives of poor producers pursuing income from biofuels feedstock production. This subsection provides a literature review on the impacts of biofuels regulatory frameworks on developing countries, as highlighted already in the previous section. The discussion here sets the context for the more in-depth analysis in Chapters 4 and 5 of the biofuels experience in Tanzania and Malaysia.

The discussion in the earlier subsections attempted to draw a comparative picture of biofuels policies and related impacts on developing countries. In Table 3.8 an attempt is made to systematically present the regulatory information to show that the biofuels regulatory environment causes the highest levels of uncertainty and negative impacts for GHG emissions and farm income. This table does not capture the political stress that is embedded within the GVC and global trade environment. To elaborate, at every stage of the production and value addition action, bargaining, cost transfer, and issues of manipulation are present. In any analysis of global trade and GVC this business reality has to be identified if we are to protect the rights and values of cultivators.

Despite the uncertainties and overly complex biofuels global trade environment, developing countries are joining the race to biofuels market capitalization. Agricultural comparative advantage dictated by land availability and low labour costs, coupled with the need to increase farm income and rural development have spurred developing countries to allow both local and foreign direct investment in the biofuels industry. The least developed countries enjoy preferential treatment from the EU and the US and are exempt from export duties under the Generalized System of Preference clause of GATT. Despite the benefits, the opportunity costs are high for developing countries if the biofuels industry fails to live up to its promises. The scenario is even worse for countries that have converted land, or taken long-term leases – for at least 40 years – on land, to plant the

Table 3.8 Impact of policy on economic, environmental, and social indicators

Instrument		Fossil fuel use reduction	GHG reduction	Farm income	Biofuels producers	Consumer surplus (food)	Consumer surplus (energy)	Government budget
Energy & Fuel Policies	Biofuel tax credit	+	<>	+	+	-	<>	-
	Biofuel mandate	+	<>	+	+	-	-	<>
	Carbon/gasoline tax	+	+	<>	<>	<>	-	+
	Efficiency standard	+	+	<>	<>	<>	+	<>
	Vehicle subsidy	<>	<>	<>	<>	<>	+	-
Agriculture & Trade Policies	Price support	+	<>	+	<>	+	+	-
	Acreage control	<>	<>	+	-	-	-	-
	Import tariff	+	<>	+	+	-	-	+
	Export subsidy	<>	<>	+	+	-	-	-
	Export quota	+	<>	-	+	+	+	<>
	Certification	-	<>	<>	<>	+	+	<>

Note: + = Positive impact, <> = Uncertain, - = Negative impact
Source: Reproduced with modifications from Rajagopal and Zilberman 2007.

inedible jatropha as they will not even be able to eat the produce if the market fails. However, it seems that biofuels demand will soar, driven by rising environmental concerns and tightening of regulations to mitigate climate change in the richer countries.

Only 18 per cent of the developing countries have biofuels policies, whereas more than 65 countries at present are involved in the biofuels GVC. As such, it is important to highlight here some common threads of threats that the biofuels feedstock industry brings to the already vulnerable agricultural sector. These threats, when ranged against countries which have no regulatory environment to protect the rights of the farmers, produce further complications.

First, the majority of developing countries involved in biofuels feedstock production initiatives have done so without considering the long-term effects (Bekunda *et al.* 2009; Biswas *et al.* 2010). Such biofuels programmes are often part of export promotion initiatives and are buttressed by foreign companies like BP, Sun Biofuels, and D1 from the UK, which are major investors in Ethiopia and Malaysia, as well as Swedish SEKAB which invested in Tanzania.[25] The countries involved have a significant pre-existing donor relationship – a theme explored in the case studies in Chapters 4 and 5. Researchers from public, private, and non-profit sectors document the impacts of biofuels on developing countries and, so far, the findings differ widely, as seen in Table 3.9.

Based on current and expected mandates, developing countries will account for an estimated 44 per cent of global demand for biodiesel and 47 per cent of bioethanol demand in 2030 (Bekunda *et al.* 2009). Developing countries are the source of agricultural commodities, but suffer from impoverishment deeply rooted in poverty and incomplete land rights. The rapid expansion of biofuels feedstock production in developing countries may add stress to land, water, and other necessary inputs which are already in short supply (Hoyos and Medvedev 2009).

Indirect land use and water utilization for biofuels certification processing is still under discussion. In the meantime, the biofuels industry adds further stress to biodiversity (see Cornelissen and Dehue 2009).[26] The inherent problem is how to control the expansion of land use for biofuels feedstock production. As shown in Figure 3.4, the land and water use for food crops grown for consumption are sometimes indistinguishable from those for crops grown for biofuels export production. For example, some of the land and water may be used directly to produce maize. As the demand for biofuels grows, a part of the harvested maize may end up in ethanol production. The transfer of maize from the food value chain to the biofuels value chain is sometimes unrealized at the time of cropping. Often the decision on how to consume harvested maize is made based on the market demand at the time. Moreover, one crop can displace another food crop. For example, maize displaced soybean on some existing cropland in mid-west America, which, in turn, may induce increased soybean production and conversion of

Table 3.9 Consequences of biofuels feedstock industry development for developing countries

Source	Affecting factor	Implications	Positive/negative
Diao et al. 2007; Kojima and Johnson 2006	National economy	Developing countries, particularly African countries can attract long-term investors and influence farmers. Help with national income, infrastructure development, and agricultural productivity. Overall push toward Millennium Development Goal (MDG) attainment.	+ve
Field et al. 2008; Cunha da Costa 2004; Searchinger 2009	Land utilization	Biofuels can reclaim existing or future abandoned agricultural lands.	+ve
Hazell and Pachauri 2006; Mulugetta 2009; Binns 2007; ICRISAT 2007; Woods 2006 Arndt et al. 2008	Local agriculture	Will improve the agricultural productivity and yield, thus improving farmers' income. Technology transfer and knowledge transfer. Local agricultural supply-chain development.	+ve
ICRISAT 2007; IEA 2004; Madubansi and Shackleton 2006	Energy security	Market liberalization following advance new technologies can bring strengthened rural development, oil security, and reduction of emissions. Local electrification and infrastructure development.	+ve
Sawe 2008; Smeets et al. 2007; van Eijck and Romijn 2008	Employment	Engage unemployed youth, improve knowledge, gender equality, and household incomes.	+ve
Cotula et al. 2010; IEA 2006; OECD/FAO 2008	Land expropriation	Food land taken over to produce biofuels feedstock.	−ve
UNEP 2008, 2009a	Carbon emission increase	Rainforest and peatland is increasingly being cleared to plant palm oil in East Asia. Exacerbation of climate change.	−ve
Arvidson 2009; de Schutter 2009; Lam et al. 2009; Mingorance 2007	Human rights	Forced eviction and other human rights abuse of minority populations in Colombia, Malaysia, Indonesia to appropriate land for palm oil for biodiesel.	−ve
Koerbitz 2007; Sobey and Watson 2008; Myers et al. 2000; Sala et al. 2009	Loss of biodiversity	Premature promotion of intensive non-food based perennial biofuels crops, exacerbation of land degradation, loss of land fertility, and disturbance of local ecology.	−ve

Source: Author.

grassland or forest land elsewhere, consuming land and water. Thus, both the direct and indirect land-use changes caused by expanded biofuels production need to be considered for a full understanding of potential environmental impacts.

The extent of land area reported for biofuels may not even reflect the likely land categories that will actually be used for producing biofuels. Meanwhile, regulatory frameworks cannot effectively categorize, assign, and monitor land use for feedstock production because of weak land tenure systems. Many studies have attempted to quantify land-use displacement due to the expansion of biofuels feedstock production in developing countries. By compiling the projected scenarios (UNEP 2009b) deforestation rates of 13 Mha per year in 2006 may rise to 286 Mha per year by 2030. Such escalation will also aggravate the already stressed water table (OECD 2006; Pimentel and Patzek 2005; UNEP 2009c).

Addressing the indistinguishable nature of land use prompted various alternative policy proposals to harmonize the global biofuels market. As highlighted in Table 3.7, none of the certification schemes include the role of existing behavioural practices, social practices, institutions, and infrastructure factors, which considerably affect harmonized labelling.[27] For example, the EU Renewable Energy Directive that sets sustainability standards for biofuels production and imports does not even mention fertilizer use (EU 2003), which along with water use, pesticides, and herbicides are serious problems for soil pollution and groundwater toxification (Harvey 2010), or practices like charcoal production by deforestation with subsequent use of that land for biofuels crop plantation.

Policy makers and scholars are now engaging in research on how to minimize the negative effects of the biofuels industry and relevant policies on developing countries. Emerging carbon markets can provide complementary revenues that make certain types of land deals more attractive, such as biofuels production or reforestation projects under a new

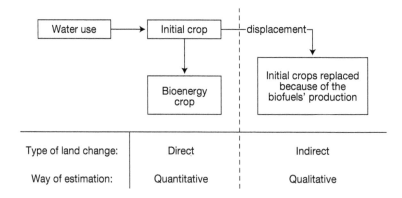

Figure 3.4 The indistinguishable nature of land and water use for food and biofuels
Source: Reproduced with modifications from RSB 2008.

mechanism for reducing emissions from deforestation and forest degradation. Strategic diplomacy through bilateral and multilateral agreements on technological cooperation can help promote green technologies and supply-chain upgrading to improve biofuels producing countries' bargaining power in the carbon market.

3.4 Conclusion

This section focused on first generation transport biofuels. The global biofuels industry is driven by innovation, globalization, and regulatory frameworks that are laying down the 'rules of the game' for biofuels value chain participants. While the literature is still divided on energy efficiency and carbon savings, there is considerable evidence of opportunity costs for developing countries; negative externalities are not addressed by integrated global policy and national institutional apparatus. Although, as Section 3.1 of this chapter shows, the history of biofuels goes far back into the early nineteenth century, the status of the current biofuels industry is still at an early stage. Nevertheless, with promising demand and market liberalization, developing countries' comparative advantage in producing biofuels feedstock, due to their lower opportunity costs of land and other production factors, make this a worthwhile adventure. This is covered in Section 3.2 as biodiesel and jatropha appear to be more promising for the emerging biofuels value chain. In Section 3.3, the chapter discusses the inconsistencies from the literature review on the global and national level apparatus used for biofuels industry expansion and their unclear impacts on developing countries.

It also attempted to set the context of a complex, dynamic, and often contradictory, market and institutional environment, within which developing countries are participating to reap benefits. Biofuels are still an untested commodity, but the industry has already grown significantly with government help and market influence. However, it is clear that the industry is not yet at a stage to compete with the fossil fuels market without substantial government support. National commitments from India, China, Brazil, and European countries to cut transportation emissions may help sustain the industry, but there are costs to the environment, the land, and human rights (Banse and Grethe 2008; Fargione *et al.* 2008; UNEP 2009a). While there are benefits to developing countries as market participants, negative effects like high production costs, high food prices, and displacement of land and water make benefits subjective to the specific crop, production and processing system, input costs, and normative policy environment. Empirical studies are necessary to draw any meaningful conclusion, as the literature review shows that there is no common ground.

The following chapters utilize the IFS framework, to overcome weaknesses in the sustainable development literature and provides a tool to conduct empirical investigation to measure and contextualize the impacts of biofuels industry development in participating developing countries.

Notes

1   Native customary land rights and customary land tenure are used interchangeably in this chapter.
2   Contract farming and outgrower schemes are used interchangeably. Borrowing a definition from the FAO, we consider 'an out-grower scheme as a contractual partnership between growers or landholders and a company for the production of commercial forest products'. Outgrower schemes vary considerably because of different treatments of inputs, costs, risks, and benefits sharing scope between growers/landholders and companies. Also, contract scope and payment timing varies widely. In other words, while growers can act independently or collectively to supply materials to the processing companies, financial benefits can be paid in credit or in advance with or without other benefits. Outgrower schemes are usually prescribed in formal contracts where producers are responsible for their land. Such schemes, heavily practiced in the forestry sector, are a popular option for the biofuels sector. Source: FAO 2001.
3   To reiterate, despite much discussion on second generation biofuels for their high energy efficiency without impact on the food market the technologies are far from being commercially viable (Paul and Ernsting 2007; Schenk *et al.* 2008).
4   For more details on the ethanol timeline see www.icminc.com/timeline/start. html
5   These cars were not flex-fuel vehicles, as are used in Brazil today. They would only run on ethanol.
6   Brazil is taking the US to the WTO for its ethanol import tariff which is hurting the expansion of biofuels usage. Like the US, other countries also still have high import tariffs and protect their costly feedstock production sectors with subsidies. This is a debate that is still unresolved. (www.ictsd.org/bridges-news/ bridges/news/us-ethanol-tariffs-subsidies-end-brazil-likely-to-continue-ethanol-imports)
7   It has been argued, however, that although it is a fact that deforestation from logging and cattle raising in the Northern Region is a problem for Brazil, it has nothing to do with the sugarcane plantation expansion, which is happening in the Southeast and Northeast regions. In fact, Brazilian authorities believe that depredated pasture area which has low carbon content can be revitalized by sugarcane plantation (de Almeida *et al.* 2007).
8   Wheat on the international market rose by 130 per cent, the price of rice rose by 74 per cent, the price of soya by 87 per cent, and the price of maize rose by 31 per cent in a single year (see FAO 2009a).
9   Ten German biofuels companies filed for bankruptcy. In the US VeraSun filed for Chapter 11 bankruptcy protection in 2007. Other major public biofuels companies include Northeast biofuels, Hereford biofuels, E3 biofuels, Earth Biofuels, and Peking biofuels. (For more information see *BiofuelsDigest* 2009.)
10 Reference scenarios are mainly modelled to show the market demand changes based on oil price and government targets and help. To learn more see IEA 2009.
11 CDM enables industrialized countries to finance low carbon emission technologies in developing countries as an alternative to more costly technologies for reducing GHG emissions from their respective countries.
12 Castor requires replantation every two years, but jatropha plantations can remain for 40 years. This is a significant difference which favours jatropha over castor.

13 Compared with other oil containing crops, jatropha is a mid-ranged oil crop. For example, the oil content of ground nut kernel is 42 per cent, rapeseed is 37 per cent, sunflower is 32 per cent and soybean is 14 per cent.

14 Output widely varies from traditional to mechanical engine driven screw presses. Most commercial plantations use engine driven screw presses, but 10 per cent of the oil produced is needed to fuel the diesel engine.

15 In 2007 Europe paid farmers a subsidy of EUR 45 per hectare for any biofuel crop produced.

16 Congress and the US EPA have set the ambitious benchmark of producing 36 billion gallons of home-grown biofuel a year by 2022, reducing dependence on volatile foreign oil.

17 See for example FAO 2008; IRGC 2008.

18 Market failure is related to incidents which prevent proper valuation and allocation of environmental assets, leading to prices that do not reflect the accurate environmental costs. Such divergence from the actual prices for goods and services leads to the loss of clean air and water, and to environmental degradation, e.g., overfishing and the depletion of the ozone layer.

19 Subsidies in the US, Canada, and the EU cost taxpayers and consumers on average USD 960 to USD 1,700 per tonne of CO_2-eq. saved. This level far exceeds the carbon value at European and US carbon markets, indicating that there are other technologies which are far more environmentally and economically cost effective. For more discussion on this see OECD 2008.

20 It is difficult to estimate job creation in the biofuels sector for several reasons. First, there are seasonal jobs in the industry; second, 'indirect' jobs' definitions are unclear and major estimates only look at the major biofuels producers based on existing capacity (i.e., operation and maintenance).

21 On 11 January 2010 Brazil revised its blending target to 20 or 25 per cent anhydrous ethanol for its proven competitive prices and environmental benefits. A 5 per cent reduction translates to about 100 million more litres available for blending (UNICA 2009).

22 With the exception of fish, fish products, and an additional number of specific products like skins, silk, wool, cotton, flax, and modified starches.

23 Argentina levies an export tax of 27.5 per cent and 24 per cent on soybean seeds and oil respectively, while biodiesel export tax is set at only 5 per cent.

24 The General Agreement on Tariffs and Trade (GATT) is core to the WTO's operations.

25 SEKAB pulled out of Tanzania in 2009 after a long controversy about their role in the country. See Arvidson 2009 for more details.

26 It has been suggested to RSB that indirect land-use impacts should be included in the biofuels standards, but instead of using GHG balance calculations based on LCA, there should be a risk-based approach. Criteria need to be defined in the RSB standards that differentiate biofuels with a reduced risk of indirect impacts from those without reduced risk (Cornelissen and Dehue 2009).

27 See, for more information on biofuels related eco-labelling and certification scheme, FAO 2008; Fontaras *et al.* 2009; UNCTAD 2008.

4   The Tanzanian biofuels experience

Biofuels industry development presents Tanzania with many opportunities as well as challenges.[1] On average, about a quarter of the Tanzanian population suffers from persistent food insecurity and extreme poverty each year (MAFC 2006), making food security a major concern. Food crops are mainly cultivated by women with hand tools, 90 per cent are rain fed, with only one harvest a year. Although no national biofuels policy has been finalized, a biofuels industry development plan has been included in the Tanzanian Development Vision 2025, Tanzania's National Strategy for Growth and Reduction of Poverty (MKUKUTA), and the National Energy Policy. In October 2009 the government suspended all biofuels investment in the country and halted land allocations for biofuels development under growing pressure from non-state agents (Browne 2009; MAFC 2009).

This chapter argues that Tanzanian underdevelopment is strongly associated with weak property rights, a misaligned decentralized governance system, and a weak infrastructural system that contributes to unplanned agro-industrialization with disastrous results for the poor. The author conducted a fieldwork research project from October to December 2008 to examine jatropha as the major feedstock of the Tanzanian biodiesel production experience. There are several reasons for selecting jatropha. First, studies suggest that biodiesel is more practical than bioethanol development since first generation biodiesel is more cost competitive and will likely dominate market development in the medium term (de Wit *et al.* 2010; IEA 2009; OECD 2008). Lamers *et al.* suggest that in the short and medium terms biodiesel will grow in the internal market, while bioethanol production is facing opposition from the major producers (2008). Second, biodiesel is gaining attention for its lower emissions, which may play a role in climate change mitigation (EUActiv 2009; Wiesenthal *et al.* 2009). Third, non-edible biodiesel feedstock crops like jatropha are gaining popularity because they are not food crops. Jatropha is also suitable for arid and semi-arid land, which is plentiful in Tanzania. Fourth, in the US and EU biodiesel subsidies are being slashed and facing threats of moratoriums, which indicates greater opportunities for biodiesel crop exports like jatropha from developing countries (Beattie 2008; Rainer 2006; van Eijck and Romijn

2008). Finally, 64 per cent of biofuels investment in Tanzania is for jatropha with a significant number of applications due to be processed at the Tanzania Investment Centre (TIC). Although the government plans to produce biofuels for national usage, until the country sets up national targets and a grid feed-in system, producing companies are focusing on exports.

The remainder of the chapter is organized as follows. Section 4.1 discusses the methodology of the research while Section 4.2 applies it to the poverty and food security situations in Tanzania. Section 4.3 presents a case study of the two districts examined in this study, Kisarawe and Bahi. Section 4.4 then discusses two biofuel companies operating in the districts, Sun Biofuels and East Africa Biodiesel, respectively. Finally, Section 4.5 concludes the chapter.

4.1 Case study description

Tanzanian farmers involved in biofuels crop production are deeply embedded in chronic, persistent poverty (Bryceson 1993; Ellis and Mdoe 2003). To analyse the complexity within which the biofuels sector operates in Tanzania, both qualitative and quantitative analytical approaches are used. This section draws descriptive and explanatory dimensions from the conceptual frameworks of political economics, institutional economics, and global governance literature.

A multisectoral approach has been taken to integrate the public, private, non-state, and non-profit actors in energy, agriculture, and national economic development plans and conservation activities in Tanzania. For this project, visits were made to Dar es Salaam, Kisarawe, and Dodoma to research bioenergy companies, in coordination with the local FAO and the Tanzania Biofuels Taskforce of the Ministry of Agriculture, Food Security, and Cooperatives from November to December 2008.

Figure 4.1 shows the national administrative institutional governance structure of Tanzania. A constructive and conscious approach was taken to trace the institutional perspective of respective authorities on assessing jatropha for biofuels production. During the time of the fieldwork, the Tanzanian economy, along with the global economy, was struck by high food and energy costs, so the interviewing process was structured to help contextualize why jatropha gained national attention as a means to attain food security and modernize the agricultural sector (Tanzania 2008a).

In addition to observing household responses and the anticipated advantages and disadvantages of having a biofuel company in the country, inquiries were made as to how people's experiences with economic and environment changes influenced their perspectives on having foreign biofuel companies in their villages. The selection of field locations and villages were made based on the twin criteria of, first, the representativeness of the rural livelihoods, broadly matching the overall Tanzanian rural environment and, second, the ability to capture agro-ecological aspects of varying kinds which makes jatropha production a suitable cash crop for the villagers. Six villages were selected from two districts – Kisarawe from the Pwani region and Bahi from the Dodoma region (previously part of the Dodoma Rural district) (see Figure 4.1). Kisarawe is semi-arid near the coast, supporting a single maize production season, while Bahi in the centre of the country is an arid region. Two biofuel companies, Sun Biofuels and East Africa Biodiesel (EABD), have started large operations there. Sun Biofuels is a British company operating in Kisarawe and EABD is led by a Kenyan, registered in Tanzania, operating in the Dodoma district. Sun Biofuels has accumulated 9,000 ha of land over 11 villages in the Kisarawe district. EABD has targeted 6,000 ha over 12 villages in the Dodoma region.

The villages selected for study are organized based on the status of jatropha operations. Marumbo, Chakenge, and Mtamba in the Kisarawe

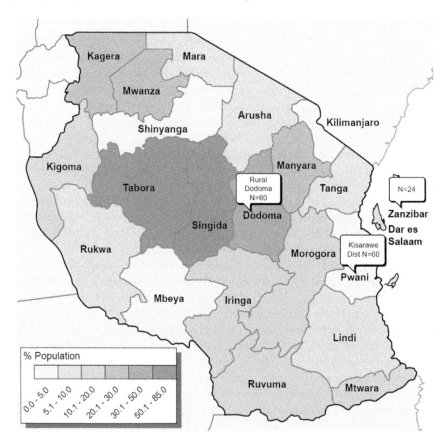

Figure 4.1 Map of case study areas and level of food insecurity
Note: Darker shade = high level of rural household food insecurity. In Dodoma, Singida and Tabora, 45–55 per cent of the households are food insecure. The Pwani region is one of least food insecure areas. Fieldwork conducted in the Bahi district of Dodoma and in the Kisarawe district of the Pwani region. Scale 1:10 m.
Source: FAO data and Naturalearthdata.com.

District were among 11 villages proposed for engagement in jatropha production by Sun Biofuels, and Mdemu, Mchito, and Chifkutwa in the Bahi district were among 12 villages proposed for engagement in jatropha by EABD. These districts are close to the major cities of Dar es Salaam (the financial capital) and Dodoma City (the national capital) but the transportation connectivity to the villages from the main towns is at a bare minimum, with earth roads making the villages quite remote and inaccessible without private transportation.

The population interviewed was chosen according to five criteria: (a) those of mixed age in a gender set to capture diversity between the youth, middle aged, and elders; (b) those who have allocated land to investors; (c) those interested in participating in the outgrower scheme or contract farming;[2] (d) those who had participated in village meetings concerning land allocation; and (e) those who are, or who will be, engaged in jatropha planting or related activities. Subject-specific questionnaires were used to guide discussions and qualitative and quantitative data collected (see examples in Appendices C, D, and E). However, for better understanding, if the questions were deemed unrealistic or inapplicable, alternative questions or scenarios were proposed to the focus group. Finally, a data triangulation process was used to validate interviews by collecting the same information from multiple sources. As mentioned, I used the ministry, farmers, and the investors for data triangulation.

4.2 National institutional and infrastructural assessment

Biofuels industry development targets are included in the Tanzanian Development Vision 2025 (Tanzania 2008a). This fits into Tanzania's MKUKUTA, introduced in June 2005. Donor countries and international development agencies like the FAO consulted with the Tanzanian government in designing the Tanzania Biofuel Guidelines in 2008. The consultancy reports showed that there is no clear biofuel blending target set by the government, but many of the benefits noted in the policy draft are guided by the objective of improving the national agricultural sector (MEM 2008). This section analyses the factors behind poverty and food insecurity and how biofuels industry investment is a fit from structural and institutional perspectives.

4.2.1 Agricultural development assessment

Traditionalism characterizes Tanzanian agriculture with farmers subjected to structural poverty and missing markets. According to the 2005 national statistics, 85 per cent of the country's poor people live in rural areas and rely on agriculture for subsistence (NBS 2006). Poverty is widespread among farmers due to scarce fertile land, water shortages, inadequate government support, and a lack of markets for their produce. Such problems are acute in arid and semi-arid areas of Tanzania where farmers are stuck in the vicious cycle of structural poverty and food insecurity (IFAD 2001).

Tanzanian food insecurity is influenced by changes in climatic conditions that cause long dry seasons, frequently leading to drought, resulting in acute starvation. Table 4.1 illustrates food self-sufficiency, where for most years with a figure below 100 per cent the root cause is weather related. In particular, years 1997/1998 and 2003/2004 saw 150 million people in food crisis. WFP reports acute food shortages during 2005/2006 and in 2007 from a long dry spell throughout the horn of Africa (WFP 2007).

Unfortunately, the government failed to invest in agricultur for many years. From 1998 to 2003, the allocation ranged from 3.5 per cent to 4 per cent of GDP, which kept the agricultural sector quite underproductive. In 2004, investment rose back up to 5.7 per cent of total government expenditure (MAFC 2006), but distribution of funds was not seen at the local level. As the case study later shows in subsections 4.3.1 and 4.3.2, the government has already accepted the fact that given the complete dependence on nature, changing weather patterns have increased food insecurity conditions for the poor in absence of integrated institutional support (Tanzania 2004).

Despite continuous international aid and Tanzanian government commitment, the country has made little progress in bolstering inadequate strategic grain reserves (SGR)[3] to 'cater for food emergencies for at least three months, with a capacity of 150,000 tonnes, which is used as a first line response in combating food emergency' (MAFC 2006). There are three interrelated issues in play here: (a) a year or two of good harvest is not enough to create a SGR for rainy days; (b) infrastructure limitations inhibit accumulating surplus from the coastal and western regions; and (c) weak, decentralized government isolates local government from central government, giving more power to the markets, which have already failed. Given these conditions, successfully building a SGR has been elusive.

Table 4.1 Domestic food crop self-sufficiency,[4] 1994/1995 to 2004/2005

Year	Production (tonnes)	Sufficiency (percentage)
1994/1995	7,719,200	95
1995/1996	8,020,700	110
1996/1997	6,181,400	117
1997/1998[5]	8,138,380	88
1998/1999	7,440,531	109
1999/2000	7,323,000	108
2000/2001	7,584,000	92
2001/2002	8,572,288	94
2002/2003	7,372,720	102
2003/2004[6]	9,000,000	88

Source: MAFC various years.

Tanzania underwent structural readjustment that decentralized the government in the 1980s, but the process was never completed, leading to significant information asymmetries (Bryceson 1993). The central government houses the Ministry of Agriculture, which channels funding to the regional administration, as shown previously in Figure 2.5. However, due to corruption, miscommunication, and political misalignment, funds do not always trickle down to the district level. Aside from incomplete decentralization, there are power struggles within the ministries that can result in loss of national income (Agrawal and Gibson 1999; Ellis and Mdoe 2003). For example, in December 2008, only seven international companies registered with the Tanzanian Tax Authority, whereas 64 biofuels companies sought land from the Ministry of Agriculture. Along with declining food exports, declining food aid, and growing food imports, Figure 4.2 shows a negative net food trade for the country. This is indicative of the poor national food security situation. The government even complacently argues for transitory food insecurity in marginal areas (MAFC 2006).

Finally, household income is a serious issue that exacerbates household food insecurity for the subsistence farmers. Even in seasons when they produce surplus, farm households are bound to sell their surplus crops immediately after harvest to middlemen to whom they have pre-existing debts for seeds, fertilizer, or cash. Most rural farmer families face competing needs of utilizing crops for food versus for sale to pay for medicine, education, or clothing. Myopic, gender correlated spending decisions also

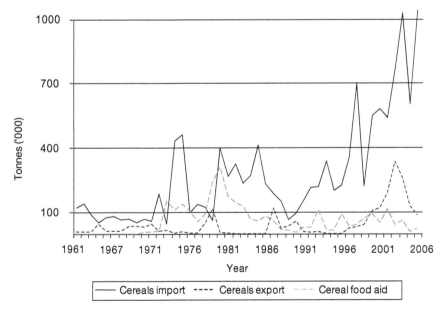

Figure 4.2 Comparison of total cereal imports, exports, and aid received, 1961–2006

Source: Author created from NBS 2007 data.

effect household level food insecurity (MAFC 2006). As a result, six to eight months of the year, peaking during the rainy season when food demand outstrips supply and prices rise, rural farmers do not have sufficient crops to eat or cash to purchase food from the market.

4.2.2 Infrastructure development assessment

Land, energy, and transportation are three integrated factors responsible for poverty, vulnerability, and insecurity creation. In order to reduce levels of poverty, vulnerability, and insecurity, the three integrated factors need to be carefully understood and analysed. In this subsection, each of the factors are further analysed within the Tanzanian context.

Despite there being an ample amount, land presents challenges deeply rooted in the land tenure system, which is embedded in the weak institutional regulatory framework. The Village Act of 1999 claims 'to recognise that all Land in Tanzania is public land vested in the President as trustee on behalf of all citizens' and states that the president can 'transfer any area of the village land to general or reserved land' both for public and private sector interests (Tanzania 1999). However, the land tenure system was never completed or fully nationalized. In effect, there are two different tenure systems coexisting, customary and statutory, causing confusion and contestation in Tanzania (Ardhi 2008; Jacobsen 1999).

The lands allocated to the biofuels companies are customary lands, signed off for 99 years, often for free or for a minimum one-time rent. These lands are the subject of contestation between the people and the government. There is no provision for judicial arbitration, and if contested, the president's rule overrides any other rule of law. For instance, with shifts in political power or changed motives of farmers, companies with investment that cannot be easily recovered could be in jeopardy. Out of such insecurity, the private sector is disinterested in structural investments, which, ironically, are the type most likely to benefit local communities involved with biofuels production. In an interview, the largest bioethanol company in Tanzania, SEKAB, from Sweden, expressed genuine concern about their multimillion dollar investment plan.[7] It is likely that other companies also worry over returns on their investments.

In the absence of an efficient, effective, economical, and transparent informative system for land administration, most villagers perceive their land as a valueless, abundant resource. Since there is no collateral system to access credit, farmers make production, investment, and land rights transfer decisions based on their own perceptions of tenure. These decisions are guided by customary law, yielding suboptimal benefits. Villages at various levels of land reforms handled the biofuels land allocation process differently, e.g., some companies utilized the TIC to delegate their demand for land to the local administrations while others directly approach the targeted villagers.

During the fieldwork, it was found that 94 per cent of villagers believed that they had 'a lot of land' and that 'land limitation is never a problem'. The villagers explained that since native land cannot be sold, there is greater economic benefit to leasing it out to a third party for investment than keeping it unused or under protected status. Since abundant, unutilized land has virtually no economic value and no protected rights, villagers often viewed leased lands as unclaimed, whereas investors understood it as a proper 99-year lease. Differences of meaning interestingly create differences in expectations, e.g., direct compensation or indirect compensation.

Aside from the land tenure system, the transportation sector is one of the major factors that exacerbate small farmers' vulnerability in the agriculture market. In Tanzania, the transportation sector significantly influences agricultural sector development and directly affects access to markets (IFAD 2001; Thum 2004). Transportation costs are two to five times higher than those of Indonesia and Pakistan, which reflects the inefficiency of the sector (NIT 2003). Tanzania does not produce its own petroleum oil and all requirements are met by imports (NIT 2003). A collective study by German Technical Cooperation (GTZ) shows that Tanzania has no regulatory framework in the petroleum industry, which results in massive tax evasion, uncontrollable increases in fuel prices and, consequently, smuggling of petroleum (GTZ 2005).[8] Moreover, the industry went into liberalization without establishing any regulatory environment or guidance policies.[9] The impact of high international prices and in-built marketing inefficiencies are due to the oligopolistic structure of the oil industry, which makes consumers particularly vulnerable.

As transaction cost theory postulates, missing markets for agricultural commodities happens because high transportation costs impinge on mobility of resources, which, over time creates an information gap in capacity building along with higher transaction costs for market participants. Accordingly, a study showed that the cost of transporting maize from/to Dar es Salaam would constitute 49 per cent to 60 per cent of the retail price. This makes it cost effective to import maize to the population-dense port city of Dar es Salaam, though prices are still too high for poor consumers (calculated from Isinika *et al.* 2005). Producers avoid expensive trips to national brokers, preferring to smuggle surplus crops across the border. According to the Ministry of Agriculture, the neighbouring countries of Kenya and Uganda consume more Tanzanian maize than Tanzania itself.

Tanzania also suffers from a major deficiency in energy consumption as 90 per cent of its population depends on solid biomass like wood fuel, wood charcoal, or forest residue and modern petroleum energy contributes only 7 per cent, the majority of which goes to transportation (Sawe 2008). Some optimistic studies argue that biofuels production has the potential to provide rural energy and substitute for costly oil imports, currently USD 1.3–1.6 billion per year, totalling 25 per cent of total foreign exchange earnings (MAFC 2009; RSB 2009). Ironically, using local biofuels for domestic consumption is not easily possible for two simple reasons. First, the domestic automobile fleet is not biofuel compatible as they are all used and out of warranty.[10] Seconds the rural electricity grid cannot easily take external energy feeds into the system (RSB 2009). However, TaTedo and other local non-profit organizations are working with jatropha and castor oil seeds to manually press seed oil to burn for lighting and cooking, thereby replacing dependency on coal and wood.

4.3   State level agro-economy and biofuels institutional assessment

This study included three months of fieldwork undertaken in the Tanzanian coastal region district of Kisarawe and in the central region district of Bahi in autumn 2008. Two biofuels companies were focused on. The first is Sun Biofuels, a UK based company, engaged in 11 villages in Kisarawe since 2006, occupying 9,000 ha of land. The second company is EABD, with 6,000 ha of land from six villages in the Bahi district since 2008. Both companies focus on jatropha cultivation, jatropha oil extraction for export, and other by-products like seedcakes, biocharcoal, and fertilizer production for local usage.

Both firms have local farmer partnership schemes, also known as outgrower schemes, where the companies provide seeds, knowledge, and a commitment to purchase crops, and the farmers give up their land, labour, and other production resources. Often, these extremely poor farmers are able to cultivate only two to four acres of land with their hand tools and no irrigation, replacing food crops like maize and cassava for a biofuels jatropha crop. Minor differences in profit sharing among schemes dictate the portion of land dedicated to jatropha as discussed later in Section 4.4.

4.3.1   Kisarawe agricultural economy

Kisarawe is one of six districts of the Pwani region on Tanzania's east coast and is bordered by the Mkuranga district in the east, the Morogoro district in the west, Dar es Salaam in the northeast, the Kibaha district to the north and the Rufiji district to the south. The native people are the Wazaramo, who can be found in official documents dating back over 100 years.[11] The population of the Kisarawe district was 95,614 with an average population growth rate of 2.1 per cent (Kisarawe 2008).[12] The area has the least off-farm income among coastal regions and 90 per cent of Kisarawe farmers work at a subsistence level (Tanzania 2007). The average household size is 4.6 members, comparable to the national average.

The district is only 40 km away from Dar es Salaam, the major trading and financial capital of the country, with a good road connection. Two railroad lines service the district, Central and TAZARA, which help support Kisarawe's potential for agro-industry development. Also, there are three permanent rivers, the Ruvu, Wami, and Rufiji, though these are inaccessible for agriculture due to poor water management. Similarly, the interior of the region is inaccessible by traders due to weak rural transportation and road systems. As a result, agricultural markets are underdeveloped or missing. The recent census shows that despite ecological suitability for crops (e.g., maize, rice, cashew, sorghum, cowpea, [sweet] potato, cotton, passion fruit, sesame, and millet) the region's yields are dropping (see Table 4.2) and only 4 per cent of the farmers use any kind of agricultural input (Tanzania 2007). Traditional agricultural system utilization causes Kisarawe to have a low land utilization at 1.5 ha/household (Tanzania 2007), which results in a per capita income of TZS 279,000, about USD 250,[13] which is half the national average.

The district is failing to sustain its major cash crop, cashew nuts. Aside from the discouraging missing market factor, young farmers perceive cashew tree cultivation as reminiscent of the village cooperative initiatives, based on equality of opportunity and self-help, established in the 1960s, which were politically rejected. Very few new cashew nut trees are being planted and cared for since the cost of inputs is high and timely availability and fair prices for the produce are limited. Cassava, which is cultivated by 53 per cent of crop growing households in the region, is slowly replacing cashew as the dominant cash crop because of its low maintenance and drought resistance (Tanzania 2007).

Furthermore, neither regional food sufficiency nor high commodity prices have helped rural farmers' livelihoods. Instead, local market prices for maize, rice, sugar, and other food crops doubled between 2005 and 2008.[14] Without additional purchasing power, rural farmers have moved deeper into impoverishment and insecurity. There are three main reasons for the low gain: (a) high cost of inputs; (b) high transportation costs; and (c) high grain processing costs. Farmers in Kisarawe suffer from food insecurity to the extent that they have had to eat seed grains, engage in barter trade, work more hours, borrow money, and take their children out of school. Many families have supplemented their household income by engaging in illegal charcoal making and poaching timber from neighbouring forests.[15] With low farm income, little off-farm employment, and no social safety nets, the Kisarawe population is stuck in a vicious cycle of poverty. Table 4.3 shows food self-sufficiency, which follows a similarly volatile trend.

Table 4.2 Major food crop yields in Kisarawe, tonnes per hectare

	1995–1996	1997–1998	1999–2000	2001–2002	2003–2004	2005–2006	*National average (t/ha) (2002/2003–2005/2006)*
Maize	0.9	0.8	0.8	0.7	0.67	0.7	5
Sorghum	1.2	1.0	0.7	2.6	0.23	1	3
Millet	0.0	0.0	—	1.7	—	—	6
Rice	1.0	1.0	1.0	1.3	0.36	0.9	5
Cassava	1.5	1.8	1.5	1.7	—	—	6

Source: Kisarawe 2008.

Table 4.3 Food production in Kisarawe (2001/2002–2006/2007)

Year	Total food production*	Total requirement	Gap or surplus	SSR**
2001/2002	373,545	909,894	−536,348	41
2002/2003	329,637	315,135	14,503	105
2003/2004	137,426	222,519	85,094	62
2004/2005[16]	152,985	228,008	−75,023	67
2005/2006	253,273	238,144	15,129	106
2006/2007	292,309	245,901	46,409	119

*Cereal and non-cereal
**Self-sufficiency ratio, based on the previous year expressed as a percentage of food production over food requirement
Source: Kisarawe 2008.

Under the current Agricultural Sector Development Programme (ASDP), the Kisarawe government is seeking to boost its local economy by introducing a new cash crop – jatropha. Regional administrators and farmers hope that having a multinational company like Sun Biofuels in the area will empower the local community to improve their infrastructure, road and water systems, and modernize the agricultural sector. The questions are to what extent and at what rate may the benefits be realized?

4.3.2 *Bahi agricultural economy*

Bahi was an administrative ward in the Dodoma Rural district of the Dodoma region that gained district status in July 2007. Due to a political conflict, the Dodoma Rural district was divided into the Chamwino and Bahi districts. Through the Local Government Act, the minister is empowered to establish new districts in order to develop, promote, and maintain effective and efficient local government (Tanzania 1982). Since Bahi is still in its restructuring and reform phase, district specific data is missing, so some data is used from Dodoma Rural that is still relevant.[17]

According to the 2002 census, the Bahi ward has a total population of 8,858 with a population growth rate of 1.6 per cent and an average household size of five. This scarcely populated district is located on the central plateau of Tanzania to the west of Dar es Salaam and close to the capital of the nation – Dodoma. The central line of the Tanzania Railway Corporation passes through the region, increasing its potential as a commercial hub.

Bahi is among the poorest, least developed, and most food-insecure districts in Tanzania. Household income was estimated at TZS 178,000 (~USD 131) compared to a national average of TZS 548,388 (~USD 400) in 2007. This is below the global absolute poverty line of a dollar a day, adjusted to 2007 purchasing power. Almost entirely dependent on subsistence agriculture and livestock farming, nearly half of the rural population is aged between 0 and 15, and so unavailable to work (Tanzania 2007).

The agricultural environment of the Bahi district can be characterized as one that has a dry savannah climate and poor soil quality. Average rainfall is relatively low (500–800 mm annually) and unpredictable, but about 85 per cent of this falls in the four months between December and March and the first sowing needs to be done by January. Of the total 153 km district road network, 40 per cent is impassable during the rainy season, which directly affects market prices and labour prices. Soils are mostly sandy, with some becoming waterlogged during the rainy season, and have a tendency to salinity because of limited outflow. The soil is locally known as *mbuga*, meaning 'cotton black soils'. There is limited use of available land suitable for agricultural activity and even less use for food and cash-crop production. About 74 per cent (596,800) of the total land area is suitable farmland, but only 32 per cent of that is utilized (Bahi 2008).

Droughts in 1997, 2000–2003, and 2006, together with climate change, negatively affected sorghum, maize, and groundnut harvests, contributing to food shortages (Tanzania 2006). The input costs of fertilizers, seeds, pesticides, tools, and oxen outpaced the profits farmers could make by using them. In most cases, middlemen or microcredit lenders filled the market gap by asking exorbitant interest rates in the form of cash or shares in the harvest. Although district level data is missing, inferences from the regional data of the 2002/2003 census show that more than 90 per cent of smallholder farmers use slash and burn and traditional farming techniques, 75 per cent of smallholder farmers do not use any form of fertilizer, and less than 13 per cent use improved seeds. Only 2 per cent of the area is under irrigation and water sources are scarce. On average, one has to walk about 3–5 km to fetch water during the dry season, and the distance is even double that for some villages. As a result of all these impediments, an average farmholding per household of 2 acres for food crops and 2 acres for cash crops has very low productivity. Table 4.4 and Table 4.5 show this in more detail.

Table 4.4 Food production in Dodoma (2001/2002–2006/2007)

Year	Total food production*	Total requirement	Gap or surplus	SSR**
2001/2002[18]	299,610	426,619	–129,009	70
2002/2003	437,974	434,166	3,808	101
2003/2004[19]	237,851	431,195	–193,344	55
2004/2005	518,074	446,694	71,380	116
2005/2006[20]	380,545	459,810	–79,265	83
2006/2007	373,687	468,869	–95,185	80

*Cereal and non-cereal
**Self-sufficiency ratio, based on the previous year
Source: MAFC 2008.

Table 4.5 Production of food crops for the 2002/2003 to 2005/2006 seasons

	Productivity (t/ha)				National average (t/ha)
Crops	2002/2003	2003/2004	2004/2005	2005/2006	(2002/2003– 2005/2006)
Millet	0.2	0.8	0.7	1.5	5
Sorghum	0.6	0.5	0.8	0.7	3
Maize	0.0	0.6	0.9	1.6	6
Paddy	0.0	4.0	3.8	3.7	5
Cassava	0.2	2.2	0.5	0.7	6

Source: Calculated from Bahi 2008 and MAFC 2008.

The central and regional governments have taken a special interest in the Bahi district to boost its economy by reforming smallholder farming preferences and introducing non-traditional crops. First, a by-law was established requiring all able-bodied people to cultivate no less than 3 ha of drought resistant crops and 1 ha of cash crops like cassava, maize, or sorghum. Next, free seeds were distributed for cashew nut production, along with donated motorized pesticide blowers to the district agriculture office for local use. Similarly, farmers are being encouraged to grow grapes, sesame, and sunflowers in Bahi. For example, small processing facilities and a wine factory were established at Hombolo to create demand for wine grapes. The government is considering a warehouse receipt system to ensure fair prices, a stable market, and transportation facilities for small farmers. Finally, within these initiatives, biofuels industry development in Bahi fits in with the local ASDP.

4.4   Biofuels companies at the local level

Within the agricultural economic experience of the case study regions, investment opportunities are embedded in the political institutional framework of the country. Did the government overlook pre-existing problems of agro-commercialization before putting biofuels on the national agenda? Will biofuels companies in Kisarawe and Bahi be able to conduct business without compromising food security directly or indirectly? Existing structural poverty and inequality coupled with an incompletely decentralized governance system creates opportunities for manipulation, marginalization, and corruption at the local level where the poor are left vulnerable.

It is not unusual for a developing country with weak institutional and regulatory systems to experience an influx of investment in a primary commodity when world market prices are high. It is also not unusual for investors to exit the industry when profits become unfavourable. In the mid-1990s, rural Tanzania saw an influx of castor and *Moringa* investments for contract farming schemes in the same regions now under jatropha investment.

Like jatropha, castor and *Moringa* are suitable for production in semi-arid and arid zones. Within a few harvests, production excitement died out as global prices dropped due to competition from other developing countries in Asia and Latin America. The Tanzanian farmers found themselves with converted land and unsold crops.[21] A similar experience revisited the jatropha farmers, stuck in chronic poverty and food insecurity, who joined the jatropha rally and then were rapidly faced with unfavourable and unfortunate realities, as explained below.

4.4.1 Sun Biofuels and Kisarawe smallholders

Sun Biofuels is a UK based shareholding company registered with the TIC to produce biofuel. The company applied to lease 18,000 ha of land from 11 villages in Kisarawe with the aim of contract farming and estate farming.[22] For the first phase, the company selected and leased about 9,000 ha of land from six villages (as listed in Table 4.6) for 99 years. The district measures 353,500 ha, of which 309,000 ha are arable and only 83,645 ha are under cultivation (Kisarawe District 2007). For all the reasons why Kisarawe is conducive to food production, it is also attractive to jatropha investors.

The villages we visited for the research project are Marumbo and Chakenge from the first phase villages, and Mtamba from the second phase. Differences were noted in details like the land acquisition and contract farming process, which created a diversified welfare experience for the farmers involved.

4.4.2 The land acquisition process

Sun Biofuels acquired land through political means. In principle, although the president has ultimate control over land, the land allocation process needs villagers' approval. The TIC forwards investment applications to the Ministry of Land for approval and sends a government attaché to facilitate the investor

Table 4.6 Sun Biofuels land acquisition 2008

Village	Village area (ha)	Area acquired for jatropha (ha)	Percentage of total village area
Vilabwa	3,637.03	379.78	10.44
Chakenge	3,074.90	1,094.31	35.59
Mtakayo	3,154.56	1,546.52	49.02
Kidugalo	2,254.54	216.21	9.59
Marumbo	7,316.18	3,268.48	44.67
Muhaga	5,761.13	1,705.48	29.60
Total	25,198.34	8,210.78	32.58

Source: Author created from Kisarawe 2008 and jatropha land data.

proposal at the district level.[23] In this process, the role of the attaché is strictly administrative to introduce the company to the local governments as shown in Figure 4.3. The company, along with the government attaché, arrived in Kisarawe to acquire land with a Member of Parliament which greatly influenced farmers' perception of the proposed investment.

Politics colluding with economics is a classic pattern of misguided decision-making processes. Only one village, Chakenge, expressed reservations and later filed a formal objection[24] that the company had earmarked more land than was provided. Unfortunately, institutional limitations left the situation unresolved until 2008, with no further information available. As Table 4.6 shows, two out of the six villages shown gave away more than 40 per cent of the total village land.

Sun Biofuels plan to use all 18,000 ha for jatropha plantation for 99 years. The possibilities of a serious backlash on infrastructural development for the village in the future and the population increase continuing at the present rate of 2.1 per cent yearly have strained the relationship between the locals and the investors. Growing discontent over biofuels and the SEKAB experience have also created ample concern over the company's profitability and the plan's sustainability.

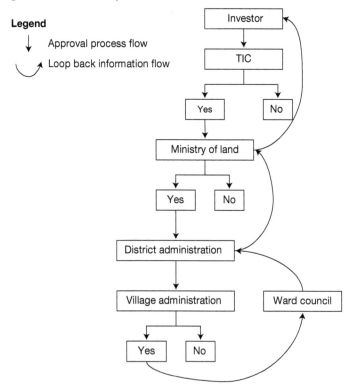

Figure 4.3 Sun Biofuels' land acquisition process in Kisarawe
Note: This flowchart gives an idea about the official land allocation system, as explained by the TIC and the Biofuels Taskforce.
Source: Author.

4.4.3 Compensation and a fair land price

It is difficult to identify fairness in compensation when information about costs is scarce, unreliable, and untestable due to a lack of regulatory frameworks. Under the certificate of the TIC, the investment implementation period was expected to start within four years of the first application, which means by September 2009 (Edwin 2007). After several initial visits to the targeted villages by company representatives in late 2006, none of the interviewed villages had seen the investors again. During the fieldwork in 2008, clear cutting the forest had already begun, prior to completion of village consultations, demarcation, and district level government approval.[25] Although requests for interviews went unanswered, later, in August 2009, the company announced that 'Sun Biofuels Tanzania has finalized the acquisition of over 8,000 ha of land in Kisarawe District' and had 'commenced land clearing operations in early June [2009]' (Sun Biofuels 2009).

There were discrepancies between the information collected from the ground, and the announcement made on the company website. There was no information about compensation made to the villagers, though their land had started to be cleared for jatropha monocropping. Some of the affected villagers only knew that their name was on a list and were not clear about their allocated land size. No contract had, as yet, been written or discussed with the village council in order to conduct any form of negotiation. However, the Land Officer for the district noted in an East African news article that the company would compensate 2,840 households. The company had earmarked USD 632,411 (Edwin 2007), yielding a one-time average payment of USD 223 per household.

When poverty is chronic, any income is better than nothing, but whether it was fair compensation is another question. When compared with the estimated rate per ha of land in Kisarawe as presented by the Ministry of Land the picture becomes skewed. An interview with the district agricultural officer indicated that the lease should be worth around USD 570 per ha, whereas Kisarawe villages were only compensated USD 77 per ha. This is an order of magnitude difference between the fair rates of income for the villagers and that reported to have been paid. Similarly, *Businessweek* stated that 'They offered the equivalent of about EUR 450,000, a ridiculous price for the 9,000 hectares (22,230 acres) that they can now use for almost a century' (Knaup 2008).

4.4.4 Employment and livelihoods

Although the company promised to create employment, confusion arose over the exact number, ranging from 1,000 to 4,000 jobs per village. From a policy standpoint, it is important to know the calculation methodology, but unfortunately, the company did not elucidate the topic. Conspicuously, people are just as happy with either of these numbers. The marginal advantage for each additional job is very high. However, analysis of company activity suggests that most of the jobs will be for clearing and preparing land, some for construction, and others for the manual labour of attending to the plants. Jatropha cultivation requires minimal operational attention. As the economic scale is attained through modernizing agricultural production systems, like vegetable oil extraction processes and distribution channels, the level of employment tends to decline.

There has been little to no development in the liberalization of the agricultural sector since 1986. Without fixing the fundamental bottlenecks of this sector as highlighted earlier, the investor will not be able to sustain a large payroll. Labour income is highly dependent on the company's profitability. *BiofuelDigest*, a major biofuel newsletter, stated that 'the company said it will pay workers USD 1095 per year for farming and harvesting and would devote an additional five per cent of its budget towards "social infrastructure"' (Lane 2009). While promises are made publicly, reports on Sun Biofuel's estimation of feasibility to become profitable seem a bit depressing when the price of a barrel of crude oil remains below USD 100 and forecasts show no repetition of USD 150 per barrel anytime soon. Hence, the benefits for the villagers of Kisarawe district are still far from being realized.

4.4.5 EABD and Bahi smallholders

It is important to understand a company's background and track record when evaluating its feasibility in the community. EABD is a private limited company registered in Tanzania, owned and operated by a Kenyan of Indian descent. Tanzania's peaceful political nature, economic prospects, and vast semi-arid lands available in Bahi attracted EABD. EABD is seeking 100,000 acres (40,000 ha) of land despite only being formed in January 2008. There are 6,000 ha and 2,246 farmers have registered for participation in an outgrower employment scheme (see Table 4.7).

EABD claims to have links with an Indian technology provider for vegetable oil conversion to biodiesel and as a supplier of capital goods. The Indian technology is argued to be low-cost technology that would bring down oil pressing costs.[27] The company expressed that the investment would be competitive even with low oil prices of USD 45 per barrel, as the conversion cost for crude jatropha oil is USD 0.15 per litre (USD 23.84 per barrel) and that for processed jatropha oil is USD 0.18 per litre (USD 28.61 per barrel). The processed oil would be then used as raw material in biodiesel factories for final grade biofuels. EABD may be profitable, but how realistic the conversion cost of USD 0.03 per litre is remains unknown since the company is reluctant to disclose details.

The company was seeking USD 4.4 million of seed money from the World Bank and other investors in 2008. The company will also apply for carbon financing from the World Bank to improve the water supply conditions for the villagers. While other promises are being made to the villagers, the land acquisition process should be considered first.

Table 4.7 Total village land areas allocated to EABD in Bahi district in 2008

Village	Area (ha)	Investors' area (ha)	Total land area (percentage)	Registered farmers
Chilungulu	7,289	614	8.4	1,015
Nguji	4,437	402	9.1	—
Misisi	7,264	305	4.2	—
Mchito	4,675	91	1.9	—
Chendege	10,095	275	2.7	—
Mayamaya	17,585	—	—	—
Mkondai	19,545	—	—	1,231
Chiftuka	31,459	1,713	5.4	—
Zejele	5,110	916	17.9	—
Magaga	525,177	320	0.1	—
Nondwa	10,842	1,331	12.3	—

Source: Author created from Bahi 2008 and investors' land data.

4.4.6 Land acquisition and controversies

EABD's land acquiring procedure did not follow the conventional process as set up by the Land Act of 1999. The company avoided the formal channel of coming to the village through the TIC and the Ministry of Land, since it found the process too long and bureaucratic. Instead, EABD depended on local networks, language skills, and tacit knowledge of African agricultural limitations. Furthermore, Bahi, as one of the least developed districts due to its semi-arid soil structure and low crop productivity, needs investment and crop diversification. The decentralized government, approached by the investors first, responded very amenably. Figure 4.4 illustrates the land acquisition steps followed by EABD.

Tapping into this need, the investor managed to receive approval for about 6,000 ha for jatropha plantation in one year. Moreover, to conduct demonstrations of the jatropha plantation, the proprietor collaborated with a couple of village primary schools, distributed seedlings, and engaged with the Mukatopora research centre to raise some test seedlings. The investor rented a plot in the national agriculture fairground to demonstrate jatropha plants.

EABD planned to distribute the first round of free seedlings to contract farmers with the first rain in December, with this first phase scheduled to end in July 2009, though no further information has been available since the moratorium. Three other phases were planned as were targets to maximize land use by introducing integrated intercropping between food and non-food crops. Phase II was scheduled to run from July 2009 to December 2010, during which EABD hoped to expand the area under cultivation to 10,000 ha. In this phase, the work to establish local extraction centres in

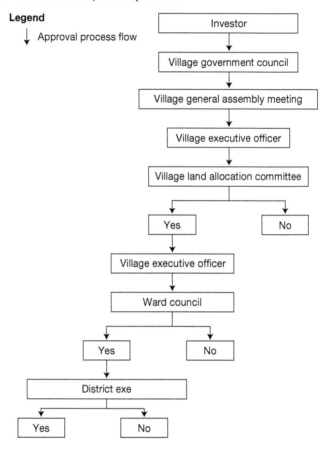

Legend

↓ Approval process flow

Figure 4.4 EABD's land acquisition process in Bahi
Note: After the district office, loop back information follows as shown in Figure 4.3.
Source: Author.

each village would begin. EABD planned to start a programme to train 10 to 12 village extension officers. If all went well, work for a refinery would begin. The technology and capital goods would be imported from India. The technology used for the refinery is a modular system which has added on capacity modules. The basic refinery converts five tons of crude jatropha oil into five tons of processed jatropha oil. According to the plan, Phase III would establish the complete biodiesel supply chain. Phase IV would be a continuation of Phase III.

Similar to the Sun Biofuels case, where local politics influenced the local farmers' decision-making processes, in the Bahi case the local government official also intervened. However, in this case, the intervention had the opposite aim: in August 2008 the Regional Commissioner (RC) publicly denounced EABD's land allocation activity[28] as illegal and ordered farmers to reject jatropha and tend to cashew nut plants instead. Despite the announcement, scepticism spread among farmers in the other villages because they did not receive the news directly from the regional administration. This started to jeopardize the investment potential for the other participating villages. Although the RC's proactive measure was the correct step, it was done in a non-administrative manner, which disturbed the local investment environment.

The intermingling of local politics with economics is common in developing countries, and often creates misinformation and misguidance in the absence of institutional clarity of goals. Another example is the case of the village of Mudemu, where 25 ha of fertile land were allocated to the investor without the consent of the owners or any formal notification to the district. It must be remembered that Bahi is already semi-arid, so each patch of fertile land is critical. While the issue was unresolved during the fieldwork time, villagers expressed deep distress as the investors threatened to move to another village if all of the requested 100 ha was not given in the desired area.

EABD planned a strategic central area annex of three connected villages. One village even gave land belonging to a neighbouring village away to EABD. The local government claims that this is not possible in principle, but in practice it happened. The land allocation process raises conflict between land use for food crops and cash crops like jatropha, which may create conflict between communities as well.

4.4.7 Compensation and a fair land price

The discussion over compensation and fair land prices is complex and politically charged. According to the Village Act of 1999, every piece of land has a value and without proper valuation, rights cannot be transferred. While this may be the law, EABD rejected any notion of paying compensation to the villagers for land. From the villagers' points of view, the responses were divided: 20 per cent of the farmers were reluctant to give up their land without proper compensation, especially if it was fertile farmland; 75 per cent of interviewees felt that giving away land without compensation would not be a problem as long as the investor kept the promises of economic development, water development, and community empowerment. A small percentage was extremely angry that the national political–economic system simply did not care about the land.

Instead of compensation, the promises that the EABD made to the participating villages were quite ambitious. The creation of labour opportunities was one of the major benefits to the community, which will be discussed in the next subsection. EABD promised to buy 50 per cent of the crops for biofuel, with the remainder given back to the community for household usage in lighting and resale. As biodiesel processing started, the by-product would be used for improved briquettes to be sold as a low-cost replacement for charcoal. Biogas would be produced from the residue and be supplied to the national grid, which would eventually electrify the villages. EABD pledged to improve water distribution systems by revitalizing the Mchito dam. Finally, 15 per cent of profits would be distributed to community development projects. Although the farmers are outgrowers, the main beneficiary of this shareholding scheme would seem to be the community.

To what extent these grand promises are viable and what the externalities are needs to be questioned and monitored closely. First and most importantly, there are no written documents listing the clauses filed with the local, district, or central government authorities. Second, much of this information came from EABD, but during data triangulation processes, data changed or contradicted the regional officers' details on several occasions. For example, in the first meeting, the profit sharing ratio was 10 per cent but in a week it had changed to 15 per cent. Information on the value of parcels of land and a propensity to establish estates close to homesteads was also conflicting. Third, there was no physical plan for any establishment until the second or third phase, and for the past year the investor had been living out of a hotel, revealing his fear to invest in physical capital. Fourth, the idea of not giving any compensation for the land used today, with the hope of future profits and other benefits is problematic and deceptive since there is no guarantee that the investment will be profitable.

It is easy to invest and divest in a country like Tanzania. With a weak regulatory framework and a weak land tenure system, investors often take advantage of the politically and economically impoverished populations and the system of information asymmetry. Policy makers, the FAO, and other stakeholders need to be proactive and vigilant to protect the rights of the poor.

4.4.8 Employment and livelihoods

There were two main ways EABD proposed to generate employment: first, by creating a labour market for the estate and factory and, second, by contract farming. An additional plan for improving income and livelihoods was to create a market for villagers to sell food crops. Initially, EABD planned to distribute semi-arid region compatible food crop seeds. To this end, an estimate of labour required was presented to the Regional Office, as seen in Table 4.8.

EABD claims to be able to employ 606,000 people for 6,000 ha in correspondence with the regional advisor. Is this figure realistic? While the regional advisor did not have the answer, EABD could not justify it. The district's available labour force of approximately 85,000 would not be able to cover the demand. Either the company would have to revise the headcount or they would require an influx of migrated labour. In principle, this would be economically positive not only for Bahi but also for other neighbouring regions. In practice, issues like transportation difficulty, labour rates,

Table 4.8 Yearly labour demand in the EABD jatropha estate

Activities	Labour headcount (1 ha)	Working days (1 ha)	Labour headcount (6,000 ha)
Land clearing	10	30	60,000
Alignment	5	10	30,000
Digging pits	25	10	150,000
Mixing manure	10	10	60,000
Planting vegetation	25	10	150,000
Irrigation (3 times/yr)	6	3	36,000
Weeding (2 times/yr)	20	10	120,000
Total	101	83	606,000

Note: The total headcount was devised by the research team from email correspondence.
Source: Meeting with Regional Agriculture Advisor.

and the nature of payments were not accounted for. Even with the modular factory plan, the project required mid-level skilled manpower, not the unskilled labour abundant in Bahi. Clearly, the accuracy of the labour estimates is dubious.

To an extent, this sad reality holds true in other central regions that have abundant, semi-arid land. Given the publicized, though dubious, plans there will be a much higher propensity among farmers to maximize their income from jatropha. If EABD were to truly keep their promises of a stable market, minimum prices, and free seeds, almost 100 per cent of the interviewed farmers were willing to compromise food production for jatropha production. Since Bahi's agricultural environment is based on traditional practices and demands manual labour, hourly labour productivity is low. Therefore, balancing labour between traditional crops and jatropha will not be as easy as predicted by the farmers at the focus group nor as is believed by government officials. Regardless of this simplistic analysis, the local government reported that farmers were already focusing solely on jatropha.

4.5 Conclusion

Tanzania has recently become a major attraction for biofuels companies for its vast, unused land. This case study has tried to contextualize the existing political, economic, and institutional situation of Tanzania within which biofuels companies operate. A long history of underproductive agricultural systems, incomplete land tenure, and underdeveloped marketing channels have undermined agro-industry development. In the last few years as the global hype on biofuels production escalated, the Tanzanian government sought to host biofuels feedstock producing companies to address long-standing rural poverty, energy security, and trade deficits. But what was missed among the promises, hopes, and desires is the actual capacity and feasibility of the country. Repeated failure to profit from cash crops signals fundamental weaknesses in the agricultural sector, namely an incomplete land tenure system, incomplete decentralization, inefficient infrastructures, and poor connectivity with the rural areas. These structural limitations hinder land utilization and reduce marginal returns – more land does not necessarily lead to more output. All of which then translate into prolonged poverty, food insecurity, and loss of human and social capital.

Failed markets need government intervention before the market can create social benefits, otherwise the market has more incentives to create social costs. Unfortunately, Tanzania has suffered from failures of government as well. For example, the government moratorium on further biofuels investment could discourage existing investments, leaving villagers worse off. Policy makers need to devise a sound mechanism to optimally balance land allocation for different uses like essential food crop production and non-edible experimental investments. A prerequisite would be an accurate land database demarcated by resources, usage, and reservation, but the government has not even created this fundamental dataset.

Economies that largely depend on the environment for economic output, such as Tanzania's dependence on agriculture, are even more vulnerable to global climate change. For instance, drought duration and intensity is increasing in Tanzania. Coupled with other exogenous forces like the global recession and food crisis, food imports and aid are becoming increasingly costly both for the nation and donors alike. If the perceived opportunity cost of biofuel crop cultivation over food crop production is low, then it makes sense for farmers to focus on jatropha, *ceteris paribus*. However, the decision is founded on misinformation promulgated by biofuels companies, leading to mistakes that adversely affect farmers' livelihoods.

Finally, while development economics can justify why, in dire impoverishment, Tanzania would allow mass production of jatropha despite its unproven, untested, and insecure productivity, it fails to explain how countries can decide on the feasibility of a new sector before going into it. This is the case in biofuels production, whose discourse is still evolving. While this chapter focused on export-oriented production from the supply side, future research should examine how malfunctioning agricultural markets and governance systems tie into international trade to further exacerbate the lives of the poor.

Notes

1 The FAO served as an advisor on Tanzania's biofuels initiative in relation to food security. I was a member of the FAO Tanzania country office as the biofuels policy expert. The actual fieldwork was supported by FAO and Commonwealth funds. This work was published in *Energy Policy*, see Habib-Mintz 2010.

2 Theoretically, contract farming is seen as a tool for the private sector to substitute for the role of the public sector in terms of providing input, extension services, credit and price support (MAFC 2006). Outgrower scheme and contract farming scheme are interchangeably used in this chapter.

3 See MAFC 2006 for more details.

4 The government reports 26 indicators to the World Food Summit Report of the United Nations to illustrate the country's status on food security. The government's 2006 report shows the table in detail. The table summarizes the weaknesses in the government in data collection, agricultural investment and diminishing human capital necessary for modernizing the agricultural system. See, for more details, MAFC 2006.

5 El Niño of 1997/1998 caused severe drought in Tanzania nationwide. A national food emergency was announced after the loss of 900,000 metric tonnes of food. The food scarcity was further worsened by global rises in food prices which made it expensive for the country to import food. The government banned food exports. Widespread loss in cattle and cash crops in northern Tanzania threatened the lives of 150 million starving people. See NDMC 1997.

6 National drought put food production at stake. Food imports, however, increase during drought years. For example, in year 2003/2004 total food imports amounted to 698,668 tons of maize, rice and wheat (MAFC 2006).

7 SEKAB shut down its business in Tanzania by the end of 2009 after the company was marred by both international and Swedish civil society criticisms over human rights and biodiversity abuse as they evicted villagers in Rufiji from the land that the president gave to them virtually for free. See SEKAB 2009.

8 Tanzania's import statistics show that 40 per cent of petrol consumption comes from imports. The total annual demand for petroleum products in Tanzania is 1.2 million tonnes. Since 1999, following the closure of the refinery plant TIPER, Tanzania stopped importing crude oils for refining (GTZ 2005). In addition, Tanzania does not produce its own petroleum oil and all requirements are met by imports (GTZ 2005). Therefore, the question that remains unanswered is from where and how the remaining 60 per cent of petroleum is becoming available in the local market. Can the emerging biofuels industry really help this cause in the context of massive smuggling?

9 In 2001 the country made the National Transportation Policy effective and allocated local resources to major road construction projects. Recently, the government has established the Energy and Water Utilities Regulatory Authority to regulate the energy and water sector in Tanzania including the technical aspects of downstream petroleum.

10 Information collected from the interviews held with the Institute of Transportation in Tanzania during the fieldwork.

11 The Kisarawe district profile was provided by the district states in which it was inaugurated in 1906 by the German colonial authorities. It covered Dar es Salaam, Mkuranga, Kibaha, and the current Kisarawe.

12 The district profile collected during the fieldwork referred to the National Sample Census of Agriculture 2002/2003 for statistical information. The latest Census is not available for the BEFS project.

13 For convenience, currency conversions in this chapter use an exchange rate of 1 US Dollar (USD) to 1,147.00 Tanzanian Shillings (TZS).

14 For instance, the price of maize flour, food purchased because of insufficient production, has risen from TZS 350/kg in 2006 to TZS 700/kg. Other foodstuffs which have seen price increases (in brackets) include rice (TZS 600/kg to TZS 1,300/kg), beans (TZS 500/kg – TZS 1,000/kg), and sugar (TZS 600/kg – TZS 1,400/kg).

15 Kisarawe is surrounded by forests and reserved land including Kazinzumbwi Forest, Ruvu South Forest Reserve, Pugu Forest Reserve, and Selous Game Reserve.

16 National level drought, coupled with high cost of food. See WFP 2007.

17 New data on Bahi has been released in the current census report of 2008. At the time of this report, the database was not available.

18 Dodoma experienced good rainfall, although the coastal region faced drought and severe loss in production in 2002/2003.

19 Two events made the food security situation worse: (a) below average rainfall put agriculture at risk; and (b) maize prices escalated, putting pressure on aid, imports, and household consumption capacity (IRIN 2004).

20 This drought continued into the next year, causing starvation for 80 per cent of the population in the region.

21 Interview with the district offices of the Ministry of Agriculture, Food Security and Cooperatives in November 2008.

22 This number varies between 18,000 ha and 20,000 ha, based on fieldwork interviews with village farmers.

23 An interview with a TIC director in December 2008 revealed that the TIC is the first point of entrance for foreign companies for land allocation. For land allocation information, the TIC depends on the Ministry of Agriculture, Food and Cooperatives. There is no detailed land bank that shows village level land, only a district level breakdown. The last land demarcation happened in the 1980s, so the data is now quite out of date.

24 The village records, interestingly, contained printouts on Sun Biofuels from an online newspaper.

25 Interview with the District Commissioner in November 2008.

26 The investor, assuming great competition in the biofuels business, was reluctant to provide any specifications about the technology and know-how. It was, therefore, difficult to make any further investigations or judgments on the quality and efficiency of the technology.

27 Mundemo village meeting held in August 2008. Other EABD villages received this news by word of mouth. There was no administrative announcement found by the research team from the regional and district office on the RC's order.

5 The Malaysian biofuels experience

The role of agriculture in economic development has been the cornerstone of the Malaysian poverty reduction strategy. As envisioned by national policy makers, growth and development successfully reduced poverty and increased social cohesion. Agricultural sector development was designed to redistribute economic and political resources, placing control in the hands of the poor. The government realized in the process that solely focusing on physical resources and capital is insufficient. The regulatory environment needed to integrate the social capital that rural communities were rich in and, through it, channel and develop existing financial and human capital. The five-year New Economic Policy (NEP) also known as the Malaysia Plan (MP) arose from this planning, formulated to encourage the development of organic entrepreneurships. National focus was particularly directed to the *bumiputera* (sons of the soil), a clause introduced in 1971 in the first NEP, created social, political and economic security programmes to reduce poverty among the *bumiputera*. *Bumiputera* belong to three categories: namely the Malays, the indigenous people of Sabah and Sarawak, and the *Orang Asli* (original people or first people). However, *bumiputera* is a politically contested term. While individual groups, because of this special category, receive preferential treatment, political leaders also sometimes use the term in a pejorative way. As a result, there are times when political leaders have underestimated poverty rates to reduce overall dependency on this provision. For instance, in 2010 a national debate broke out in Sarawak when the national government underestimated the poverty rate and evoked large-scale controversy (Wong 2010a).

Although there are unresolved debates in the country as to how much poverty has been reduced among the *bumiputera*, agricultural sector development has been aimed at integrating poor smallholders by allocating equity to them. The key to this process was based on production and export of palm oil and palm oil products. Smallholders retain a 41 per cent share of their palm oil sector hectares and the state-led land development projects created livelihood opportunities for the rural poor in the palm oil industry in the 1970s (Simeh and Ahmad 2001). Along with other political–economic changes that the country undertook during this time, agricultural commercialization and the integration of smallholders in the process helped reduce national poverty. The incidence of smallholder poverty dropped from 30 per cent in the 1970s to nearly 3 per cent in 2008 (Ariffin 2008).

The total population of Malaysia is 28.2 million of which 79.9 per cent live in Peninsular Malaysia, 11.0 per cent in Sabah, and 9.1 per cent in Sarawak (DOS 2000). Of these, the ethnic composition of the population is about 58 per cent *bumiputera*, 24 per cent Chinese, 7 per cent Indian, and 11 per cent categorized as 'Others', which also includes non-citizens (DOS 2000, 2009). However, non-Malay *bumiputera* areas, like Sarawak, remain disproportionately impoverished with 42 per cent of the population below the poverty line (Mulakala 2008). The 2005 census recorded about 2 million people, with more than 40 ethnic groups spread through 11 divisions: Iban (29 per cent)[1], Chinese (26 per cent), Malay (22 per cent), Bidayuh (8 per cent), Melanaus (5 per cent), OragUlu (5 per cent), and other *bumiputera* 6 per cent (Malaysia 2008). Illiteracy and food insecurity is a constant issue in Sarawak.

Aside from the central government's focus on eradicating poverty, global attention is on the preservation of peatland, which, once destroyed, takes about 145 years to replenish with carbon, and the state government envisions taking advantage of the carbon trading platform by being the custodian of the global carbon sink and a producer of renewable energy. Recently, in the midst of the major global food price hike, in February 2008 the Sarawak Corridor of Renewable Energy (SCORE) was launched, which was a part of the NEP plan, and came into effect in 2010 (Lane 2008). Both the national and state government focused on a joint-venture-based commercial development in Sarawak to promote successful renewable energy investment by 2020 for domestic and export purposes. Under renewable energy sector development, along with palm oil, jatropha has been chosen as an oil crop to produce biodiesel for export, while the domestic market, institutions and infrastructures (roads, storage, and engines) are ready to facilitate consumption. This is an important contextual change happening in Malaysia, within which this research took place.

To what extent these objectives concerning Sarawak will be fulfilled and jatropha-based biofuels industry development will play a role is unknown. To find the answers, three important factors need considering: (a) 10 million NCR lands,[2] often blamed for underinvestment in the agricultural sector – in 2007 the state government announced 1.5 million ha of land, mostly underutilized and without title, which were open for private sector investment for agricultural plantation projects (Wong 2010b); (b) the One Malaysia concept, buttressing the social capital environment for *bumiputera* and non-*bumiputera* to become economic partners – in 2008 this concept was officially introduced with the aim of integrating Peninsular Malaysia and the two Borneo states (Sabah and Sarawak) under uniform political–economic environment; and (c) all levels of institutional quality and capacity to address economic urgency and social protection mechanisms which influence individual decision-making processes when participating in the biofuels value chain.

The remainder of this chapter is structured as follows. Section 5.1 discusses the case study, including application of the IFS framework. Section 5.2 analyses national political economics to determine how the biofuels industry development fits into the national and state level agricultural and energy sector development plan. Section 5.3 introduces case study locations and the specifics of their agro-economies within which jatropha investments and productions are taking place. In Section 5.4, two companies operating in the global jatropha value chain are discussed to weigh the potential benefits and threats that companies introduce to jatropha producing communities. This section develops analysis based on the IFS and traces global-, national-, state- and local-level interactions in commercial jatropha production in Sarawak. Finally, Section 5.5 concludes the Chapter.

5.1   Case study description

As mentioned, there are controversies around poverty levels in Sarawak, and it is important to understand each level of the GVC embedded in Malaysia, including the progress, opportunities, and constraints experienced by individuals in pursuit of viability and improving livelihoods. The national government invested USD 103 billion in the SCORE development plan, which includes heavy investment in jatropha and palm-based biodiesel production, in 2008 in Sarawak to help achieve Sarawakian livelihood targets (Lane 2008). To what extent the targets by the government and the jatropha companies have succeeded in creating income and not further stressing peatland conversion is a key focus for the fieldwork. To offer comparative perspectives between mainland Malaysia and the island part of Malaysia (Sarawak and Sabah), the research was conducted on both sides of the country, as indicated in Figure 5.1.

The IFS framework is utilized to examine how the biofuels domestic supply chain is developing and to conduct participatory poverty assessments and stakeholder consultations into differences between mainland Malaysia and the island states of Malaysia. Such combined assessments will help capture institutional blockages, geographical concentrations of power and structural characteristics for actually reducing local poverty by producing jatropha feedstock for the biofuels value chain. Two companies, Bionas and Alam Widuri Sdn Bhd (AWSD), operating in two districts of Sarawak – Sri Aman and Serian, respectively – were chosen to configure the relevant regulatory frameworks and support institutions to conduct a multidisciplinary based horizontal and vertical analysis.

In addition to institutional investigations, in-depth interviews were held within focus groups to identify the plans and roles of two biofuel, companies active in Sarawak. The field locations and villages were selected, using the methodology discussed in Section 2.4, considering: (a) rural livelihoods

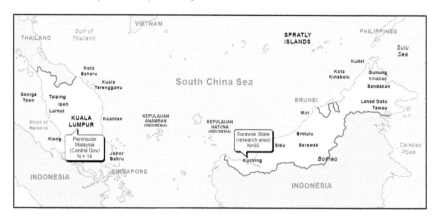

Figure 5.1 Research map of Malaysia
Note: Scale 1:10 m.
Source: Naturalearthdata.com.

representative of the overall Malaysian rural environment; (b) the ability to characterize agro-ecological trends that make jatropha production an attractive cash-crop option for villagers; and (c) accessibility, since Sarawak is a difficult region to access geographically and institutionally as the decentralized state government has tight control over the social research environment. Six villages were selected from two districts – Sri Aman and Serian. It is important to note that the fieldwork coincided with the Gawai festival time in Serian, during which people refrain from any task that may disrupt good fortune. Therefore, it was not possible to hold focus groups. Instead, one-to-one interviews were conducted with 20 individuals from the three villages, who were the community leaders and were playing leading roles in the collective decision-making process on jatropha plantation. State level institutional interviews were also held with nine government officers involved in agriculture, land, extension service, and energy fields.

Sri Aman District, in the Sri Aman division, is 193 km from Kuching, the political and economic capital of Sarawak, and has a large non-Muslim Iban ethnic group majority. Serian District, in the Samarahan division, is about 65 km from Kuching and has a large Bidayuh majority along with Chinese and Iban groups. Both the Iban and Bidayuh observe customary land rights and have benefited from the early 1970s livelihood creation efforts of the Sarawak Land Consolidation and Rehabilitation Authority (SALCRA) through the developing value chain of rubber and palm oil. Since the agro-ecology of these districts falls under peatland, which is not suitable for palm plantations,[3] inhabitants are forced to relocate out of their villages in search of employment. Two biofuels companies, Bionas and Alam Widuri Sdn Bhd (AWSB), have started operations in the area. Bionas, a Malay-owned international enterprise, has an aggressive plan of jatropha expansion to 1.2 million ha, whereas AWSB is a smaller company spearheaded by a Chinese priest, mainly operating through an outgrower scheme.

5.2 National institutional and infrastructural assessment

Concern over food security was the impetus behind Malaysia modernizing and intensifying the agricultural sector. In the 1980s, the state supported robust agricultural growth, while in the 1990s, the private sector led rapid agricultural modernization and commercialization (Siamwallah 1996). After a lull, interest in agriculture returned in a major way as the third engine of growth in the Ninth Malaysia Plan (9MP), focusing on the frontiers of renewable energy and biotechnology (Malaysia 2006). The plan set out an ambitious growth rate of 5 per cent for agriculture and 5.2 per cent for agro-based industry[4] by 2010 with an emphasis on export promotion, and a 5 per cent biodiesel blending mandate in the national transportation sector (AFP 2010).[5] Accordingly, 92 licenses were issued in 2007–2008 to promote commercial investments in biofuels, though only 12 recipients were operating at the time of the fieldwork. Subsections 5.2.1 and 5.2.2 explore the plans in greater detail through the agricultural and transport energy sectors, respectively.

5.2.1 Agricultural development assessment

Malaysia's policy regime is sensitive to rural industrialization and private sector growth. A major shift in agricultural policy took place with the National Agricultural Policy (NAP) in the 1990s which replaced the NAP of 1984. The focus was on rural capacity building for agro-industry development, unlike the 1984 plan which focused on subsidies and migration (Sivalingam 1993). Consistent with current policy, the government gradually withdrew from providing subsidized services, land development, and agricultural loans. It facilitated a greater role for the private sector and deregulated factor markets, which resulted in more efficient resource allocation. The government designed a market oriented land development scheme, the Federal Land Development Authority (FELDA), which was a successful public–private scheme for poverty reduction.

It is difficult to find food insecurity data in Malaysia as such records are not in the public domain. Although national food security has increased over time, it has stagnated in the Borneo region. Two prominent studies on rural food consumption patterns show that, between 1984 and 1997, the mean energy intake of 1,874 kcal, broken down into 12 per cent from protein, 18 per cent from fats and 70 per cent from carbohydrates, did not change (Chee *et al.* 1997; Chong *et al.* 1984). Note that this is less than the FAO recommended daily allowance of 2,200 kcal (MAFC 2008). Food insecurity is still a national problem, despite the nation's achievements in poverty reduction. Between 1975 and 2005 total arable land grew 5 per cent annually as forest clearing and frontier expansion continued. Permanent land devoted to cash crops (mainly palm oil) grew by 837 per cent, or 46 per cent annually, whereas rice cultivation declined by about 10 per cent in the same period (Kamil 2005). Malaysia reached 73 per cent self-sufficiency for rice in 2008 and aimed to reach 83 per cent in 2010 to reduce its dependency on imported rice (Tey 2010).

Under the threat of a global food crisis, the government launched a renewed interest in revitalizing food crop agriculture and rice granaries in 2008 and identified Sarawak as the new rice zone, as shown in Figure 5.2 (Malaysia 2008). Sarawak was targeted for four interrelated reasons:

- Sarawak State government has declared that there are 1.5 million ha of NCR land, mostly underutilized and without title, which can be used for agricultural plantation projects.
- About 77 per cent of the palm plantation is mature in Sarawak, and the rural poor dependent on plantations need an urgent agricultural revitalization and modernization plan to reduce rural poverty.
- To achieve self-sufficiency in rice, the country needs more land to produce rice. Overly crowded and developed Peninsular Malaysia is looking at Sarawak to provide that space.
- Cheap Indonesian labour is easily available in Sarawak as it borders Indonesia. This makes labour intensive rice cultivation suitable.

Sarawak has the lowest palm oil yield per hectare at 3.3 t/ha and a low overall agricultural yield. This is due to unsuitable soil conditions, aging farmers, and poor institutional support (e.g., access to credit, extension services). Therefore, the rate of poverty reduction through the expansion of the agricultural sector has been relatively slow. Recently, jatropha has gained popularity and momentum due to its suitability for poor quality soil, low inputs, and attractive market price.

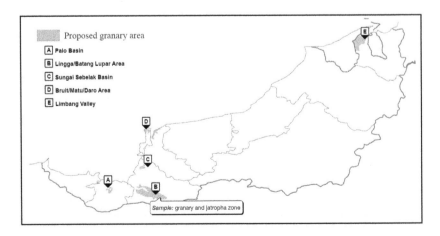

Figure 5.2 Proposed granary area in Sarawak
Note: Scale 1:10 m. Granary area estimate based on DID 2010b.
Source: Naturalearthdata.com.

Though the government provides price control and subsidies, paddy farmers report this to be insufficient as cross-border rice imports depress farm-gate prices beyond the government's decree. Rice production is chronically inefficient and argued by some to be a deadweight loss to society (Lopez 2007). These deadweight losses constitute a serious misallocation of scarce resources, and encourage a move away from food production to palm oil production. When a national rice crisis threatened public unrest in 2008, the government undertook a barter scheme and called for emergency rice, oil, and sugar stockpiling in exchange for palm oil with bordering countries, such as Thailand (John and Damis 2008).

While the private sector was tasked with cash-crop industry development, and the government promoted rice production to meet self-sufficiency targets, MPOB expressed scepticism over jatropha investment (see Table 5.1). Worryingly, the biofuels value chain may conflict with rice production

Table 5.1 Comparative economic returns from jatropha, oil palm, and rubber in Malaysia

Factor	Jatropha	Oil palm	Rubber
1. Immature/establishment			
• Per ha	RMY 6,300	RMY 2,580	RMY 11,900
• Per year	RMY 252	RMY 103	RMY 476
• Per unit yield	RMY 42/t seed	RM5.7/t FFB	RMY 0.34/kg DR
2. Mature (RMY/year)			
• Per ha	RMY 2,955	RMY 3,201	RMY 3,038
• Per unit yield	RMY 493/t seed (RMY 1,970/t oil)	RMY 176/t FFB (RMY 880/t oil)	RMY 2.17/kg DR
• Labour requirements	105 MD	41 MD	80 MD
3. Total (RMY/year)			
• Per ha	RMY 3,207	RMY 3,304	RMY 3,514
• Per unit yield	RMY 535/t seed (RMY 2,240/t oil)	RMY 182/t FFB (RMY 910/t oil)	RMY 2.51/kg DR
4. Return/ha @ price	RMY 500/t seed	RMY 550/t FFB	RMY 6,677/kg DR
• Gross	RMY 3,000	RMY 10,010	RMY 10,034
• Net	–(RMY 207)	RMY 6,706	RMY 6,790
• Family Return	RMY 2,418	RMY 7,723	RMY 8,790

Notes: RMY – Ringgits (Malaysian currency). Currency is not converted here as the target is to show the actual return on investment.
MD – Men per day. Number of labourers used per day in the plantation. (Most labourers are men.)
FFB – Fresh fruit bunches. About 10 to 12 bunches per year are produced by each palm tree. Each bunch can have 1,000 to 3,000 fruits which weight between 40 and 70 pounds.
Source: MARDI 2002.

initiatives in determining land use in Sarawak. By looking closely, it appears that Figure 5.2 shows that two of the targeted biofuels areas fall in the granary zone, noted as Zone B. This point is revisited later. Will granary development reduce poverty and improve food security significantly?

5.2.2 Infrastructure development assessment

Transportation energy, the transportation sector and land rights are fundamental factors of infrastructural conditions of a country. National energy markets underperform if the transportation sector is not functional and easily accessible through good connectivity, adequate vehicles, and energy distribution systems.

After the 1997 Asian financial crisis, the Malaysian economy grew rapidly and the country realized the need to tap into domestic hydrocarbons and cut back on imported fossil fuels, which drain foreign savings (see Figure 5.3). National exploration of untapped gas and coal mines decreased dependency on fossil fuels from 90 per cent in 1980 to 60 per cent in 2005. In 2001, the Four-Fuel Diversification Policy was revised into a Five-Fuel Policy as part of the 8MP, adding biofuels to the energy supply mix. Renewable energy is

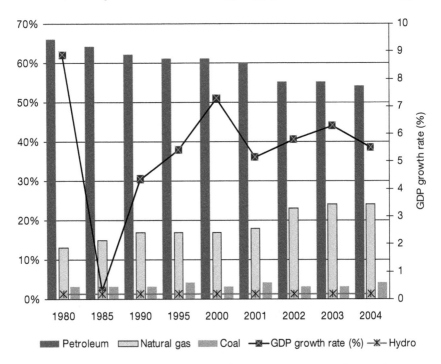

Figure 5.3 Energy demand and GDP growth rate (1980–2004) reflecting changes in the energy mix

Note: GDP/breakdown at constant 1990 prices in US Dollars.

Source: Author created with data from Isa 2007 and Malaysia 2008.

targeted to contribute to the country's electricity supply, as the demand for electricity was estimated to rise 20 per cent by 2010 (EIB 2005). As the national economy grows, demand for energy grows, so national energy policy constantly focuses on ways to improve the energy mix and market situation.

In 2008, the Ministry of Energy began implementing the National Biofuel Policy passed in 2006. This policy, spearheaded by the Minister of Plantation Industries and Commodities, aims to enact specific legislation on biofuels. This initiative connects the Five-Fuel Diversification Policy with the national industrial plan and the Ministry of Agriculture to strengthen the palm oil industry and expand its market leadership. There are five strategic points (MPIC 2006):

- Supply B5[6] biofuels for transportation
- Distribute B5 biofuels for industries
- Improve biofuels technologies
- Promote worldwide Malaysian biofuel
- Use clean biofuel, which is environmentally sustainable.

The Malaysian Biofuel Industry Act 2007 (Act 666) was enacted in July 2007 and scheduled to enforce a blending target B5, but it has changed several times already. The global financial crisis and high energy price has reduced the government's capacity to provide subsidies and other market incentives to promote biofuels consumption domestically. Moreover, the severe economic recession of 2008–2009 experienced in the EU severely hampered the import demand for biodiesel from Malaysia. This experience reasserted the national initiative to improve the national energy infrastructure to develop the domestic market for biofuels. Biodiesel is included in the list of products/activities that are encouraged under the Promotion of Investments Act 1986 and so producer companies are eligible for Pioneer Status or Investment Tax Allowance as infant industry incentives. A new investment receives a 100 per cent tax exemption for Pioneer Status business models for a ten-year period and a 60 per cent Reinvestment Allowance (RA) on machinery expenditure for improving energy conservation (European Commission 2013; MPOC 2007a, 2007a). The government reduced annual road taxes for diesel engine capacities less than 1,600 cubic cm (cc), which can also run on biodiesel (Hoh 2009). Reduction in road tax is a relatively new incentive, since the recovery from the financial crisis. With the lower cost per unit of diesel and aggressive expansion of national carmaker PROTON sales, the number of diesel-run vehicles will likely increase (Idris 2004; Prathaban 2006). Although current estimates on actual diesel vehicle increases were unavailable, the government is negotiating with automobile manufacturers to extend warranties to include biodiesel usage (Prathaban 2006).

It is nationally known that transportation infrastructure development and capacity building are precursors to sustainable economic development and human welfare. Most of Malaysia is well connected through road systems. Nationally, the automotive industry has been rising consistently at the rate of 1.1 per cent for four reasons: (a) the National Highway Development Plan has been increasing the road network; (b) all Malaysia Plans are also steadily increasing public investment in the transportation development sector; (c) the national auto manufacturing industry – PROTON; and (d) indigenous oil reserves which have helped reduce imported oil costs.

According to the Asia Pacific Energy Research Centre energy demand in road transport is projected to continue to grow at an annual rate of 3.5 per cent up to 2020. However, the fuel type growth rate shows significant differences, with gasoline growing at 2.9 per cent per year, and diesel at 4.2 per cent per year for both transportation and agricultural usage (APEC 2006). The increased demand for diesel is in line with the earlier assumption made in the introductory section on why the biodiesel market has a longer-term lifespan and higher potential for developing countries.

Unlike Peninsular Malaysia where the transportation system has boomed, Sarawak has seen sluggish growth in transportation infrastructure development. This in turn has hampered the agricultural and industrial development in the region by imposing high transportation costs and slow returns on private investment. There are two main factors behind the sluggishness – the first is the dependency on the natural inland water route system, which is inefficient and slow in trafficking people and goods from one point to another. Although recently the federal government took note of this and developed a Pan-Borneo road system connecting the major urban centres of Sarawak, private investment to extend the highways into trunk roads to reach rural areas has remained slow. The second reason is NCR lands: under NCR, in accordance with land law, land cannot be sold, so NCR lands cannot be used as collateral. As a result, Sarawak has 1.4 million hectares of NCR land which is unused and without title (Bulan 2007; Wong 2010b). Development of infrastructures is very much at the mercy of the government, and on the private commercial farming which receives special legal protections for their social investment, including investment in infrastructures like paving roads, building bridges, or culverts.

5.3 State level agro-economy and biofuels institutional assessment

Sarawak is poised to be the next agricultural hub of Malaysia, contributing to the region's acceptance of federal government interventions in its decentralized governance domain. Sarawak's state government is willing to support the national food security agenda, whereas the neighbouring state of Sabah is resisting federal interference in its territory. Sarawak and Sabah are the poorest regions of the country and closely resemble developing countries.

Food cultivation is undertaken by aging farmers and considered a household activity for women among an illiterate and impoverished population. The younger generations are moving away from the agricultural sector to the service and industrial sectors. Agricultural sector income is very low, foreign labour has put downward pressure on wages and, without access to education, rural area youth prefer employment in the growing manufacturing sector.

Sarawak contains about 30 per cent of national lands, but its 2.5 million people represent only 9 per cent of the country's population. Sarawak is known for its ethnic diversity, natural resources, destruction of carbon-rich peatland areas, unplanned palm plantations, and logging activities (Cramb and Wills 1990; DOS 2008; Windle 2008). Since 1976 a direct government intervention has been active in raising the standard of living of rural people. Some level of success was achieved with the implementation of *in situ* land development programmes through the introduction of palm and rubber plantations under SALCRA.[7] SALCRA also included social programmes focusing on education, mind development, dietary training, better housing, access to roads, and road development.[8] After 30 years of operation, about 77 per cent of the plantations are mature, the farmers are aged and the youth are reluctant to join in the plantation, which is more work and less pay compared to the booming off-farm factory jobs and government jobs in Kuching. While urban migration among the youth has become a problem for rural areas, unresolved issues of poverty and income inequality (Gini coefficient 0.44) are the causes behind environmental destruction observed in the rainforest (Cooke 2006; UNEP 2007).

Sarawak's land tenure system and quality can partly explain the unresolved issue of poverty and partly explain the attraction toward biodiesel industry development. Aside from NCR lands, Malaysia has 7.6 million hectares[9] of marginal soil, of which 2 million hectares are in Sarawak (Sai 2002). There

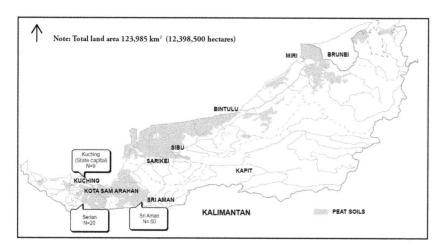

Figure 5.4 Sarawak map with distribution of peat soil and study areas
Note: Scale 1:10 m. Peat area reproduced based on MARDI 2002.
Source: Naturalearthdata.com.

are about 1.7 million hectares of peatland in Sarawak accounting for 13 per cent of the state's total land area (see Figure 5.4) (DID 2010a). Unfertile peatland, coupled with a climate which is warm,[10] highly humid,[11] and rain prone[12] – causing flooding, obstructing perennial cultivation and disrupting transportation – has historically made land in Sarawak unattractive to private sector investors. Jatropha plantations, which can grow in marginal soils, is attractive to private sector interventions to improve such land's utility. Along with land, anticipated global demand, high income potential, and social-business models provide a win–win situation for Sarawakians. Finally, jatropha plantation schemes as introduced by private investors are in line with the NEP, SCORE and state plans to develop two million hectares of unused land by 2020.

The rest of the section identifies, within the given state level context, how biofuels companies are introducing jatropha plantations to Sarawak and influencing individual farmers to participate in commercial farming schemes. The analysis is drawn from three existing institutional dimensions: access to land ownership, social capital, and government social safety nets.

5.3.1   Sri Aman agro-economy and space for jatropha

The Iban play an important role in the transformation of Sarawak's socio-economic development. The Iban are the largest group of non-Muslim natives and under the new discourse they are included in the *bumiputera* list. They dwell in *rumahpanjai* (longhouses) built close to river banks, practice shifting cultivation and own the largest share of NCR rights. Sarawak scholars consider that about 35 per cent of Iban are found in the Sri Aman area, which has about 4,000 registered longhouses (Ngidang 2007).[13] The sheer volume of Iban NCR land ownership and their communal living patterns have empowered the group politically.

As indicated, NCR lands are operated within the informal institutional domain. To explain further, consider that the Iban believe that the Earth God, *Pulang Gana,* owns all things and controls the success of the Iban agricultural economy. A poor agricultural ecosystem is partly responsible for underutilization of the customary lands.

There exists a cultural factor which provides insight on why communities would leave their land untouched: agricultural land is merely borrowed from the *Pulang Gana* (Cramb 2009; Ngidang 2007). So, ideally, the land needs to be returned in the condition it was found, which implies undisturbed land. This has a huge environmental significance, as the biodiversity remains intact and the community share the costs of underproductive land. Such cultural beliefs also provide a barrier to implementing the Land Code, but their rural economy has transformed from subsistence farming to an actively engaged agro-economy participating in global commodities markets (Cramb 2009). Such anthropological issues are important considerations for understanding why and how land-use change may or may not happen.

While poverty estimates are unreliable, the perception is that poverty and hunger are less acute, partly because of diversity in income sources. The farm income distribution ratio is: 59 per cent pepper, 20 per cent paddy, 7 per cent oil palm, 3 per cent rubber, 3 per cent SALCRA, with the rest being made up of orchard, livestock, and cocoa (Ngidang 2007). Ngidang reported that 77 per cent of households engage in agriculture, although agriculture contributes only 36 per cent of income with 64 per cent derived from non-farm activities in the capital city (Kuching), 193 km away (2007).

Three villages were studied in the field for this research, which are about 80 per cent Iban. Table 5.2 summarizes data collected from local villagers on site. Urbanization is popular among the youth, while 80 per cent of families have an average of six members and still have someone in the longhouse. Older, undereducated farmers' decisions are influenced by the urbanite Ibans who are considered more knowledgeable and networked with the political system.[14] Use of social capital benefits the wider Iban society significantly. Several studies found that in response to long, persistent poverty farmers in this area quickly adapt to changing their crop preference to maximize gains from commodity prices which are channelled to them through networks (Windle and Cramb 1997; Windle 2008). However, poverty is widespread in rural Iban households with 53 per cent earning less than half of the national poverty line of RMY 600 per month (Ngidang 2007). Among the rural poor, who are, generally, the older generation, palm plantations and logging are less attractive for income, with jatropha gaining prominence due to its high demand and low labour intensity.

It was also observed that in Iban communities NCR lands create opportunities for farmers to experiment with new crops or techniques, without subjecting themselves to commercial loss as the high food price is putting pressure on household income and consumption.[15] The Iban population have benefited from the SALCRA initiative as literacy is high among them and exposure to commercial information, through having access to media like TV, radio, and newspapers, has empowered their decision-making processes. Moreover, collective crop diversification decisions are better than individual decisions. Finally, the inter-ethnic politicking empowers one community over the other as they have a representative in government and this is an important political-anthropological aspect to channel economic activity. As a result, it currently appears that more districts in the rice zone are interested in joining the state-led rice cultivation programme, including Sri Aman (see Figure 5.2, Zone B). Although 80 per cent of farmers utilize SALCRA schemes, and are confident in the government's ability, 10 per cent are involved in jatropha plantation. Shareholding schemes of jatropha companies are also more interested in including the educated, politically connected Ibans.

Table 5.2 Summary of three Sri Aman villages

Village, sub-district	Tarmac road	Average income/year	Longhouse (LH), doors (D), families (F), household size (HHM)	Major crops	Jatropha households (percentage of total village households)	Bionas Land request	Existing agro-investment	Concern over food vs fuel conflict
Gua, Pantu (N=20)	100%	RMY 7,000/ USD 583	LH: 3 D: 20 F: 250+ HHM: ~6	Oil palm, pepper, rice	100+ (~40%)	10,000 ha	Dayakhash	Maybe (43%)
Tnentulang, Pantu (N=20)	100%	RMY 3,000/ USD 250	LH: 2 D: 18 F: 80+ HHM: ~5	Oil palm, pineapple	10+ (~12.5%)	1,000 ha	Dayakhash	Some (75%)
Sarok, LubokAntu (N=20)	100%	RMY 10,000/ USD 833	LH: 1 D: 42 F: 100+ HHM: ~5	Oil palm, rice	20+ (~20%)	1,000 ha	SALCRA	None

Note: LH – Number of longhouses, D – Number of doors, F – Number of families, HHM – Average number of household members.
Source: Author created from fieldwork data.

5.3.2 Serian agro-economy and space for jatropha

Serian is the capital of Serian District, situated between Kuching Division and to the west of Sri Aman. Serian is only 65 km from Kuching and is commercially well connected by roads (60 per cent) and accessible by water routes. Serian's population is 82,042, out of which 67 per cent are Bidayuh, and the rest are mainly Iban, Chinese, and Malay (DOS 2008). The Bidayuh, known as 'land Dayaks', are native to the island and are in the middle of a legal dispute to be included in *bumiputera* actions. Although the majority of Bidayuh are farmers, they have high levels of education and income. Like Sri Aman, Serian has benefited from SALCRA schemes since the 1970s and now suffers from matured plantations, aged farmers, and urbanization of the youth.

In Serian villages, jatropha is viewed as an alternative to declining rubber estates. Similar to Sri Aman, Serian's proximity to Kuching contributes to rapid urban migration of the young population, leaving behind older farmers. The jatropha crop movement only started in 2007 and, by 2009, the villagers had mixed comments on the crop. While the younger generation supports jatropha companies who make price guarantees without taking over land or participating in binding government projects, the older farmers who labour in the aged government plantations find it difficult to trust commercial companies. Nevertheless, the expansion of jatropha cropping is happening through social networks here, as seen in Iban society, with the youth convincing elders to try jatropha cultivation, or senior village members or farmers creating cooperatives, like Koperasi Pembangunan Jatropha SerianBerhad (the Serian Jatropha Cooperative) which was started in 2009. The cooperative is attracting the educated, the well-connected, and government employees to join the farming scheme. Under the Ministry of Cooperatives and Entrepreneurs, and in accordance with state bylaws, the cooperative has 2,000 members and an institutional structure that ensures a balance between food and fuel crops by providing grants for jatropha crops, education, and buyback guarantees. These are the conditions within which jatropha plantations are being introduced to the rural households.

Although the experience of jatropha commerce among Sri Aman and Serian villagers should be examined again in a few years, the extent that jatropha cropping may directly compete with the food production, rather than contribute to local poverty reduction, needs to be investigated through the lens of value chain analysis of the relevant companies. The next section conducts an IFS analysis of the jatropha value chain embedded in Sarawak.

Table 5.3 Summary of three Serian villages

Village name (focus group number)	Significant ethnic group	Households: number of families (average number of household members)	Average household income/year	Average land available per household for food crops	Major cash crops	Number of households that have joined the jatropha company	Existing agro-investment	Concern over food vs fuel conflict
Bunagaga (N=8)	Bidayuh	100 (~4)	RMY 10,000/ USD 833	5 acres	Pepper, rubber	40	SALCRA	Significant (80%)
KamMuaraAhi (N=7)	Chinese	30 (~5)	RMY 3,000/ USD 250	5 acres	Paddy, durian	20	SALCRA, remittances	Maybe (47%)
PaonGhat (N=5)	Bidayuh	100 (~5.5)	RMY 5,000/ USD 416	5 acres	Rubber, durian, rice	20	SALCRA	Significant (73%)

Source: Author's fieldwork collected in 2009.

5.4 Biofuels companies at the local level

Despite broad national achievements, poverty incidences are highly prevalent among indigenous groups living in inaccessible rural areas, dependent on agricultural income and suffering from inadequate market opportunities (Cramb and Wills 1990; King 1992; Rasul and Thapa 2003). Growing inequality caused by Sarawak development policy encourages poor Sarawakians to join biofuels companies. Jatropha, as a non-food crop with high market potential and growing global demand, is regarded as the next big cash crop for smallholders. Fieldwork research at the ground level through focus groups with the various jatropha supply-chain nodes found inadequate evidence to argue that jatropha will directly conflict with the local food security situation. Competition between companies yields variations in agricultural system planting schemes and business models. Two Sarawak districts were selected for case studies, Sri Aman and Serian, where the two largest biofuels companies, Bionas and AWSB, respectively, operate. Note that other smaller companies operate in these districts and the majority of households still practice shifting cultivation. Therefore, allocating a large tract of land to a non-edible crop is risky and this is fairly well understood by the villages visited.

The state government has demarcated land for rice (see Figure 5.2) under the national granary locations identified in Sarawak. The government accordingly provides targeted training and subsidies to promote rice cultivation. Therefore, there is no apparent conflict between food and fuel, but there are other threats like peatland exploitation. IFS analysis conducted on two jatropha diesel companies competing in the neighbouring districts of Sri Aman and Serian found that companies capitalize on local socio-economic and ethnic conditions and promise income opportunity incentives for cooperation to achieve economies of scale in production.

5.4.1 Bionas and Sri Aman

Bionas is a subsidiary of the Bionas Agropolitan Technology Corridor (BATC) holding company, a Malaysian registered corporation. It is a leading jatropha producer in Malaysia with global ambitions. The company was founded in 2007 by a Malay businessman from Johor who aims to eradicate Malaysia's rural poverty and has aggressively promoted the jatropha business since. According to the Chief Executive Officer of Bionas, by the end of 2011, the company hoped to cultivate 1.3 million ha of jatropha plantations in Malaysia and complete press mill and refinery facilities to start selling in local and international markets, with a further 1.6 billion ringgit invested by 2015.[16] The company, along with a downstream business plan, began an upstream programme. Bionas Murabahah Sdn Bhd was established mid-2009 as a special purpose investment vehicle to encourage global investments in sustainable jatropha diesel production in Malaysia.[17]

During the interviews the company's mission was stressed. This mission is 'to contribute in enhancing the economy of rural communities with the objective of eradicating poverty', which means that it operates in the poorest regions: Sabah, Sarawak, Trengganu, and Kelantan. By way of the Islamic *Musyarakah* – a joint-venture concept – BATC will develop jatropha plantations with contracted farmers in rural areas and create job opportunities. There are already 263 appointed nurseries, which are used as the main marketing tool for the company. Under Phase 1, 200,000 ha of land were offered to entrepreneurs to purchase jatropha seedlings, bags, uniforms, and plantation fertilizers from Bionas-registered nurseries, for RMY 3,000 per one unit plot (0.20 ha). The suggested number of trees per hectare was 800. The selling price for jatropha seeds to BATC was marked as RMY 4,500 which would be paid to participants in deferred payments plus a *hibah* (gift) of RMY 750.00 based on a 2+1 year designed tenancy.[18]

The poor see the Malay-owned Bionas as an opportunity to receive secondary benefits from the *bumiputera* clause. The company understands the need to improve local entrepreneurship among the poor. The benefits trickle down to producers, as Bionas's business plan seeks to build shareholder and stakeholder relationships with local partners. Shareholder schemes invite financial or land-based investments, whereas stakeholder relationships are fostered by promoting Bionas's business practices. In Sarawak villages, nurseries are the main medium of downstream supply-chain management. The Bionas nurseries, often operated by community leaders, attract people of their own community and ethnic groups. Nurseries deliver seedlings, financial support, and training programmes for participating partners. It is the social capital, within which the Sarawak economic structure exists, that Bionas tapped into to expand jatropha development.

Economic efficiency is gained when transaction costs are low, which, over time, indicates economy of scale and profitability. Bionas aims to reduce transaction costs and have greater control in the supply chain. One of the factors for this is the land, which provides both opportunities and challenges. Since there is no market for customary lands, access depends on socio-political networks. If communities agree, access to land is a great advantage for the commercial venture. At the same time, there is a risk for the community and the company as there is no legal protection if either party decides to exit the contract. Commercial property development has been very weak in Sarawak, and a movement to replace the SALCRA scheme, which jatropha companies are tapping into, is under way.

What makes SALCRA scheme conclusive to Jatropha expansion, is the way the palm plantations moved away from public goods development to for-profit. This influenced the influx of cheap Indonesian workers, which put downward pressure on local wages. Urbanization has drawn out the youth, leaving the older population behind in the longhouses with limited production capacity. Despite thousands of hectares of inherited village lands, each family practices subsistence farming on a limited area of 2 ha. In time, the vast unused lands are likely to be captured by the government under the land development clause. Hence, Iban households are excited about jatropha not only to supplement their income, but also to utilize their land holdings. There is no data available on the size of the land, but interviewed farmers are confident that they will not plant jatropha on their paddy land, but in unused or reclaimed lands.

Strong social benefits contribute to jatropha expansion in the Iban community. While Bionas offers a RMY 0.85 per kg jatropha buyback price, edible crops like pineapple, watermelon, and maize give higher returns to farmers. Yet, farmers are attracted to Bionas. There are presently no conflicts between food and fuel, if Sri Aman's longhouses continue to maintain their affiliation with a Malay-owned company and reclaim customary lands. This arrangement provides the benefits of jatropha to the local community, which in return reduces transaction costs for Bionas.

Finally, commercial-scale harvesting is different from harvesting for personal consumption. Commercial-scale 'whole-crop harvesting' is a system where all fruits are accessible and ripen simultaneously. But jatropha's non-synchronization of flowering/fruit ripening and the position of the fruits within the canopy impede whole-crop harvesting. The way the canopy develops remains a concern for investors looking to maximize the output of each plant with minimum labour and time. The harvesting process remains labour intensive. Bionas argues that an individual can tend about 5 ha of jatropha, while tending other crops, because their high quality seedlings need little attention, but Malaysian Agricultural Research and Development Institute (MARDI) researchers counter that 88 per cent of production costs are from labour (105 labour days), as broken down in Table 5.4.

5.4.2 AWSB and Serian

AWSB[19] is a Malaysian company launched in 2007, spearheaded in Sarawak by a Chinese priest with jatropha business experience in Indonesia.[20] AWSB aims to collaborate with communities to establish up to 100,000 ha of jatropha plantation throughout Sarawak. The company profile is complex and controversial. AWSB sits between its parent holding company, Alam Widuri Group, and its own subsidiary biofuels companies. On the ground, the subsidiaries use religious platforms for expansion. Non-Muslims are reached through small churches, while an Islamic-named company follows Islamic-leaning political lines.

As discussed earlier, despite coverage under the *bumiputera* clause, Sarawak's indigenous population is often marginalized from federal government benefits. For the locals, having a joint-venture opportunity with a private company is promising to improve their unused lands' utility and improve local income. AWSB identified that by having joint ventures with the indigenous population it can attract government grants. Within the frame of social capital, AWSB attracts both political leaders and local village

Table 5.4 Jatropha plantation cost structure

Immature stage cost/ha			
Item	Labour (daily rate)	Materials (RMY)	Cost (RMY)
(a) First year			
• Land preparation	27	—	675
• Planting/replacing	10	1,900	2,150
• Weeding	40	—	1,000
• Manuring	5	900	1,025
(b) Second year	40	—	1,000
• Weeding/pruning	5	330	455
• Manuring			
Total	127	3,130	6,305

Mature stage cost/ha			
Item	Labour (daily rate)	Material (RMY)	Cost (RMY)
(a) Upkeep			
• Weeding/pruning	40	—	1,000
• Manuring	5	330	455
(b) Harvesting			
• Picking/depodding/ drying/transporting	60	—	1,500
Total	105	330	2,955

Source: Reproduced from Sivapragasam 2008.

leaders to promote jatropha. The business plan seeks to promote rural entrepreneurship by providing an opportunity for a joint venture with AWSB, as farmers create associations, which are eligible to receive government funding under the state's objective to develop a cooperative environment.

AWSB has a three-pronged supply-chain governance and development scheme. First, it is set up to spearhead jatropha R&D in Sarawak. Collaborations include local organizations like MARDI, Universiti Malaysia Sarawak (UNIMAS),[21] and Universiti Teknologi MARA, and internationally with Labland Biodiesel Ltd., India. Further collaborations are in the pipeline with organizations in India, Singapore, and other countries. Second, AWSB promotes a joint venture based on jatropha production with large landowners and community leaders to ensure local leadership support for the company. Third, individual small landholders can become contract farmers at a fixed buyback price. Finally, collected raw materials are to be processed at AWSB's refinery then exported.

Various ethnic groups respond to jatropha plantation differently, much of which can be categorized from a social capital perspective. For example, Malay representatives appear less convinced about AWSB's promotion claims, whereas AWSB was keen to foster more entrepreneurial relationships with Malay communities to take advantage of the national *bumiputera* clause. Serian Bidayuh groups were receptive to investing in jatropha as an experiment, the Chinese are keen investors, and the comparatively poor

Iban living in *villages* simply could not afford to buy seedlings at RMY 2 each. Interviewees involved in jatropha cultivation hold jobs like retired soldier, school headmaster, village committee chairman, extension officer, and factory worker. Engagement of AWSB is promoted as a catalyst process for indigenous community development mainly to receive state recognition, grants, and other support for their agricultural sector which is opening up for private interventions.

Several issues were raised by the interviewees about the authenticity of AWSB and its failed promises. The main issues were over the quality of seedlings, buyback contracts, and the company's social responsibility. AWSB nursery seedlings required much more water and fertilizers (8 kg of fertilizer) to survive, which is costly for the farmers. AWSD advertised that their seeds come from three trees that the priest planted six years ago from selective seeds brought from Indonesia. It was also claimed that while other jatropha seeds provide 30 per cent to 33 per cent oil, AWSD's seeds can produce up to 37 per cent and with more research this can be increased to 50 per cent. Per tree, per year, the planting costs are RMY 13 and management costs RMY 18. With AWSD's recommended 1,111 seedlings per hectare, farmers with a-few-month-old trees found that the investment cost was more than RMY 34,000. Some were optimistic because AWSB promised a buyback price of RMY 10/kg. In the first month of harvesting, one hectare should yield about 300 kg of seeds, which translates to RMY 3,000. Two harvests were promised in a week for a year-old plant, which is actually labour intensive and infeasible according to local experts. Along with the unsubstantiated productivity estimation, the high labour demand and need to employ Indonesians were adding to the already politically conflicted labour market. In a nutshell, this finding contradicts with the company's position on jatropha being a low-input and low-labour crop.

Sceptics argue that the buyback price has no written contract and that it is too high compared to other competitors, such as Bionas. Also, a few villagers' own research found that AWSB promised different buyback prices in different areas. For example in Sibu and Nuntun, buyback was RMY 2/kg. There were even rumours that RMY 10/kg may even drop to RMY 0.60/kg because the company is financially strapped following the global recession. Furthermore, registered farmers were concerned about the company's social responsibility because the company binds contracts to register designated land for jatropha.

5.4.3 *Comparing Bionas and AWSB planting practices*

Aside from the competitive advantage in maximizing social capital to access NCR lands and economic benefits of the *bumiputera* clause, jatropha business models are closely linked with production economies of scale. This subsection compares the planting techniques, aimed at production economies of scale that the two companies promoted among the villagers. The information compared in this sub section was collected from the farmers, company representatives, the village extension officers, and independent researchers.

The planting practices promoted in the district are inconsistent, with Bionas advocating 800 trees per hectare and AWSB targeting 1,111. The Sarawak extension officers indicated that the soil structure cannot support 1,111 plants in one hectare. Eight hundred plants per hectare is feasible, but given the plant's 30-year lifespan, spacing is critical. Scientists from UNIMAS and MARDI are running tests on the quality of major companies' seeds. Seeds distributed by Bionas and AWSB were tested and it was found that the seed quality for both was low with only a 30 per cent germination rate found. It was also noted that the seed oil content was about 33 per cent, which could be increased to 50 per cent under strict nursing. UNIMAS plant biologists believed that a hybrid process that would take about five years could stabilize the best quality seed genes and multiply them for mass production. Aside from the hypothesis about the ecotype quality of jatropha plants, adequate spacing, and ample sunshine and water are required to maximize jatropha production.

Furthermore, marginalized and unused NCR lands are mainly peatland. Since jatropha can be planted in peatland, and native communities are claiming ownership on unused land, peatlands are being cleared. This appeared to be a sensitive matter, as the informal institutional analysis already highlighted, the belief that land is borrowed from God leaves the Iban feeling apprehensive about destroying peatland or community forests. However, the economic crisis and high food costs are influencing the farmers' collective decisions on how to integrate jatropha in their farming system. The AWSB has already cleared more than 200,000 hectares of land and about one third of that is peatland. Bionas is moving into the frontier of the Sarawak district which is predominantly peatland based. For Sarawak, where deforestation is a major problem, without proof of a sustainable business plan, there should be some injunction from the regulatory framework to stop aggressive jatropha plantation expansion. MPOB and the agricultural scientists expressed fear that imported hybrid seeds could affect the natural pest management system by introducing foreign pests and diseases. For labour and land, without a vigilant land regulatory body, jatropha expansion in remote parts of Sarawak may complicate the already stressed agro-political system. Unplanned jatropha cultivation may stimulate an influx of informal labour from Indonesia to support plantations, which will contribute to socio-political and economic stress. Smallholder income depends on family labour, but if they cannot compete with cheap migrant labour, then there will be serious political repercussions.

5.5   Conclusion

Sarawak is one of Malaysia's poorest regions, occupied by 9.1 per cent of the population, having been subjected to unequal development and unresolved governance differences between the central and the local system. This research found that commercial ventures are taking advantage of that policy gap. Jatropha expansion is happening through social network channels that are particularly strong among the older and poorer natives, who rely on remittances instead of state-promoted palm estates. The palm estates have matured and replanting requires both physical and economic capital.

Limited in both respects, the rural Sarawak population finds commercial jatropha an attractive alternative for its low input and high demand. Many farmers are avoiding participation in the government subsidized palm replanting schemes in order to join the jatropha sector. Bionas has set a standard for contract farming by distributing written contracts whereas the other companies use informal networking to engage with local farmers, the response to which can best be gauged by the local farmers' receptiveness. Companies are doing whatever needs to be done to attract producers because the industry's sustainability ultimately lies in adequate supplies of feedstock to process into biodiesel. In terms of land, Sarawakians are not only clearing NCR forests, but also monocropping this unproven commodity, which is likely to create ecological complications.

Given the strong institutional structure in place to eradicate rural poverty and the national focus on food security, jatropha plantations cannot replace the importance of food security. The extent to which farmers will alter farming practices to integrate jatropha into their production decisions. It is justified for farmers to use jatropha cultivation to diversify their household income, protect their customary land, and bring social development. But the various contract farming schemes that companies use in the name of poverty reduction appear predominantly profit driven. This approach largely remains unattractive to poor farming communities and hence, in the absence of formal government guidance on jatropha, farmers depend on their social networks.

Both of the companies studied are keen to leverage the *bumiputera* clause and state entitlements. Hence, the poorest participate in jatropha plantations, committing investments and hoping for an income from an unproven crop. The buyback prices, which differ between companies, incentivize farmers and capture commitments to produce jatropha. Despite high returns, the majority of the jatropha farmers are reluctant to give up their existing food and cash-crop lands, but instead plant jatropha on marginal lands. Jatropha still requires irrigation, pesticides, and fertilizers for high productivity, but being planted in the marginal lands introduces two dilemmas. Farmers need to buy or source inputs for jatropha plants or utilize intensive monocropping to maximize the investment output. Both options are unattractive for farmers at this point who, despite all their dissatisfaction with the government, rely heavily on them for direction and depend on collective decision-making processes from their community. Social capital is very strong in Sarawak, which makes jatropha less likely to conflict with existing agricultural systems or rapidly destroy the rich ecosystem of the land. Having said this, if poverty deepens due to economic reasons, or the agricultural market fluctuates for palm and rice, the farming community may convert more land for jatropha. This can only be tested in time.

In summary, the jatropha industry is still at an early stage and farmers are not fully convinced whether private jatropha initiatives are competitive with the public palm oil industry while national food production policy tightens requirements for crop land share. To attain the same scale of production as other crops, along with soil quality, jatropha need regular investment in inputs and labour. While a sustainable biodiesel sector is still at a developmental stage, a competitive environment has already set in, but the impact of it is unclear given the strong positive influence of social capital and effective socio-political governance structure. Although there is no evidence of conflict between food and fuel under careful Malaysian institutional arrangements, the vulnerability from insufficient food production and informal land rights of Sarawak requires future study of the impact in the region as the global biofuels value chain matures in Malaysia.

Notes

1   A term used since the Sarawak Interpretation Ordinance in 2004 when the state government banned the use of the word 'Dayak' in official communication. Thus 'Sea Dayak' has been changed to 'Iban', 'Land Dayak' has become 'Bidayuh' and 'Murut' is now 'Lun Bawang'. But in Federal Article 161a (7) 'Iban, Bidayuhs and Lun Bawang' are not listed. Thus they are considered as non-natives under the Federal Constitution. The legal implication of this is huge when it comes to benefiting from the *bumiputera* policies. (See 'The Broken Shield, 2009. Is Iban a *bumiputera* or not?' *The Borneo Post*.) This point will be mentioned again in the analysis.
2   In Sarawak land belongs to the state and its people. The Land Code of 1958 has a colonial legacy and is a major obstacle to private investment in land development. Under this code, land rights cannot be traded in the land market, but can be exchanged only as a form of grant, lease or gift (e.g. marriage dowry) (Cramb 2009).
3   Peatland costs 40 per cent more in land development, as it needs to be drained and Ph balanced. Also, it involves higher maintenance costs compared to mineral soil, not to mention the environmental criticisms the planters face. Peatlands are considered last resorts for palm plantations. In 2002, MARDI published documents on how to make peatland useful for agricultural use, since the populations living on such land were the poorest due to unfavourable agricultural opportunities. See MARDI 2002.
4   This is an ambitious target because the Eighth Malaysia Plan (8MP) forecasted a growth rate of 3 per cent, which was then revised to 2 per cent in the midterm review. Similarly, in the 7MP the agricultural target was set out at 2.4 per cent, revised down to 1.9 per cent in the midterm review, and actually only achieved 1.2 per cent.
5   According to personal interviews with MPOB experts in 2009 on biofuels, it became clear that the high level of market barriers seen in the EU market and subsidized gasoline market will make it hard for the Malaysian biodiesel

industry to be competitive. In early 2010 the government announced a delay in its plan to blend 5 per cent biodiesel with fossil diesel until 2011.

6   B5 means a 5 per cent biodiesel blend in a unit of fossil diesel. The mixer can be as much as 100 per cent, in which case the term is B100.

7   Between 1976 and when this report was written, a total of 45,000 hectares of NCR land had been planted with oil palm. About 14,000 participants are involved in the scheme, of which slightly more than 50 per cent are Iban and the rest are Bidayuh. A total of RMY 100 million worth of dividends have been distributed among the scheme participants. In this study, major beneficiaries of SALCRA projects are from Sri Aman and Betong Divisions. Also, with the implementation of the farm schemes, longhouse communities are road-linked to town centres, government facilities and rural clinic and services centres. See Ngidang 2007.

8   The programmes are the: (a) Mind Development Programme (Program Pembangunan Minda Insan – PMI); (b) Training and Education Programme (Program Latihan dan Pendidikan – PLP); (c) Supplementary Balanced Food Programme (Program Makanan Tambahan Seimbang – PMTS); (d) Income Increase Programme (Program Peningkatan Pendapatan; (e) Housing Support Programme (Program Bantuan Rumah – PBR); (f) Integrated Urban Community Advancement Programme (Program Pemajuan Masyarakat Bandar Bersepadu – PPMB); (g) PreSchool Building Programme (Program Bangunan TASKA); (h) Bumiputera Trust Fund (Amanah Saham Bumiputera Sejahtera); and (i) In-situ Community Development Programme (Program Pembangunan Masyarakat Setempat – PPMS).

9   Peninsular Malaysia has 1.3 Mha, Sabah 4.3 Mha, and Sarawak 2 Mha of marginal soils (Sai 2002).

10   Averaging a daily minimum of 23° C and a maximum of 32° C.

11   Humidity levels can average around 70 per cent in the mid-afternoon.

12   Rainfall averaging from 2,500 to 4,000 mm per annum. November to January is the monsoon and June to August is known for its dryness, relative to the height of the area.

13   For more about Iban culture, see Cramb 2009.

14   Similar levels of social cohesion, interactions and dependency between generations were found in Soda 2007.

15   For an anthropological study, see Cramb 2009.

16   Projected during the interviews by the Bionas CEO, who is a *bumiputera* businessman.

17   Visit the Bionas website for more information on the company at www.bionas. com.my

18   The country's land law allows only three-year tenancies.

19   Company website www.alamwiduri.com/corporate_profile.php

20   Informants mentioned that the priest lost RMY 3 million in the jatropha business in Indonesia.

21   Interviews with UNIMAS and MARDI denied any affiliation with AWSB, supplying instead rather contradictory information about the company and its vitality as the company is financially struggling. However, the financial status information was unavailable for verification.

6 Looking forward while leaning backward

This book empirically tests the extent to which non-edible, drought resistant, first generation biofuels crops like jatropha could contribute to energy security, climate change mitigation, and poverty reduction, and subsequently help to improve the agricultural sector in developing countries and to ease food insecurity. At the heart of this research is contextualization of 'the rules of the game in a society or, more formally... the humanly devised constraints that shape human interaction' (North 1990: 3). One of the distinguishing features of this quotation is that developed or high income countries' institutional capacity to articulate and enforce consistent rules of the game is greater than that in developing countries. Developing countries involved in complex diplomatic relationships find their national policies being influenced by foreign interests playing the roles of investors, consumers, and aid donors. North's notion of humanly devised constraints that shape human interaction forms the core of the IFS framework proposed to analyse how rules and policies condition the political environment, market arrangements, and individuals' decisions in a given context. This chapter utilizes the theoretical framework presented in Chapter 2 to analyse the case studies. The context-specific analysis developed in Chapters 4 and 5 is combined to make observations on results and lessons for the future. The comparative case study analysis between Tanzania and Malaysia provide evidence for these three points through the lens of multidisciplinary research on the biofuels industry development and its impact on food security.

The remainder of the chapter is organized as follows: in Section 6.1 a comparison is drawn between the factors that made Tanzania and Malaysia attractive for biofuels feedstock production; Section 6.2 comparatively analyses Tanzanian and Malaysian agro-economic regulatory frameworks to highlight how poverty and food insecurity issues are addressed over time; and Section 6.3 uses a livelihood perspective on decentralized governance and market systems to analyse biofuels investment and production opportunity perceptions by locals in the case study villages. Finally, this chapter concludes the book by summarizing the findings based on reassessing the food versus fuels debate and offering an invitation to review the policy informing tools for complex commodities and the emerging GVC, within which we aim to build a sustainable world.

6.1   International political economy of biofuels and jatropha

Communities and institutions have multiple, nested, and overlapping definitions and interactions, which necessitate multi-scalar coordination in order to address poverty, food security, and climate change actions. The multi-scalar approach bridges differences between community, district, and national level priorities which are interwoven and require a participatory approach (Barrett *et al.* 2001). The IFS is used here to analyse rural poverty reduction, agricultural sector improvements, and biofuels market participation without reducing food security.

This section compares the factors making Tanzania and Malaysia attractive for biofuels feedstock production and investments. In the broader scale of international economics, biofuels industry expansion in African and Asian countries follows a specific line of interest of modern global trade: access to cheap land for agricultural commodity cultivation. In a buyer-driven agromarket, agriculturally developing countries have little power of price, policy, or distribution systems. This topic is discussed at length in the Chapter 3 literature review. Here, focus is placed on the two case study countries in the international biofuels market supplying jatropha oil. Of the various feedstocks, estimates showed a very strong global growth for jatropha plantations to grow tenfold in 2015 reaching 12.5 million ha of land (GEXSI 2008; REN21 2009). This leaves the question of how 12.5 million ha of land will be accommodated within the global agricultural land system.

6.1.1   *The buyer factor: the international agro-economy of biofuels*

The question critical to the research: can biofuels crop production for commercial export generally be a 'win–win' situation for all countries that enter the market? At the time of this research, the jatropha industry was in its very early stages, covering a global area estimated at 900,000 ha (GEXSI 2008). Jatropha is a new and complex agricultural phenomenon that expanded into important sectors of an economy, namely energy and investment.

As mentioned earlier, the tropical zone is suitable for biodiesel crops like palm oil and jatropha. However, although jatropha investors have attracted the rural population in the semi-arid and unproductive zones in developing countries where the most vulnerable and undernourished population resides, it appears that the economic scale of production was not necessarily attained during the promised time frame. There is a close connection between food insecurity and structural poverty, which translates into cheap land and labour, and a relatively easy environment for FDI. This point was underscored by the 1994 World Bank report (World Bank 1994). In terms of timing, biofuels production reached a height in terms of interest from the national governments, approximately, 2005. Around that time the global oil price started to creep up and began worrying both developed and developing countries. While developed countries' worry translated into a search for oil substitution and alternative technologies, in developing countries with land this translated into a flow of investments in the agriculture sector to capture land and feedstock for biofuels processing (Clancy 2013).

Such conditions, coupled with a relatively stable political environment started to attract a particular types of developing country such as Mozambique, Tanzania, Kenya, Malaysia, India, and others. Some developing countries became attractive producers of biofuels feedstocks, which translated into FDI. Cross-country econometric evidence indicates that GDP growth generated in agriculture is at least twice as effective in reducing poverty as growth generated in other sectors (World Bank 2008a). From a political economy perspective, biofuels have the potential to generate employment in rural areas, make use of unused land, diversify the agricultural sector, and trigger agricultural growth with implications for poverty reduction. Furthermore, long depressed commodity prices have eroded productivity of the agricultural sector but, since 2007, the sector has seen prices rise, placing tropical developing agricultural countries in the perfect situation to undertake biodiesel crop production for commercial export (FAO 2008).

The focus of tropical developing countries situated in rich but fragile biodiversity zones on export-oriented agro-business is bringing their own and foreign interests in the agricultural sector into conflict with environmental protection. To understand the global biofuels value chain, it is important to understand the differences between producer and consumer countries and the interactions between the agro-economy and the agro-environment.

As mentioned already, tropical agrarian economies like Tanzania and Malaysia are based on primary commodities, but face different levels of income elasticity, institutional capacity, and human development levels among producers, which affects their export earnings. In theory, demand for primary food crops like nuts and cocoa will rise less than output from producing developing countries. Over time, supply outpacing demand pushes down primary commodity prices, which then drives down agricultural sector productivity due to a lack of return on investment. For example, half of Tanzania's population, of which 80 per cent are rural farmers, is food insecure. Since the late 1990s, the country has started experiencing declining terms of trade and a regression in major cash-crop sectors like cashew, tobacco, cotton, and sisal due to drops in international primary commodity prices (Tanzania 2008b).[1] More than 90 per cent of the country's arable land is underutilized, with over 80 per cent of its population in agriculture engaged in vulnerable employment – unpaid work or subsistence farming – making the cost of feedstock production low (World Bank 2009a).

Low land prices, cheap labour, and market friendly rural development policies are making Tanzania an appropriate country for foreign investors to target. Furthermore, low price elasticity of demand induced Tanzania to make national priorities to revitalize the agricultural sector in order to remove structural poverty and food insecurity from rural areas (see Tanzania 2008a).

In contrast, Malaysia is a leader for rapid poverty reduction through state-led projects. In the 1970s, half of its population was impoverished, while in 2001 only about 3 per cent lived in poverty. One of the major reasons behind the impressive reduction is the commercialization of major cash crops like palm, rubber, cocoa, and pepper in participation with the poor through FELDA and SALCRA. Palm oil, a high-value-added crop with inelastic demand from the international market, made a threefold contribution to Malaysia – the national economy, agricultural sector development, and agro-commercial standards (Ariffin 2008). As a result, in the 1980s export-led agro-policies on the one hand increased public investment in cash crops and on the other hand encouraged investment in upgrading the agricultural value chain and biotechnology. Over time, rural participants in the national programme benefited immensely, while the country leapt into industrial sector development. Malaysia became a leader in value-added agricultural commodities, laying the foundation for its entrance into the global biofuels market (World Bank 2010b).

Biofuels crops like jatropha were introduced to the country by foreign investors as a cash crop, but the complex interactions of biodiversity loss from foreign crops were overlooked. Studies found that the ability of current biofuels crops to compensate for the loss of native plants are minimal and limited knowledge is shared between producers, exporters, and the consumers on the loss of biodiversity and the spread of invasive pests or species (Hertel *et al.* 2010; Naylor *et al.* 2007; Taheripour *et al.* 2010). Similarly, jatropha proponents in Tanzania who promote intercropping pay little attention to the fact that semi-arid and arid zones have their own unique ecosystems from which the native populations of animals and a variety of flora can be lost.[2] In Malaysia, having already utilized available land for cash crops, peatlands are being converted to produce biofuels crops. Jatropha production on such land not only threatens to destabilize the stored carbon, but also threatens to pollute the soil and water as there is a negative trade-off between crop productivity and input demand, e.g., water, fertilizer, and pesticides.

Given the wider debate on biofuels, as discussed in Chapter 2, it is clear that there is no consistency in findings and claims on the biofuels industry outcomes on human health, economies, and the environment. From a human health perspective, bringing new crops into developing countries and intensifying their cultivation has led to the introduction of more nitrate, phosphate, and pesticides, potentially exacerbating the already weak human capital and health services. Jatropha is, in fact, highly toxic,[3] and the fruit has an irritant sap that can be fatal when in contact with humans and animals (FDA 2008). In 2005, Western Australia banned *Jatropha gossypifolia* as an invasive species due to its high toxicity to people and animals (MacIntyre 2007). Burning land and post-harvest biomass can contribute to smoke pollution which has yet to be measured by scientists, but clearly has environmental impacts. The effects of jatropha cultivation and harvesting are far more complicated than Western buyers and the policy makers have considered. Finally, even in Malaysia, despite having sophisticated plantation management systems, little consideration is given in the National Biofuel Policy discourse on the rebound effects of efficiency and loss of household economics. In other words, as the efficiency of engines operating with unprocessed biofuels increases, the demand for biofuels crops will also increase. Although, increased use of biofuels crops may decrease transportation emissions, the secondary effects of biofuels crop production are not properly understood and calculated within current models. The carbon savings, welfare gains, improved land use, technology transfers, and skills development in developing countries are questionable, while the buyer-driven global biofuels industry promotes higher blending targets, investment support (e.g., carbon credits) and sets quality standards.

6.1.2 *The seller factor: the national agro-economy of biofuels*

Different products require different levels of productive factors and countries have different production factor advantages. For example, agricultural products require more labour per unit than manufactured goods, which instead require more machine time per worker than most primary commodities. However, because the labour required in agriculture is relatively lower-skilled, the cost of human labour is low. The average labour to land cultivation ratio is about two to three workers per hectare, but jatropha requires only one worker for every ten hectares of land, because the crop is less labour intensive. This translates to even less labour demand and cost per hectare of land, in comparison to other cash crops.

Investors are attracted to Tanzania mainly for its relative factor advantages of abundant unused arable land and cheap labour, despite its fluctuating investment environment. For Malaysia, although labour and land costs are relatively more expensive than in Tanzania, the biofuels investment environment is stable and there are spillover effects of good agricultural management practices, biotechnology, and market governance systems. According to the World Bank, it takes 29 days, a 12-step process, and a minimum investment of 39 per cent of annual per capita income to set up a business in Tanzania, compared to Malaysia where it takes 11 days, a 9-step processes, and no minimum cost (World Bank 2010a).

Figure 6.1 shows that the Tanzanian business climate may be more difficult than Malaysia's, but is comparable to that in India and China, two leading countries in the biofuels sector. The data is from the World Bank's

Figure 6.1 Web of 'doing business' in selected countries in 2007 (Low 0–High 100)
Note: Ranking scaled by log⁵.
Source: Author created using World Bank 2010a data.

Doing Business report. Although the report is subjective and incomplete, it significantly influences foreigners' decisions concerning investment in developing countries because of the report's insights into the regulatory frameworks and institutional structures.

Such knowledge of the business environment, underlined by political and economic conditions, translates into the FDI inflows that each country attracts. According to the World Bank's Governance and Anticorruption indicator, Tanzania's political stability ranked in the 35th percentile in 2008 while Malaysia was in the 50th percentile.[4] Although the World Bank claims that this ranking does not influence its development assistance funding decisions, FDI inflows to developing countries are influenced by perceptions of political processes, stability, and transparency, often expressed in such a ranking.[5] Between 2004 and 2008, FDI inflows to Malaysia grew by 86 per cent; inflows in India grew by 441 per cent in the same period; inflows in the USA showed a 184 per cent growth; but in Tanzania the growth was only 51 per cent. In practice, it is very difficult to quantify the influence a national political environment has on such international FDI.

Donor partnership schemes, foreign governments, and their national private companies operate under a public–private partnership business model. For example, Tanzania's biofuels sector, domestic regulatory frameworks, and international market presence are built and influenced by numerous donor countries and multilateral agencies stakeholders, in line with their economic and political relationship with the country. For example, SIDA provided funding that enabled Tanzania's National Biofuel Task Force to conduct initial meetings, while GTZ commissioned the most comprehensive study on the prospects of biofuels in Tanzania. It was identified that sometimes because of the long-standing relationship between Tanzania with Germany and Sweden as two important development donor partners international interests are not aligned with domestic goals and the people's needs. A key example is the GTZ development assistance study to measure and analyse whether the Tanzanian transportation system was suitable for biofuels usage. The goal was to help the country reduce its imported oil dependency, but its conclusion, that converting the national transportation infrastructure to suit biofuels is a costly proposal, should have been intuitively apparent. It is clearly risky for a low income, food deficit, highly indebted, poor country like Tanzania to enter a highly unproven sector like first generation biofuels feedstock production, such as the case with land grabbing.

Land grabbing is a growing global practice and a point of concern. Much of it is influenced by two facts: first, the assumption that investors will better utilize land than leaving it idle; and second, the power play between poor landowners, mainly under customary land title, manipulated by politicians that benefit from foreign financial gains. In both Tanzanian and Malaysian villages, growth in FDI often helps with the election process. Tanzania has been subjected to land grabbing for biofuels production, with land often purchased at unfair prices. The large tracts of land are owned by the community under customary land rights or native land rights, but the land rights transfer process is plagued by corruption (Cotula *et al.* 2010). In 2009, Tanzania halted all foreign biofuels investments until it passed the National Biofuels Policy and completed establishing its regulatory framework. In the same year, the World Wildlife Foundation (WWF) reported illegal logging and land clearing projects in Malaysia for biofuels, which raised global attention (Smolker *et al.* 2009), particularly concerning jatropha plantations on peatlands, which are unsuitable for palm plantations.

Nevertheless, investor countries' subsidies and biofuels blending targets coupled with producer countries' export-led policies, tax breaks, and biofuels policies create push and pull factors for international and national oil and agribusiness companies to invest in the biofuels industry. Companies including Shell, Neste Oil, Greenergy International, BioX, Cargill, and Archer Daniels Midland are involved in the sector, but their operations are in partnership with public companies and local governments. Fifty countries have identified jatropha–specific policies, with Asia leading the field with publicly funded jatropha research projects (GEXSI 2008).[6] Malaysia is developing hybrid seeds that will be suitable for intercropping with a variety of crops, and that can be easily pruned, managed, and harvested.

Unfortunately, African countries are seeing a greater tendency for monocropping of jatropha among smallholders and commercial landholders. Lands are being cleared, taken over, and converted for jatropha plantations under public–private partnerships. The larger question in the current context is how to control the expansion of land use for biofuels feedstock production while maintaining a sustainable global commercial interest on jatropha feedstock outsourcing from developing countries.

Many studies attempted to quantify displacement of land use due to biofuels feedstock production expansion in developing countries. By compiling the projected scenarios, according to UNEP, the global deforestation rate of 13 million hectares per year may rise to 286 million hectares per year by 2030 (UNEP 2009b). Water use, fertilizer use, and the use of pesticides and herbicides are serious problems, causing soil pollution and groundwater toxification (Harvey 2010). All of these may aggravate the already stressed water table and soil quality in agricultural countries (OECD 2006; Pimentel and Patzek 2005; UNEP 2009c). Given the diversity in standards observed in Chapter 3, Subsection 3.3.2, the RSB, founded by the WWF, proposed definitions for direct and indirect land use to create a standardized biofuels certification. The discussion on how to account for indirect land use and water utilization for biofuels certification is still under discussion (Cornelissen and Dehue 2009).[7] This institution is also working on guidelines and better management practices for jatropha plantations with global jatropha leaders. These instruments are being designed to ensure a triple bottom line (profit, people, and planet) in the global jatropha business environment. Unfortunately, none of the certification schemes have been examined in the context of existing behavioural, social practice, institutional, and infrastructure factors, which considerably affect labelling legislation.[8]

6.2 National institutional economy of biofuels and jatropha

This section compares the Tanzanian and Malaysian institutional and regulatory frameworks to assess the differential benefits of biofuels sector development, specifically through the jatropha GVC. It is widely understood that there are many variables that can cause differential performances of a commodity between countries, among which, the national regulatory and political institutional structures have the greatest influence on agro-industrial outcomes. This is primarily due to information asymmetries within regulatory structures, which affect the nature and quality of markets. Investors strive to minimize input costs, while neglecting environmental and social externalities. Resource abuse prevails in land, labour, and water consumption, which are deemed cheap resources. Abuse undercuts the benefits that agro-industries like biofuels bring to the people in producer countries, with land grabbing, labour rights abuses, and overconsumption of water as just a few examples.

This is a case for public intervention through standards on resource usage, for example, setting price ceilings and taxes. However, these policies are frowned upon by market liberalists. Moreover, problems arise in practice when public intervention is weak, such as when institutional structures lag behind market changes, are uncoordinated or contradict authority between agencies. For example, deforestation legislation may contradict urban expansion plans. Furthermore, weak property rights systems exacerbate the negative outcomes of export-led agro-market expansion strategies. The private sector has little incentive to invest in fixed capital (e.g., machinery, factories) and even less in health, education, and infrastructure development, although promises are often made in business proposals. Conversely, their interest is high in exploiting cheap natural resources. Since governments control the local environment within which agro-industry businesses operate, and by extension these businesses' behaviour, and because environments can vary significantly as seen earlier, differences in benefits from biofuels industry development are likely to occur between Tanzania and Malaysia.

6.2.1 Biofuels embedded in the national political economy

Economic growth is an outcome of cumulative and sustained changes of the institutions working in an economy. It is widely agreed that better institutions are correlated with less income volatility, i.e., smaller fluctuations in per capita income. As Figure 6.2 shows from a snapshot analysis of Malaysian and Tanazanian institutional quality over time, there is a reasonable expectation that poor farmers in Malaysia would have better protection from any shocks than their Tanzanian counterparts. This kind of relational assumption, although it may not be the complete truth, holds enough evidence to justify a conservative or liberal approach to market reforms such as promoting an unproven crop like jatropha to join the global biofuels value chain.

It is important to remember that there may be periodic shifts in political power or changes in the national economic environment, like a financial crisis, that could trigger institutional instability. For example, after the financial crisis of 1997, the Malaysian government's regulatory capacity was brought into question while real per capita GDP dropped. In contrast, Tanzania, despite having about ten times smaller per capita income, has improved its overall institutional quality rank over time.

Nevertheless, the patterns observed in this data suggest that a feedback loop may run from institutions to the outcomes and from outcomes to possible sources of institutional variation. While the aggregate GDP showed a small but positive growth rate in Tanzania, Malaysia experienced some income and institutional volatility following the Asian financial crisis which partially explains some variation (Amsden 2001). Institutional change is typically very slow, even taking decades depending upon rates of economic growth, knowledge growth, and technological adaptation. As institutional economist

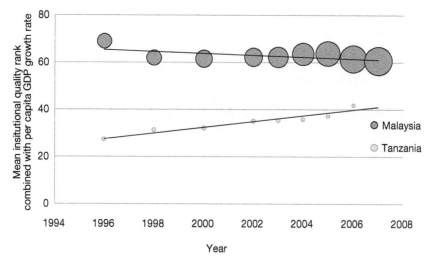

Figure 6.2 Institutional quality rank and real per capita GDP growth (1996–2008)
Note: The circle diameters represent the quality of institutions measured against GDP per capita (the bigger the circle, the better the quality). It is not intended here to show any causal relationship, rather, the focus is on the trend of quality improvement over time. Constant prices, adjusted according to exchange rates by year, were derived from the growth rates of the consumer price index.
Source: Author created. Institutional quality rank data from World Bank 2009b; real GDP per capita data from Heston *et al.* 2009.

Veblen pointed out 'Institutions are products of the past process, are adapted to past circumstances, and are therefore never in full accord with the requirements of the present' (Veblen 2008: 148). As the IFS framework points out, institutional economic research finds deep historical origins in the divergence of institutions and hence income, including factors such as colonial power allocation, the nature of colonial resource allocation, legal systems, patterns of resource endowment, and infrastructural connectivity. The two countries selected for this research have very different institutional political economies but have some very basic cultural similarities.

Specifically, both Tanzania and Malaysia have diverse socio-cultural and religious systems, with a Muslim majority. Both of the countries have a British colonial history, the legacy of which moulded their legal systems on English Common Law. Currently, the Tanzanian political economy is a democratic republic and Malaysia has a democratic federal system. Both countries gained independence within five years of each other, Malaysia in 1957 and Tanzania and 1961, and started their nation state building projects under the principles of consociationalism – communal interests are resolved in the framework of a grand social coalition – and both of the developmental states face challenges from growing inequality between races, genders and income groups. While the Tanzanian project failed to materialize the full potential of bridging the differences between interest groups, Malaysia, with its religiously and ethnically divided political rhetoric and preferential treatments of the Malay population, created a fragile political environment.

The two countries share some similarities with regard to marginalized rural poverty and food insecurity. Take, for instance, the Malaysian state of Sarawak and the Tanzanian districts of Kisarawe and Dodoma. The former is independently governed and geographically separated from the mainland, while the latter were isolated from the central government during the 1990s' decentralization process. On an economic level, Sarawak is comparable to Tanzania's overall developmental condition, as mentioned in the case study section; Sarawak's governance sovereignty was separated from that of Peninsular Malaysia until recently, as shown in Chapter 5. As a result, while Peninsular Malaysia's poverty rate, malnutrition, and illiteracy rate declined rapidly, Sarawak continues to suffer from a high prevalence of malnutrition, low education rates, and poor health care provision. Like Tanzania, the state of Sarawak remained highly dependent on agricultural growth rates for its state income. However, when the two countries are compared, the Sarawak state institutional system has provided more social benefits to its people, which over time have increased their relative well-being standards more than those of their Tanzanian counterparts.

Malaysia and Tanzania both have a biofuels policy, but no crop-specific considerations – a significant omission since crops are divided into edible and non-edible designations and operate within distinctive demand structures. While edible biofuels crops like soy, palm, and sugarcane have a market beyond biofuels, jatropha, *Moringa,* and others are limited to the single market. Since the biofuels market is niche, it has higher transaction and opportunity costs. Furthermore, feedstock producing countries are experiencing a new era in their commercial agricultural systems. Aside from estate farming, outgrower schemes are being widely introduced by foreign companies to secure feedstock consumption while at the same time ensuring they appear socially responsible. As the case studies discussed, sample contracts provided to farmers, or farmer organizations, by biofuels companies contained three main promises: (a) a buyback guarantee; (b) a buy back price based on the international market price; and (c) profit sharing, conditional to the company's earnings.

Many important contract clauses like production costs, transportation costs, conflict resolution, exit clauses, and others were missing from the observed contractual agreements. Such missing elements have the potential for conflict. Aside from missing elements, it was also observed that contract clauses were sometimes too ambitious in their specifications, ignoring the contract recipients' comprehension capacity. For example, companies in Sarawak have both an outgrower scheme and a shareholder scheme where villagers or individuals can participate in the production of seedlings, distribution of seedlings, cultivation, and transportation logistics. The contract documents given to shareholders have complicated terms and conditions and an elaborate business model. Although, it was observed that the population who were involved in the early phase of jatropha expansion were relatively educated, most of them were using their meagre savings to invest in the company. This raises questions concerning the villagers' understanding, knowledge, and rights, as well as legal implications if conditions are not fulfilled. Similarly, in Tanzania, the foreign investors were using the outgrower scheme models. In Swahili there is no direct translation of this term, which, in effect, introduced misguided interpretations, as different locals perceived the term differently.

The inherent conflict between food crops and cash crops is present within commercial biofuels feedstock production. Both Malaysia and Tanzania are fitting jatropha within their existing value-added agricultural sectors. While maintaining leadership in the palm oil market, Malaysia is also attracting foreign jatropha investors like D1, BP, and other oil companies. Two main aspects are driving jatropha industry development in Malaysia. On the one hand, the government sees the crop as an opportunity to diversify the aging palm oil sector and eradicate chronic poverty from Sarawak. On the other hand, jatropha investors are pursuing spillover effects from advanced agricultural management, biotechnology, and cheap migrant labour from rubber and palm plantations.

The 9MP sets out an ambitious plan to grow the agricultural sector at 5 per cent and agro-based industry at 5.2 per cent. Along with this ambition the National Biofuels Policy (2005) identified biofuels to be the fifth element in the Five-Fuel Diversification Policy.[9] To promote this sector, the government listed jatropha as a key biofuels crop, controlled under the Promotion of Investment Act 1986 to receive Pioneer Status, Investment Tax Allowance, and RA for five to ten years. The national government may also introduce biofuels consumer subsidies and eliminate fossil fuel subsidies. Sarawak is attractive for jatropha production because of its poor quality peat soil, which is not suitable for palm oil, and abundant cheap labour from Indonesia. At the state level, jatropha is included in the Sarawak renewable energy plans and important political figures are personally promoting the crop in their constituencies, native villages, and within their clans. During the research period, it was noticed that educated Sarawakians were interested in examining the value of jatropha before engaging in mass production. As the price of fossil fuel is projected to rally again, enthusiasm remains steady among poor smallholders to join the rally of jatropha plantations and there is no apparent conflict between food and jatropha, or between jatropha and palm oil plantations.

In contrast, although Tanzania did not have a national biofuels policy until 2009, it quickly became one of the top biofuels producing countries, mainly for jatropha. Even with the policy, the state does little to protect the rights of outgrower scheme participants. The outgrower scheme is popular in Tanzania's value-added agricultural system, wherein 80 per cent of farmers are illiterate and work on a subsistence basis. Ironically, even oral explanations for the outgrower scheme are difficult, since Tanzania has 15 to 20 clans, each with a slightly different dialect and oral knowledge about agricultural systems. Nevertheless, all levels of the national and local regulatory system of the agro-industry believe that jatropha will replace their dying cashew and sisal industries, while rescuing the declining agricultural sector and helping reduce rural poverty. In exchange for abundant arid land, private companies promise to reduce the public sector burden to improve social services, build infrastructure, and create employment opportunities. Unfortunately, as Veblen identified, current institutions are not capable of producing outcomes for the present as they are built on the past (Veblen 2008). Tanzania suffers from an incomplete decentralization process, multiple land tenure systems, and inadequate infrastructure, which all contribute to high transaction costs for buyers and sellers.

While the foreign companies investing in Tanzania forge vertical integration to gain expertise and develop innovative processes and products, they are still faced with political–economic imperatives to maintain productivity. To achieve sustainability and productivity, companies need to overcome the inherent complexity of coordinating resources within the regulatory and institutional frameworks. It is not only expensive, but also, in some cases, impossible to change the environment within which business takes place. For example, it is expensive and premature for Sun Biofuels to commit to pave village roads to reduce transportation costs, or even invest in a large factory for biofuels processing, as the global economy and the biofuels market are facing turbulent times. For Sun Biofuels, an outgrower scheme with minimum investment maximizes its rate of return.

As shown in Chapter 4, companies in Tanzania aim to gain economies of scale by transferring and minimizing transaction costs down the value chain. Similarly, within the context of long-standing local-level party politics, confusion over land rights and unclear regulatory apparatus to protect poor farmers' rights may negatively affect the poor (Mulakala 2008; Ngidang 2007; Sivapragasam 2008; Stephanie and Soraya 2008). In Malaysia, given the national vigilance over the biofuels market, little evidence suggests that biofuels investments are contributing to national food security or helping to reduce poverty. However, it was possible to gather enough case stories from the smallholders to show that the food versus fuel threat is inherent in the current biofuels expansion model. The first generation biofuels market has potential utility as one of the solutions for renewable energy, and the GVC governance is becoming competitive. Therefore, the integration of small farmers into the GVC may increase exposure to global price volatility, trade discrimination, and potential conflicts between crop use as food or fuel as the biofuels feedstock market enjoys higher prices over prices of food or traditional cash crops. However, given the fact that food crops prices are also rising, the counterimpacts are also unknown.

6.2.2   Policy building blocks

The dichotomy between the market and the state is spurious, and the notion that all, or even most, public interventions are inefficient is simplistic. States consist of a variety of institutional arrangements – regulatory agencies, sponsoring departments, and legislative bodies, to name a few – which have a large variety of goals, processes, and consequences. There are important interdependencies between some forms of state intervention and associational governance. For example, in Tanzania the Ministry of Agriculture and Cooperatives and the Ministry of Energy and Minerals came into conflict with each other on their objectives to promote the biofuels industry. The cross-utility of biofuels feedstock crop introduced a new level of regulatory institutional challenge that remained unresolved in 2009. Interestingly, when 65 per cent of biofuels companies operating in Tanzania were export oriented, it was discovered that the Ministry of Trade and Industry was not a member of the national biofuels investment taskforce, commissioned to develop the National Biofuels Policy.

One outcome of the confusion was found during the National Biofuels Policy evaluation process, where the TIC, which was designed to be a one stop shop for investors and the government to monitor the industry, was actually just a welcome centre. Another example comes from the Tanzania Revenue Authority, which lists only a handful of the 65 biofuels companies identified by the Tanzania Biofuels Taskforce. Furthermore, the case studies made it clear that large foreign investors like SEKAB and Sun Biofuels used as much presidential power as possible to acquire tens of thousands of hectares of customary land. Under the Land Act of 1999, customary land rights can be overruled by presidential decree, such as occurred when the TIC set up a land bank of 2.5 million hectares identified as suitable for agrofuel investment. Table 6.1 links foreign company investments from Tanzanian donor countries with land grants for biofuels initiatives, which includes customary land and even a WWF recognized global biodiversity zone.[10]

The way the Malaysian central government delegates its functions; the regulations and monitoring mechanisms of the agricultural sector, the energy sector, public versus private investments, and the property rights regime have been factors of conflict between the Sarawak indigenous population, the state government, and the central government. Such nested conflicts are critical considerations when making effective institutions. Sarawak and Sabah have indigenous majorities and separate land laws enacted by the local legislatures, which are observed by the state, though separate from the Malaysian federal jurisdiction. However, the energy and renewable energy sectors are under sole control of the central government, creating fertile ground for conflict as the government pursues its ambitious energy initiatives.

Governmental agencies that contribute to the policy are the Ministry of Energy, Green Technology and Water, the Energy Commission and the

Table 6.1 Observed company profiles in Tanzania

Company and main crop	Country of origin and donor rank*	Local share and investments	Agricultural schemes	Contract disclosed	Land area requested (ha)	Land area granted (ha)
SEKAB (Sugarcane)	Sweden Rank 7	PPP USD 500m	Estate and outgrower	No	20,000–200,000	20,000 (first phase)
BioMassive	Netherlands Rank 6	Shareholder USD 3.4m	None	No	55,000–100,000	50,000
Bioshape (Jatropha)	Netherlands Rank 6	None USD 1.3m	Estate and outgrower	No	81,000	37,000
Sun Biofuels (Jatropha)	UK Rank 2	1 per cent share USD 20m	Estate and outgrower	No	18,000	8,000

*Donor countries ranked by CIA 2010
Source: Author collection from company interviews, websites, and public announcements of IPO sales.

Malaysian Energy Centre, mainly targeted to source renewable energy from biomass and palm oil waste. Interestingly, Sarawak's palm oil industry is state-owned, but the sector is declining and biomass sourced from palm waste is limited. Hence, under the SCORE initiative, the focus is on hydropower, natural gas, and biofuels. Although SCORE was designed along with the federal government's National Renewable Energy long-term objectives, conflicts arise with customary land allocations for renewable energy projects. Jatropha is slowly becoming an attractive cash crop in Sarawak as palm oil plantations age and require a long maturation for income generation, but this has yet to be endorsed by the national government. Hence the expansion of jatropha remains a private effort, dependent on social capital and, in the absence of a state-level public policy to regulate its expansion to replace villagers' primary commodities earnings – once heavily dependent on palm oil, it may threaten the balance of the local food sector. Nevertheless, in comparison to Tanzania, Sarawakian villagers were less vulnerable to jatropha investment expansion for two key reasons. First, a national entity either owns or has a high partnership share in investments in Sarawak, protected under the National Investment Policy. Second, there are 19 social security policies in place to financially help the poor, providing education, medical services, community infrastructure development funds, and so on.

In sum, this section looked at the unequal power of economic agents, which affects production and employment levels, distribution of income, as well as wealth and knowledge. Unlike the neoliberal economics model, no optimum distribution of income or social benefits is obtained, instead cumulative inequality is generated. Markets and investors operating in poor agrarian economies which lack redistributive regulatory frameworks are associated with local collusion and speculation, and are likely to deviate from the ideal objectives and targets that they set forth. Some agents have more resources, power, and information than others, through which they capture market benefits while passing down rents without providing benefits in exchange.

6.3 The local socio-political economy of biofuels and jatropha

What do biofuels crops mean for individuals involved in the biofuels value chain? Why produce first generation biofuels feedstock when there is existing food insecurity? These are fundamental questions investigated throughout this research. Figure 6.3 summarizes the diverse yet representative perspectives collected during fieldwork in Malaysia and Tanzania. The agents' representations, concerns, and solutions to the food versus biofuels debate are very much tied to their representative characteristics of socio-economic and political status. While the buyers are foreign multinationals like oil, auto, air, and industrial manufacturers, the intermediary agents are mainly local entrepreneurs working with the poorest and marginalized populations. The complete value chain operation is embedded in the social system of politics (Polanyi 1944). Intangible resources like knowledge of market subtleties, brand names, and regulatory bodies are of little utility to poor producers. The large investors can create international market imperfections through targets and price setting, market segmentation, bypassing local barriers to entry, providing financial incentives, and exerting bargaining power over developing countries. This finding is in line with the expected behaviour of actors in the biofuels value chain.

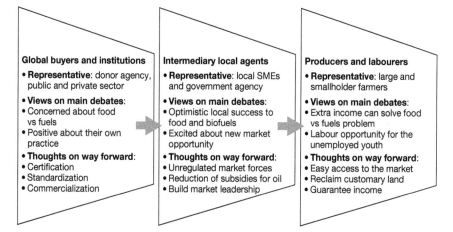

Figure 6.3 Generalized views of representative agents in the biofuels value chain
Source: Author.

6.3.1   Security as a dilemma

Participants give different weights to the preferred function they undertake to engage with the biofuels value chain, compare to other economic activities such as on-farm and off-farm activities. These weights are dynamic, reflecting the histories, respective positions in the social ladder, economic status, and internal political structures of networks. Such differences in positions on biofuels are also reflected at the country level, given each nation state's position in the global economy. While the nation state is concerned with being labelled 'green' and having foreign income, intermediary agents are mostly keen on entrepreneurial empowerment, while poor farmers or labourers want to solve their security dilemma, which is rooted in the absence of functioning agricultural, land, and labour markets. Since jatropha companies are targeting semi-arid regions or unused tracts of land, they are interacting with the poorest populations of both countries.

The case studies of this research look at the extent to which jatropha fits with the local agro-economic system. Unfortunately, while Tanzania suffers from poor data quality and availability, the Malaysian government is very sensitive about sharing national data on household livelihoods, food security, and poverty. Talking about poverty is largely taboo in Malaysia, but it is commonly highlighted by Tanzanian respondents. Interestingly, poverty status was found to be effectively correlated with institutional effectiveness and political stability. In Sarawak, 95 per cent of respondents were openly critical about their government, but in Tanzania, political questions appeared highly sensitive. In both countries much of the criticism is related to growing income inequalities in society. Table 6.2 shows that, although Malaysia has reduced hardcore poverty, its Gini coefficient is higher than Tanzania's. While rural population empowerment helped people voice their views, villagers in Tanzania are deep into poverty and much more vulnerable and timid about the political process, which has been so ineffective in improving their livelihoods. Such differences between the poor from the two different regions suggests that the integration of the biofuels value chain with the existing agricultural value chain will result in different experiences, and hence outcomes. Global trade policy and commercial renewable investment perspectives should be considered carefully by local governments when approving any biofuels business opportunity.

Table 6.2 Hardcore poverty reduction does not mean reducing inequality

	Malaysia, Sarawak		Tanzania	
	Hardcore poverty (%)	Gini coefficient	Hardcore poverty (%)	Gini coefficient
1991	3.22	47.65	72.59	33.83
2004	1.54	37.91	88.53	34.62

Source: Author compiled from Jin 2006 and World Bank 2009a data.

There are stark differences between the studied areas on basic questions like access to fertilizers, improved seeds, extension services, and the transportation system. Such agricultural services and subsidies are managed locally in Tanzania and Malaysia by public, private, and civil society organizations. The relative outreach of the subsidy programme varies and hence special attention was given to this topic during the fieldwork. Table 6.3 shows the percentage of informants who thought they were benefiting, compiled from biofuels participants gathered in focus groups.

Institutions should contribute to making conducive market environments by reducing transaction costs and improving social benefits. Table 6.3 shows the steep distinction between the qualities of the agro-economic livelihoods of the poorest Malaysian farmers in comparison to the farmers of Tanzania. Development literature provides ample evidence that Malaysia has been exemplary in reducing poverty. The state and federal governments introduced numerous programmes to address poverty through various five-year plans. In the plans for Sarawak, people-oriented programmes were launched which targeted specific problem areas. The key programmes covered infrastructure, human development, economic services, and welfare. These programmes were also re-categorized as educational, mind developmental, dietary, housing, urban behaviour, and community strength development specific, as mentioned in Section 5.3. The state indirectly addressed poverty through its rural and land development programmes, which were designed after the federal government's FELDA scheme. All the participating villagers in the SALCRA have access to water, energy sources, child and adult educational outlets, agricultural markets, land for food production, and a two-bedroomed house (Berma *et al.* 2006). Most households have one or two members of the family working in the city who send remittances. Having a constant connection with the city benefits the villagers not only with remittances, but also with enlightening information. Hence, Malaysian people were more opinionated and concerned than their Tanzanian counterparts in every aspect of the livelihood changes that a new investment might bring.

While the Sarawak government is now focusing on new poverty schemes, like providing inflation adjusted allowances, boosting low interest bearing

Table 6.3 Access to institutional support for agricultural activities

Indicators	Malaysia, Sarawak districts		Tanzania districts	
Access to:	Sri Aman	Serian	Bahi	Kisarawe
Extension services	90%	95%	5%	3%
Improved seeds	87%	93%	0%	1%
Irrigation	95%	97%	3%	2%
Public transportation	100%	100%	17%	30%

Note: Numbers are rounded.
Source: Author created from fieldwork.

microcredit sources, microinsurance plans, and so on, Tanzanian villagers are still deep in the darkness of underdevelopment. All six of the Tanzanian villages visited shared major similarities. On average women and children walked two to three hours to fetch water; more than 90 per cent were subsistence farmers dependent on rain and slash and burn cultivation; 90 per cent were illiterate; and there was no access to electricity despite close proximity to a large urban area. Kisarawe villagers appeared to be engaged in illegal charcoal making from the preserved forest situated in their locality to meet the shortfall of their income from subsistence farming. Moreover, based on IPCC assessment, as discussed in Chapters 2, 5, and 6, the income from farming is constantly under threat due to worsening predictability of seasonal rainfall, growing desertification, and weak microeconomic performance in the region. In Sarawak, the impacts of climate change were not as prominent as those observed in Tanzania. Moreover, exports of food crops are discouraged, consumer subsidies and a higher degree of agricultural management system provide rather a safer platform for non-edible cash crops like the jatropha industry to take place. In comparison, villagers in Tanzania were more vulnerable to the web of poverty, with 80 per cent of income spent on food, compared to their Malaysian counterparts with their government safety nets.

6.3.2   Food security solutions and jatropha

Achieving food security requires precautionary long-term, cautionary mid-term, and immediate actions. In the midst of high food prices, the Malaysian government focused on production-centric policies to increase its self-sustainability level, while on the other hand attempting to correct market policies that encouraged exports. In contrast, the Tanzanian government increased its food imports. In 2008, under the National Food Security plan, the national government and the Sarawak government identified five granary areas in the eastern and western basin and valley areas accounting for 38,000 ha of land to cultivate rice.[11] At the same time, Tanzania focused on export-oriented biofuels investments. High food prices affected almost everyone interviewed in Tanzania, but were unknown in Malaysia, except for a few who were unhappy with the rice export ban.

Threats to local food security are institutionally influenced, localized, and context specific. In the Tanzanian villages studied, both those with and without jatropha cultivation experienced food insecurity. With jatropha there were two options to consider: either improving household income to improve food security, or worsening food insecurity by giving away arable land. These options are not mutually exclusive. Poverty coupled with growing inequality and insecurity leaves little option for the vulnerable, who are then inclined to trust anyone who offers a solution. Considering that hindsight is 20-20, the way to break the poverty cycle is to introduce a new commodity, a new market, and a new dimension to the economy. Although jatropha offers exactly these benefits, the unknown factors are much too many to ignore. The apparent differences and similarities in the two case study regions are summarized in Table 6.4.

Human agencies when buttressed by education and market information find it easier to introduce a new system to complement existing livelihoods. In Malaysia, about 65 per cent of the interviewees, of which 95 per cent have at least one household member in the city and access to a variety of market information on jatropha, responded that jatropha cultivation would bring in extra income, but *would not take over* their food crop lands or their original income generating crops like white corn, palm oil, and pepper corn production. The majority of Tanzania's respondents were excited about jatropha and ready to convert fertile land to jatropha if companies provided good prices and regular buyback. In some villages in Kisarawe, lands were being allocated away to other villages. Such enthusiasm is fuelled by illiteracy, information asymmetry, and lack of control over transaction costs forced on the farmers due to weak infrastructure and institutional support. In both Malaysian and Tanzanian villages, respondents often overlooked possible future conflict over land rights, which was already a contentious topic. Most importantly, access to transportation and agricultural markets were fundamental factors in the farmers' jatropha production decision-making processes. Contract farming schemes which give assurance to smallholders that the harvest will be collected by buyers at a farm-gate price won commitments from smallholders in both cases.

In both Tanzania and Sarawak, 77 per cent of households expressed concern over aging farmers and existing farming practices which do not attract the youth. To them, private company-backed jatropha appeared a stronger opportunity for young farmers, who often seek off-farm employment to compensate for lost farm income. Also, much of the unused land could be reclaimed by the community by planting jatropha. The companies invested in these villages have understood these sentiments and are working to also promote jatropha as a social crop. Notice in Table 6.5 how these companies view the benefits they are bringing to villages.

Table 6.4 Comparing variables between Tanzanian and Malaysian experiences

	Sri Aman and Serian, Sarawak, Malaysia	Bahi and Kisarawe, Tanzania
Land tenure system	Customary	Customary
Urban migration	Rapid, agriculture aging	Rapid, agriculture aging
Governance system	Decentralized	Decentralized
Poverty level	~0.3% (2008)	~78% (2007)
Agriculturally dependent population	14%	90%
Extension services	Effective agricultural subsidy, localized extension services	Ineffective agricultural subsidy, urbanized extension services

Source: Author.

Table 6.5 A broad comparative sketch of business plans

	Variables	Sun Biofuels	EABD	Bionas	AWSB
Similarities	Income	X	X	X	X
	Reclaim land	X	X	X	X
Differences	Infrastructures		X	X	
	Social		X		X
	Local environment			X	X

Source: Author.

When public institutions fail to fulfil basic needs, persistent poverty further marginalizes the poor, creating a political and policy vacuum where market forces gain strength. The underlying forces of institutional market governance systems become weak and the situation of the vulnerable population is exacerbated. As a result, the impacts of jatropha industry development in Tanzania has rather more negative prospects than in Sarawak, Malaysia, where the market mechanisms are monitored both by national and local governance systems. Nevertheless, caution is required for jatropha plantation expansion in Sarawak, given its poverty level and inclination to exploit carbon-rich peatland, in order to protect agricultural land. This book has looked at the extent to which such interference is meaningful and its relationship to underlying symptoms. Within this topic, institutional effectiveness influences individuals' inclinations to participate with the private sector and how slowly the private sector integrates with the public sector.

6.4 Conclusion

Development literature promotes primary commodity-based industries as an economic platform for less developed countries to integrate their labour rich agricultural economies with the global market to provide export earnings, employment, and livelihoods (Cramer 1999; Gwynne 1999). The global agro-industry market has reached a crossroads wherein market liberalization clashes with globalization, and globalization clashes with climate change. In the middle of all this, about one-third of the global population's livelihoods depend on global primary commodity value chains.

While trade literature explains how developing countries are beholden to buyer-driven regulations that manifest themselves in market diversions, price erosions, and long-term momentum loss, climate change literature, similarly, examines how climate change increases the frequency and intensity of natural disasters which undermine the lives and production systems of poor primary commodity producers. More recently, the global agenda recognized social and economic aspects of poverty and underlying causes of disaster risks and found that strengthening existing livelihood strategies is an important element of reducing climate change vulnerability. Within this context, this research investigated the extent to which biofuels crops, as a new primary commodity, create chains of actions that contribute to long-standing poverty and food insecurity. To explore these issues, this book investigated the complex interactions that exist among the energy market, climate financing, and the global agro-trade environment within the context of renewable energy industry development in Tanzania and Malaysia. In the biofuels market, focus was placed on jatropha production as a non-edible crop to explore its relationship to food security.

Literature on the welfare gains or losses for biofuels value chain development is thin; this research aims to help fill that gap. Development of the supply chain in the case studies appeared to be simple or incomplete with three main components, producers, pre- and post-processing agents, and consumers. The unskilled, poor population is at the bottom of the value chain. Their numbers will grow if global and national targets to promote biofuels continue to grow. Despite the popular view that jatropha company contract farming schemes will help generate income and employment opportunities for poor labourers and smallholders, this research argues the opposite. Jatropha development has yet to revitalize agricultural livelihoods and reduce poverty because the business models are influenced by national regulatory frameworks, within which property rights are weakly applied. According to GTAP and general equilibrium policy models, biofuels plantations will increase demand for land, which will increase land prices and help to reduce landowner poverty (Hertel *et al.* 2010). But, as discussed, lands targeted by biofuels producers are fertile and owned under unresolved customary land rights. The assumption is that land prices will rise and trickle down to increase the income of the owners, but this does not happen smoothly. Because of jatropha, many customary lands are being reclaimed by the rural communities, but that does not make them richer in monetary terms, as the local communities already own hundreds of hectares of land anyway, which are not tradable.

Next, this study examined how the spillover effects to develop other small industries from biofuels are limited and crop specific. For example, while sugarcane and palm oil plantations' outputs can be sold in two large markets, food and biofuels, crops like jatropha and *Moringa* have one main output, biofuels, and some smaller by-products. Companies aim first to maximize the output/profit ratio before considering setting up factories to produce by-products like soap. Instead, commercial companies are installing modular presses to extract oil from jatropha seeds in these countries. Oil content in jatropha fruits is still at about 30 per cent and companies claim that one person can harvest about four hectares of land, as the fruit does not all ripen at the same time. To process the pressed oil into biodiesel, the commercial biodiesel factories are planned to be located on site, from where it is easy and cheap to export biodiesel. Claims for a high labour demand to harvest, process, or help with the development of skilled labour are still unproven. Furthermore, literature reviews show that the jatropha contribution to climate change mitigation is unproven as large-scale biofuels crop plantations not only threaten biodiversity, they also cause land use change by taking over arid lands. There is no guarantee that this will help with the energy security strategies targeted by consumers in developed countries, as biofuels can only replace a mere 3 per cent of the total fossil energy consumed (see discussion in Chapter 2).

Indicative planning is needed to integrate a new agro-industry into the existing agricultural system. Economic problems are essentially structural and institutional – institutional not only in the economic growth framework, but also in the ideology and culture within which markets and societies prevail, plus in the purposes and the goals to which people aspire. The general type of economic order that emerges from society will have extremely important cultural and information-purveying functions, as best illustrated in Michael Best's (1990) work on the US car market. He showed how both the cultural texture and the information signals within society changed. It became both desirable and rational for individuals to own and use cars, and the socio-economic system became locked into that style and pattern of industry and life. To move away from fossil fuel dependency, the socio-economic system needs such restriction and reinforcement of cultural texture and preference change that is not only economic but also a part of life. At present, the world is trying to seek a cheaper source of renewable energy, instead of changing the demand structure. This is creating unnecessary pressure on agents in the value chain, which is hurtling down with great force onto the lowest node – the poorest producers.

A completely decentralized, private enterprise system is not the best way to promote long-term investment projects. In fact, in most advanced capitalist countries, including the US, a great number of important technological innovations emanate from institutions, such as universities, which rely a great deal on state funding. For biofuels, the role of national governments is imperative to balance human welfare with technological innovation. Aware of the drawbacks of first generation biofuels, the global biotechnology sector is investing heavily in second and third generation biofuels. The discovery of cellulosic biofuel algae made headlines and generated optimism similar to that for first generation biofuels. However, as the demand for biofuels is estimated to grow with the decline of global fossil fuels subsidies, high prices, and growing economic development, large-scale production will start exposing uncertain threats including waste management, changing biodiversity, and resource management. It will also take time to reverse the negative impact of first generation biofuels production. There is, however, considerable fear that developing countries may leap into the second and third generation biofuels as they may find it difficult to overcome the structural limitations to first generation biofuels. Given the global urgency to tackle climate change while supporting ongoing economic growth, which is significantly dependent on the transportation system, the expansion of biofuels crops is likely to continue. If risks and uncertainties are not adequately and systematically addressed through institutional apparatuses, even the best biofuels crops or processes have the potential to threaten, exacerbate, and further damage the livelihoods of the poor, agricultural sectors, and natural biodiversity.

Developing countries often market themselves as desirable hosts to foreign biofuels companies against competing countries in the region. As Western buyers are proponents of decentralized governance systems which empower the private sector, incomplete or uncoordinated decentralized governance systems can be more problematic for rural development than otherwise anticipated in the theory. This was experienced in Tanzania and Sarawak, where ownership of industry development was lost and the people were subjected to the actions of foreign investors while customary land rights were jeopardized. The government of Tanzania realized the negative effects of unplanned, unscreened, and unfeasible biofuels industry expansion, and after four years of an intensive influx of foreign investments, the government put a hold on expansion. This was a wise and timely move. Nevertheless, the country could not push the operating companies out, leaving behind the potential impact on livelihoods discussed in the case study. Even in a decentralized system, governments *can* play a positive role in internal market creation activities like commodity research and technology development to shield the poor from market exploitation. Consequently, it is highlighted here that, for Malaysia, the impacts of biofuels industry development on food security are not as negative as in Tanzania because of the Malaysian higher socio-economic security, which is an important starting point, global trade relationships, capable national institutions, and local-level agencies run by the local people.

With the current demand for biofuels, propagation of crops, emerging alternative technological solutions, declining demand for fossil fuel, and cheaper fuel prices, one needs to be realistic about long-term effects. Besides imperfect knowledge on biofuels crop science, unrealistic blending targets, and unreachable climate treaties, the fundamentals of the global system have been shaken during the course of this research project. Examination proves that the results presented here do not contradict the initial argument that we need to improve our assessment tools to better understand complexities around global commodities like biofuels. The IFS is one such framework, presented here with evidence from the case studies, which reveals that better understanding about the socio-economic and political processes of local to global institutions can complement quantitative models of market projections. Scenario building exercises are important, but they should not be taken so seriously that we denounce the reality, which is dynamic, complex, and contradictory at times.

The global market for basic commodities has collapsed under unsustainable business practices and exponential demands since 2008. The world has not completely recovered. At the time of finishing this book, another shock to the global economy was under way from the fear of the Russian economy crashing as the global oil price continued to decline and prices began to rise for basic commodities like food in Europe. One more example where it appears the market is not the prestigious arbiter between policy failure and welfare failure, where regulatory institutions become bystanders. Instead, the market, which is socially embedded, is manoeuvred by individual agencies, which are related to power, privilege, and relationships with institutions that dictate economic outcomes of agricultural markets, rather than the anonymous forces of supply and demand.

As observed in Tanzania, the imposition of central planning without adhering to respective changes elsewhere in the micro- to meso-society and market levels, will fail to bring substantial results from the first generation biofuels industry development. The complexity and variety within the economic process requires a multiplicity of regulatory systems at different levels of the economy to successfully integrate changing modes of global economies into the national system. Industrialization, be it that of agriculture or manufacturing, involves poor populations in its value chain and takes place within the context of national and supranational institutional involvement – which is partly indicative, partly regulatory, and partly directive in character – in tackling poverty, insecurity, and the ongoing deprivation of the poor. The task of development economists is to apply the wider literature on, and experience of, planning, industrial organization, financial structures, and the management of production in a way that is appropriate for the economic and social objectives of a given commodity, its value chain, and the agents embedded in the institutional environment.

The concerted application of institutional economics in development has yet to be mainstreamed. To tackle practical problems, one requires detailed and painstaking study of institutions and their development, along with the success and failure each has in achieving development goals over time. For example, this jatropha-based biofuels study looked at the agricultural, infrastructural, and energy sector institutional development history along with the core focus of the countries' plans in terms of agricultural and energy sector development. All of these topics are essential to any country's food security, energy security, and climate change mitigation strategy. At the theoretical level, such an approach applies interdisciplinary scholarship which is neither fashionable nor encouraged at present by the structure or goals of academia. It requires lateral thinking and a change in mindset that is often frowned upon by specialists and experts for sometimes lacking in formal and quantitative elegance and glamour. Social science is practically concerned with human welfare, but not all welfare factors (e.g., health, education, and access to services) can be classified, categorized, and quantified. These elements are interchangeable and intertwined with, and interdependent on, multilateral institutions, which are constantly changing and evolving. Hence, instead of taking a social problem as a unit of analysis, problems need to be seen as un-dimensional and interwoven with other problems of mass unemployment, poverty, information asymmetry, repeated target failures, and now climate change. A new dimensional institutional economics may well prove useful, such as the IFS, which looks into the value chain of a commodity as it passes through the market (de)regulatory frameworks and touches economic agents who are part of the institutional structure consisting of society, politics, economy, ecology, and climate.

According to the *Nature Chemical Biology* 2010 report it is clear that, regardless of whether policy makers or social scientists engage in the practical conversation of change, the bio-based society is quickly coming of age. Bioethanol and other biofuels are changing the way land is used and engines are designed. Engineered bacteria are increasing production of useful commodity chemicals, ranging from amino acids to polymer precursors. A growing number of production-scale biorefineries are under construction and in operation. As chemical biologists step forward to contribute, exciting new fundamental discoveries and applications seem capable of converting bioproducts from fiction into fact and affect food and energy security condition locally to globally.

Notes

1 Terms of trade basically refers to export growth rate. Tanzanian crop export growth rates have declined from 7 per cent per year in the 1990s to a mere 2 per cent in recent years.
2 Similar studies should be carried out in countries where mass production of biofuels crops is being targeted to fuel the Western transportation system (Landis *et al.* 2008).
3 The major toxins are lectin, saponin, carcinogenic phorbol, and a trypsin inhibitor.
4 The Worldwide Governance Indicators (WGI) report displays a country's performance for all available years between 1996 and 2008 in six governance dimensions: (a) Voice and Accountability; (b) Political Stability and Lack of Violence/Terrorism; (c) Government Effectiveness,; (d) Regulatory Quality; (e) Rule of Law; and (f) Control of Corruption. The country level data on each of the six indicators were extracted from other institutional and research studies. Percentile ranks indicate the percentage of countries worldwide that rate below the selected country. Higher values thus indicate better governance ratings and a more stable political environment. The margins of error correspond to a 90 per cent confidence interval. This means that there is a 90 per cent probability that governance is within the indicated range. Relevant links for country level studies: www.govindicators.org, www.worldbank.org/wbi/governance/
5 There are 20 major sources of indexes available which rank countries based on their political institutional quality. These are found in the methodology index of the WGI. All of these indexes are based on subjective indicators. The World Bank has taken efforts to systematically synthesize the indexes and hence produced the WGI. There is ample research on the World Bank website indicating how independent research shows that investment decisions are highly influenced by the governance perceptions shown in ranking indexes.
6 Of the projects analysed in Asia, 85 per cent are involved with jatropha research, compared to 54 per cent in Latin America and only 36 per cent in Africa.
7 It has been suggested to the RSB that indirect land-use impacts should be included in the biofuels standards, but instead of using GHG balance calculation based on LCA, there should be a risk-based approach. Criteria need to be

defined in the RSB standards that differentiate biofuels with a reduced risk of indirect impacts from those without a reduced risk (Cornelissen and Dehue 2009).

8 For more info on biofuels-related eco-labelling and certification schemes see FAO 2008; Fontaras *et al.* 2009; UNCTAD 2008.
9 Refer back to the Malaysia case study, Chapter 5.
10 Kilwa, a miombo biome district, belongs to the Global 200 WWF list of important biodiversity eco-regions of the world. A part of this forest, several thousand hectares, has been given to Bioshape, and has been cleared already.
11 The strategic granary programme has been criticized for the land allocation exercised over customary land owned by locals. See the map in Figure 5.2.

Appendices

Appendix A Production capacity, future targets, and biofuels policies in selected countries

Country	Current capacity	Future targets – quantity and year	Main sources for biofuel	Biofuel policies (explicit)	Main trade policy for biofuel
US	18.4 billion litres of ethanol (2006), 284 million litres of biodiesel (2005)	28 billion litres of ethanol by 2012 and 1 billion litres of cellulosic ethanol by 2013	Maize and, in the future, cellulosic sources	Excise tax credit, mandatory blending, capital grants, vehicle subsidies	Import tariff of USD 0.1427 per litre ethanol plus ad valorem tariff with some exemption for Caribbean countries
Brazil	17.5 billion litres (2006)	25 per cent blending of ethanol (which has been in effect for a long time), 2.4 billion litres of biodiesel by 2013	Sugarcane, soybean	Mandatory blending, capital subsidies, vehicle subsidies	20 per cent ad valorem import tariff on ethanol (waived in cases of domestic shortage)
EU	3.6 billion litres of biodiesel (2005), 1.6 billion litres of ethanol (2006)	5.75 per cent of transportation fuel on energy basis by 2010	Rapeseed, sunflower, wheat, sugar beet and barley	Excise tax credit (beginning to be phased out), carbon tax credit, mandatory blending, capital grants and funding for R&D	Ad valorem duty of 6.5 per cent on biodiesel and an import tariff of USD 0.26 per litre on ethanol (the latter is waived for some categories of countries)
China	1.2 billion litres of ethanol (2006)	na*	Maize, cassava, sugarcane	Subsidies and tax breaks but only for non-grain feedstock	Import tariff of 30 per cent on ethanol
Colombia	400 million litres of ethanol (2006)	10 per cent ethanol blending in cities exceeding 500,000 people since 2006	Sugarcane, oil palm	Mandatory blending, tax breaks for sugarcane plantations, capital subsidies	Ad valorem import tariff of 15 per cent on ethanol and 10 per cent on biodiesel

Country	Current capacity	Future targets – quantity and year	Biofuel policies (explicit)	Main sources for biofuel	Main trade policy for biofuel
Indonesia	340 million litres of biodiesel (2006)	10 per cent ethanol and 10 per cent biodiesel effective April 2006	Mandatory blending, capital subsidies	Oil palm	Lower export tax for processed oils compared to crude palm oil
Malaysia	340 million litres of biodiesel (2006)	5 per cent biodiesel from April 2007	Mandatory blending, capital subsidies	Oil palm	Lower export tax for processed oils compared to crude palm oil
Thailand	330 million litres of ethanol (2006)	Na	Price subsidy, capital subsidies	Cassava, sugarcane molasses	Import tariff of 2.5 baht per litre and ad valorem tariff of 5 per cent on biodiesel
Canada	240 million litres of ethanol (2006)	5 per cent ethanol by 2010 and 2 per cent biodiesel by 2012	Mandatory blending, excise tax credit, capital subsidies	Maize and wheat	Import tariff of USD 0.1228 for ethanol and USD 0.11 for biodiesel (lower tariffs and exemptions for selected countries)
Argentina	204 million litres of ethanol (2006)	5 per cent biofuel by 2010	Excise tax credit, mandatory blending, export tax exemption on biofuel blends	Soybean	Low export tax (5 per cent) for soy biodiesel compared to soybeans (23.5 per cent) and soy oil (20 per cent)
India	200 million litres of ethanol (2006)	5 per cent ethanol in selected cities and 10 per cent biodiesel by 2012**	Mandatory blending for ethanol, capital subsidies	Sugarcane molasses, jatropha (in the future)	Ad valorem duty of 199 per cent on CIF value of denatured ethanol and 59 per cent duty on un-denatured ethanol

Appendix A *continued*

Country	Current capacity	Future targets – quantity and year	Main sources for biofuel	Biofuel policies (explicit)	Main trade policy for biofuel
Australia	170 million litres of ethanol	350 million litres of biofuel by 2010	Wheat and molasses	Producer subsidy, capital grants, vehicle standard	Import tariff of USD 0.31 per litre on both ethanol and biodiesel
Japan	Insignificant	360 million litres by 2010 and 10 per cent biofuel by 2030	Imported ethanol	excise tax credit	Ad valorem import duty of 23.8 per cent on fuel ethanol (to be lowered to 10 per cent by 2010)

* Data not found
** Biodiesel policy has not yet passed into law in India and is merely a government preference at this point
Note: Agricultural policies that affect production of biofuels crops are not covered here.
Source: Reproduced from Rajagopal and Zilberman 2007.

Appendix B Biofuels blending targets and production required to meet the targets

Country	Fuel ethanol plus biodiesel 2005–2007				Blending mandates		Biofuel targets	Volumes required per year	
	Billion litres	Percentage (%)	Mt	PJ	Bioethanol	Biodiesel	Biofuels total	Bioethanol	Biodiesel
Canada	0.781	1.67	0.62	17	E5 by 2010	B2 by 2012	–	–	–
USA	21.946	46.86	17.41	473	–	–	20 per cent by 2022	130 billion litres by 2022*	–
EU Total	7.563	16.15	6.64	226	–	–	10 per cent by 2020	–	–
Australia	0.262	0.56	0.22	8	Regional only	–	–	–	–
Japan	0.000	0.00	0.00	0	–	–	5 per cent by 2030	6 billion litres by 2030	–
South Africa	0.000	0.00	0.00	0	E8–E10 proposed	B2–B5 proposed	4.5 per cent biofuels	–	–
Ethiopia	0.002	0.00	0.00	0	–	–	–	–	–
Mozambique	0.001	0.00	0.00	0	–	–	–	–	–
Tanzania	0.004	0.01	0.00	0	–	–	–	–	–
Brazil	13.657	29.16	10.80	290	E22 to E25 exist	B5 by 2013	–	–	–
Columbia	0.268	0.57	0.21	6	E10 existing	B5 by 2008	–	–	2.5 billion litres by 2013

Appendix B *continued*

Country	Fuel ethanol plus biodiesel 2005–2007				Blending mandates		Biofuel targets	Volumes required per year	
	Billion litres	Percentage (%)	Mt	PJ	Bioethanol	Biodiesel	Biofuels total	Bioethanol	Biodiesel
Peru	0.000	0.00	0.00	0	E7.8 by 2010	B5 by 2010	–	–	–
China	1.565	3.34	1.24	33	E10 in 9 provinces	–	–	13 billion litres by 2020	–
India	0.544	1.16 t	0.45	15	E10 in 13 regions	–	–	–	2.3 billion litres by 2020
Indonesia	0.047	0.10	0.04	2	–	–	–	–	–
Malaysia	0.000	0.00	0.00	0	–	B5 by 2008	–	–	–
Philippines	0.017	0.04 t	0.01	0	E10 by 2011	B2 by 2011	–	–	–
Thailand	0.134	0.29	0.11	3	E10 by 2007	3 per cent share by 2011	–	–	–
Turkey	0.043	0.09 t	0.03	1	–	–	–	–	–
World Total	46.834	100.0	37.63	1073	–	–	–	–	–
Argentina	–	–	–	–	E5 by 2010	B5 by 2010	–	–	–
Bolivia	–	–	–	–	–	B20 by 2015	–	–	–
Croatia	–	–	–	–	–	–	5.75 per cent by 2010	–	–

Country	Fuel ethanol plus biodiesel 2005–2007				Blending mandates		Biofuel targets	Volumes required per year	
	Billion litres	Percentage (%)	Mt	PJ	Bioethanol	Biodiesel	Biofuels total	Bioethanol	Biodiesel
Dominican Republic	–	–	–	–	E15 by 2015	B2 by 2015	–	–	–
New Zealand	–	–	–	–	–	–	3.4 per cent by 2012	–	–
Paraguay	–	–	–	–	–	B5 by 2009	–	–	–
Uruguay	–	–	–	–	E5 by 2014	B5 by 2012	–	–	–
Belgium	–	–	–	–	–	–	5.75 per cent by 2010	–	–
France	–	–	–	–	–	–	10 per cent by 2015	–	–
Germany	–	–	–	–	E2 by 2007	B4.4 by 2007	12–15 per cent by 2020	1.45 billion litres by 2020	8.3 billion litres by 2020
Italy	–	–	–	–	E1	B1	–	–	–
Portugal	–	–	–	–	–	–	10 per cent by 2010	–	–
UK	–	–	–	–	E5 by 2010	B5 by 2010	–	–	–

Note 1: Mandates and blending quota may refer to shares based either on volume or energy content (which is often not clear). According to the lead author of the REN21 (2007) report, blending mandates generally refer to volume, while percentage targets generally refer to share of transport energy content, but the UNEP author assumes that there are exceptions and is not absolutely sure about it (UNEP personal communication by email from Mr. Martinot, 21 October 2008). In the case of biodiesel, shares referring to energy content require about 10 per cent more volume, and even, in the case of ethanol, 50 per cent more volume, as the energy content of these biofuels is lower than that of fossil fuels.
* of which *ca.* 50 billion litres are from corn-based ethanol and *ca.* 80 billion litres are from cellulosic ethanol
Note 2: The 10 per cent biofuels target of the EU for 2020 refers to 10 per cent energy from all renewables sources in all forms of transport.
Source: Reproduced from UNEP 2009c.

Appendix C Institutional level questionnaires

The following questionnaire was used in both Malaysia and Tanzania with limited necessary changes made to take account of the local and livelihood differences between the two countries.

Declaration

Any information shared will remain *confidential* and will only be used for research purposes. If you would like to know more about the privacy, confidentiality and ethics of this project, please contact me at [insert contact details].

1 Please provide details of your name and institution.
2 What does the government of your country get from having biofuels companies?
3 Is there any thoughts monitor if the companies are keeping its social and economic promises made to the villagers?
4 What is the history of the institution?
5 What is the income source?
6 Does the institution carry out performance evaluation? If so, what kind and for what?
7 How are land prices decided?
8 What is the definition of land used, unused, or underused? Please provide any data.
9 Do land rights control and monitoring systems exist?
10 What is the current food production and consumption situation?
11 What are the main issues that affect the food availability, accessibility, and usability? (Give time to respond to each one)
12 What percentage of the farmers use fertilizers, improved seeds, and pesticide? Why so low or high?
13 How has the price of inputs changed since the financial crisis? What percentage of the price?
14 Does land pricing affect the input cost?
15 Who do the farmers sell their crops to? Do you monitor them?
16 Do you use a biofuels crop promotion map or system? How does food crop promotion differ from that of non-food crops?
17 To what extent are farmers ready to take on biofuels crops?
18 How do crop promotions identify whether the actual benefits are being realized by the farmers?
19 What is the subsidy pattern for the food and non-food producers? What percentage of the farmers receive that?
20 Does crop promotion work with the crop market? Who would be the relevant person to speak to about land rights, water rights, and farmers' rights?

21 How do you feel about the biofuels policy initiatives taken by the government?
22 What kind of biofuels related plan does the district level government have in mind?

Appendix D Company level questionnaire

The following questionnaire was used in both Malaysia and Tanzania with limited necessary changes made to take account of the local and livelihood differences between the two countries.

Declaration

Any information shared will remain *confidential* and will only be used for research purposes. If you would like to know more about the privacy, confidentiality, and ethics of this project, please contact me at [insert contact details].

General

1 Please provide details of your name and company.
2 What is the history of your company? When and why did you enter into the biofuels/agro-export business?
3 What is the total market capitalization of your company (e.g., ha of land, businesses, total equity, and total assets)?
4 Where are your plantations and processing factories?

Human resources

5 How many plantation workers do you have? What percentage are full-time and what percentage are part-time?
6 How do you acquire workers? What percentage are local and what percentage are foreigners?
7 What are the differences between local and migrant workers? Is it convenient or inconvenient for the company from the legal, wage, productivity, and other terms perspective?
8 How are seeds, fertilizers, and pesticides collected? Which is the largest cost to production?
9 Can you do without them? To what extent?

Land

10 How did you select land locations? How did you acquire ownership?
11 What kind of land rights does the company have? Who used to own the land before?
12 What is the total land area? What is the average yield from 1 ha of land?
13 Do you engage in any social activities with the local people? Do you help them with their food production? If so, how?
14 Do you see any land-use conflicts between food and fuel crops?

Company relationships

15 What kinds of benefits do you receive from the government, e.g., subsidies or technical assistance? How could this be changed for the better?
16 What kind of agricultural system do you follow for production (e.g. contract farming or outgrower scheme)? How many members are involved in this system?
17 Do you have any contracts with local, state, or federal government on compensation, marketing, input distribution, or other items?

Marketing channel and pricing

18 What is your supply chain like and who is involved in the value chain? (e.g., is it all done by the company, or is some part of the supply chain controlled by the company while the other parts are controlled by third parties?)
19 Where do you sell your product (e.g., locally or internationally)? If both, what is the percentile breakdown?
20 How do you price your commodity?
21 Have you made any profit? If not, in how many years, and under what conditions do you hope to make a profit?
22 How are the current fuel price fluctuations and international financial crises affecting you?

Policy and current situation

23 What are your thoughts about the national biofuel policy? How do you see it affecting your business?
24 What needs to be improved or changed to foster the growth in this industry (e.g., more government intervention or less)?

Appendix E Questionnaire for smallholders, contract farmers, and labourers

The following questionnaire was used in both Malaysia and Tanzania with limited necessary changes made to take account of the local and livelihood differences between the two countries.

Declaration

Any information shared will remain *confidential* and will only be used for research purposes. If you would like to know more about the privacy, confidentiality, and ethics of this project, please contact me at [insert contact details].

Household and community level

Group: _____

Village Name: _____

Ward Name: _____

District Name:_____

Contact 1: _____

Contact 2: _____

Contact 3: _____

About the respondents

Name/HH number	Age (a)	Gender (b)	Marital status * (c)	Household heads? ** (d)	Education *** (e)	Job and hours **** (f)	Ethnic group ***** (g)
		M/F		Yes (1) No (0)			

1 Are you native to this land? ☐ Yes (1)   ☐ No (0)
  If 'No', from where _____ and when (average number of decades ago)? _____
2 What is the total number of persons usually residing in the household?
  _____
3 How far do you walk to collect food and fuel? _____
4 How do you feel about your livelihoods?
  ☐ Happy
  ☐ Sometimes happy
  ☐ Sometimes unhappy

☐ Unhappy
☐ Miserable

5 How many members of the family are working? _____

6 Are they working:
☐ on the family farm_____,
☐ outside with the community on a farm _____,
☐ by themselves (owner of a separate farm or businesses) _____,
☐ off-farm _____?

7 Is the family income:
☐ sufficient,
☐ somewhat sufficient,
☐ somewhat insufficient,
☐ insufficient,
☐ other?

8 Are/were you a member of any cooperatives?
Yes (1) No (2)

9 If so, what benefit do/did you receive from them for what crop?

10 What is an outgrower scheme? Do you have any experience of outgrower schemes for other crops? (*Note whether they mention any differences.*)

11 What is your agricultural practice? (*Please ask them to raise hands. Write the percentage, or a fraction, such as 8/10, next to the criterion.*)
☐ Subsistence _____
☐ Commercial and mechanized _____
☐ Sharecropping _____
☐ Slash and burn _____
☐ Other _____

12 Why do you use certain agricultural practices? (*Please give them the reasons and ask them to raise their hands if they fall into that criterion. The same person can raise their hand for all.*)
☐ Not interested in trying other practices
☐ Not enough labour and tools
☐ Not enough land
☐ Not enough money to buy inputs
☐ No/limited market to sell additional crop
☐ No/limited storage
☐ Loss due to anti-social and illegal activities
☐ Other _____

13 How do you access your farming inputs?
☐ From the market, buying at your own cost
☐ From the middlemen (*Ask under what scheme.*)
☐ From a microcredit scheme (*Ask the interest rate.*)
☐ From the trader, provided in advance (*Ask under what scheme and how regularly.*)
☐ From a farmers' association (*Ask under what scheme.*)
☐ Other _____

14 Has anyone heard about the biofuels crops (e.g., cassava, sugarcane, jatropha, and palm oil)? _____ (number) (*Please have them raise their hands.*)

    ☐   If yes, what do you think about the crop and the companies? (*Identify social, political, economic, and structural [infrastructure, education] issues.*)

Advantages	Disadvantages

    ☐   If not, are you interested in finding out more about it? Why?

15 How were you initially contacted about this project? What are your experiences with biofuel companies coming into your region?

16 How did you feel about the companies requesting land from you? (*Please have them raise hands for the list.*)

    ☐   Proud

    ☐   Happy

    ☐   Strange

    ☐   Upset to see foreign companies taking the land

    ☐   Nothing

    (*For the majority feelings ask why.*)

17 How many have started or are planning jatropha plantation? _____

18 For those of you who have started jatropha production, how do you make sure that enough food crops are produced. *(Here it would be interesting to find out land, labour, input, and time share details from the person. Please note qualitative information.*)

19 Were you present at the meeting? Yes _____ No _____ (*Enter the number.*)

20 What was the land acquisition process? How many hours did it take and with how many people? (*Please try to get them to identify the main actors who led the meeting decisions. Also, ask if they were given anything on the spot.*)

21 Do you know the size of your village and how many hectares of land were given to the company? (*Obtain the data from them.*)

22 How was the land acquisition process? (*Please identify their concerns if they express any, like the land appraisal was not transparent, adequate information was not shared, questions were not answered, and any others they may raise.*)

23 Have you seen the contract? Yes _____ No _____ (*Enter the number.*)

24 Who wrote the contract? Who has the copy in the village? (*We need to collect a copy.*)

25 Do you know when the contract will cease? Years _____, or under what condition _____

26 Do you know for how many years the land has been given away? Years _____

27 Have you discussed your village's rights and legal protections? If so, what?

(*These are points seen in other contracts. Please give the discussion points and probe them to think about whether such issues were raised.*)

- ☐ Seeds were provided by the company *but* at whose cost?
- ☐ For how many years?
- ☐ Will there be other input support (fertilizer, pesticides, or irrigation)?
- ☐ Who will bear the cost of the inputs?
- ☐ If the company fails, do the villagers get any compensation?
- ☐ Do villagers have any rights over the company?
- ☐ Where will the company get its water from? Will they pay for it? To whom?
- ☐ How will the price be determined?

28 How have the villagers been compensated?

Compensation process	Details (amount, year, duration)	Comments
One off		
Consecutive years (?)		
For the life of the land		
By providing social services		
Other		

29 Do you feel that you were fairly treated? Why, or why not?

30 Which individuals played the biggest role in the decision-making process? What was your role?

31 In an outgrower scheme, where companies only provide the market access, who, in your opinion, should deliver your inputs, training, and credit for changing farming practices? Why?

- ☐ Companies
- ☐ Self
- ☐ Input cooperatives
- ☐ Government

32 In the last two years did you face any change in your food prices? If so, in which commodities and by how much? (*First, make a list of the main crops and then get the percentage or multiplication factor of the change.*)

1.
2.
3.
4.

33   What is the staple food? _____

34   How are you coping with this high price?
- ☐   Eating less
- ☐   Working more hours in the farm
- ☐   Have taken on off-farm jobs
- ☐   Seeking help (From whom?) _____
- ☐   Have taken children out of school
- ☐   Making children work
- ☐   No effect
- ☐   Other _____

35   Do you know why prices are high? Is this *unusual?*

36   Are you malnourished or do you face food deficits in the family? (*Please survey all ten people and ask them for how many years they think this has been the case.*)

Number	Yes (1) No (2)	Years	Key reason
1			
2			
3			
4			
5			
6			
7			
8			
9			
10			

Comment:

37   What are the major income sources of your household? (*There could be multiple earning sources, please rank according to the highest income and lowest income source.*)

Sector	Rank	Income percentage	Income and average hours
☐ Plantation	1		
☐ Agricultural labour			
☐ Food cultivation			
☐ Livestock farming			
☐ Service			
☐ Business/industry			
☐ Self-employed			
☐ House rent			
☐ Remittance			
☐ Others (specify)			
		Total	Total

Flipchart exercise

Do you consume imported food? What percentage of your monthly budget goes on food and fuel?

Please provide information about use of produced or bought food and vegetables in the household.

Total household budget ____ (per month) Total food budget Total fuel budget (kerosene?)	Quantity used per month *		Cost **
	In kilograms, litres	As a percentage	
Household production			
Purchase Local percentage ____ Imported percentage ____			Local percentage ____ Imported percentage ____
Borrow			
Donation			
Other Total usage			

Crop production mapping (only the top three crops)

Main Crops	Land size	Yield t/ha		Production cost		Sale price		Consumption	
		High season	Low season	High season	Low season	High season	Low season	Family percentage	Sales market percentage
1 person: crop names									

Compare jatropha with other crops

	Average yield/1 ha	Average land	Average labour	Average water
Jatropha				
Crop 1				
Crop 2				
Crop 3				

Input mapping

What are the major inputs for farming (e.g., fertilizer, labour, land, and pesticide)?

Input name (for major common crop)	Cost or cost share (price/per unit)	Sources of payment (1. Self. 2. Gov. 3. NGOs. 4. Pvt comp.)	Problems
Land			
Labour			
Fertilizer			
Pesticide			
Transportation/marketing			
Crop processing			
Other			
	Total cost		

Production lost

In the past 12 months have you lost any harvest?

Yes (1) _____ No (0) _____

Why?

Reason	Priority	Loss in money	Solutions	Institutional support (1–low, 5–most)	Community support (1–low, 5–most)
Bad weather					
Changing cropping pattern					
Inefficient technical skill					
Insect, fire, rotten					
Finance crisis					
Stolen					
Loss in transportation/ storage					
Other					

Problems with agricultural system

What are the major problems with the current agricultural system? List them and rank them.

Sector	Problems	Possible solutions, implemented by whom
Agro-export sector		
Food production		
Pricing		
Distribution		
Other		

Bibliography

AAFC (2005), 'Vegetable Oils: Competition in a Changing Market', *Bi-weekly Bulletin*, Volume 18, Number 11 (Ottawa, Canada: Agriculture and Agri-food Canada).

Acemoglu, D., Johnson, S., and Robinson, J. (2001), 'Colonial Origins of Comparative Development: An Empirical Investigation', *American Economic Review*, 91, 1369–401.

—— (2006), 'Understanding Prosperity and Poverty: Geography, Institutions and the Reversal of Fortune', in A. Banerjee, D. Mookherjee, and R. Bénabou (eds), *Understanding Poverty* (Oxford, UK: Oxford Publisher), 37–62.

Acemoglu, D., Bautista, M.A., Querubin, P., and Robinson, J.A. (2008), 'Economic and Political Inequality in Development: The Case of Cundinamarca, Colombia', in Elhanan Helpman, ed., *Institutions and Economic Performance* (Cambridge, MA, US: Harvard University Press), 181–245.

Achten, W.M.J., Maes, W.H., Aerts, R., Verchot, L., Trabucco, A., Mathijs, E., Singh, V.P., Muys, B. (2010), '*Jatropha*: From Global Hype to Local Opportunity', *Journal of Arid Environments*, 74 (1), 164–5.

Adenäuer, M. (2008), 'CAPRI versus AGLINK-COSIMO, Two Partial Equilibrium Models – Two Baseline Approaches', *12th Congress of the European Association of Agricultural Economists – EAAE 2008* (University of Bonn, Bonn, Germany).

AFP (2008), 'EU to Open Anti-Dumping Probe into US Biodiesel Imports', *Agence France-Presse*, June 12, 2008.

—— (2010), 'Malaysia to Switch to Biofuel Next Year', *Agence France-Presse*, March 24, 2010.

Agrawal, A. and Gibson, C.C. (1999), 'Enchantment and Disenchantment: The Role of Community in Natural Resource Conservation', *World Development*, 27 (4), 629–49.

Aksoy, A. and Isik-Dikmelik, A. (2008), 'Are Low Food Prices Pro-Poor? Net Food Buyers and Sellers in Low-Income Countries', *World Bank Policy Research Working Paper* (Washington DC: World Bank).

Altenburg, T. and Christian, V.D. (2006), 'The "New Minimalist Approach" to Private-Sector Development: A Critical Assessment', *Development Policy Review*, 24 (4), 387–411.

Amsden, A. (2001), *The Rise of "The Rest": Challenges to the West from Late-Industrializing Economies* (New York: Oxford University Press).

Andresen, N.A. (2008), 'Public Choice Theory, Semi-authoritarian Regimes and Energy Prices: A Preliminary Report', *RUSSCASP Working Paper* (October

2008; Lysaker, Norway: Russian and Caspian energy developments and their implications for Norway and Norwegian actors).

Aoki, M. (2001), *Toward a Comparative Institutional Analysis* (Cambridge, US: MIT Press).

APEC (2006), 'Malaysia', *APEC Energy Demand and Supply Outlook 2006 – Projections to 2030 Economy Review* (Tokyo: Asia Pacific Energy Research Centre).

Appaduri, A. (2004), *The Capacity to Aspire*, V. Rao and W. Walton (eds) (Culture and Public Action; Stanford, US: Stanford University Press).

Ardhi, H. (2008), 'The Agrofuel Industry in Tanzania: A Critical Enquiry into Challenges and Opportunities' (March 2008; Dar es Salaam: Land Rights Research and Resources Institute).

Ariffin, T. (2008), 'Successful Agricultural Commodity Development and Diversification Strategies – the Case of Malaysia', *UNCTAD Secretary-General's High-Level Multi-Stakeholder Dialogue on Commodities in the context of UNCTAD XII.*

Arndt, C., Rui, B., Finn, T., James, T., and Rafael, U. (2008), 'Biofuels, Poverty, and Growth: A Computable General Equilibrium Analysis of Mozambique', *IFPRI Discussion Paper* (Washington, DC: International Food Policy Research Institute).

Arts, B. and Tatenhove, J.V. (2004), 'Policy and Power: A Conceptual Framework between the "Old" and "New" Policy Idioms', *Policy Sciences,* 37 (3/4), 339–56.

Arvidson, A. (2009), 'Biofuels Initiatives in Tanzania Deserve Careful Consideration', *The Guardian,* March 24, 2009.

Bahi (2008), 'Bahi District Profile 2007/08' (Bahi, Tanzania: District Commissioner Office).

Baland, J.M. and Platteau, J.P. (1996), *Halting Degradation of Natural Resources: Is There a Role for Rural Communities?* (Oxford, UK: Clarendon Press).

Balat, M. and Balat, H. (2009), 'Recent Trends in Global Production and Utilization of Bio-Ethanol Fuel', *Applied Energy,* 86 (11), 2273–82.

Banerjee, A. and Iyer, L. (2005), 'History, Institutions and Economic Performance: The Legacy of Colonial Land Tenure Systems in India', *American Economic Review,* 95, 1109: 213.

Banse, M. and Grethe, H. (2008), 'Effects of a Potential New Biofuel Directive on EU Land Use and Agricultural Markets', *Modelling of Agricultural and Rural Development Policies* (Seville, Spain: Paper Prepared for the European Association of Agricultural Economists 107th Seminar).

Bardhan, P. (2005a), 'Institutions Matter, but Which Ones?' *Economics of Transition,* 13, 499–532.

—— (2005b), 'Theory or Empirics in Development Economics', *Economic and Political Weekly,* 40 (October 1, 2005), 4333–5.

—— (2006), 'Globalization and Rural Poverty', *World Development,* 34 (8), 1393–404.

Barnes, J. and Kaplinsky, R. (1999), 'Globalization and Trade Policy Reform: Whither the Automobile Components Sector in South Africa' (Brighton, UK: Institute of Development Studies, University of Sussex).

Barnes, J., Kaplinsky, R., and Morris, M. (2003), 'Industrial Policy in Developing Countries: Developing Dynamic Comparative Advantage in the South Africa Automobile Sector' (Brighton, UK: Institute of Development Studies, University of Sussex).

Barrett, C.B., Brandon, K., Gibson, C., and Gjertsen, H. (2001), 'Conserving Tropical Biodiversity amid Weak Institutions', *BioScience*, 51 (6), 497–502.

Bassett, T. and Winter-Nelson, A. (2010), *The Atlas of World Hunger* (Chicago, US: University of Chicago Press).

Beattie, A. (2008), 'Tanzania Blows Hot and Cold Over Biofuels', *Financial Times*, May 28, 2008, sec. Global Economy.

Beer, T., Grant, T., and Campbell, P.K. (2007), *The Greenhouse and Air Quality Emissions of Biodiesel Blends in Australia* (Aspendale, Australia: CSIRO Marine and Atmospheric Research).

Bekunda, M., Palm, C.A., de Fraiture, C., Leadley, P., Maene, L., Martinelli, L.A., McNeely, J., Otto, M., Ravindranath, N.H., Victoria, R.L., Watson, H., and Woods, J. (2009), 'Biofuels and Developing Countries', in R.W.H.a.S. Bringezu (ed.), *Biofuels: Environmental Consequences and Interactions with Changing Land Use* (Gummersbach, Germany: Proceedings of the Scientific Committee on Problems of the Environment (SCOPE) International Biofuels Project Rapid Assessment).

Bento, A. and Jacobsen, M. (2007), 'Ricardian Rents, Environmental Policy and the Double Dividend Hypothesis', *Journal of Environment, Economics, and Management*, 53 (1), 17–31.

Berma, M., Shahadan, F., and Gapor, S. (2006), 'Alleviating Bumiputera Poverty in Sarawak: Reflections and Proposal', *The Malaysian Research Group 4th International Conference* (June 19–21, 2006; Salford, UK).

Bernard, R. (1995), *Research Methodology in Anthropology* (London: Altamira and Sage Publication).

Best, M.H. (1990), *The New Competition: Institutions of Industrial Restructuring* (Cambridge, MA, US: Harvard University Press).

bin Othman, M.R. (2006), 'Highway Network Development Plan for Malaysia', *PIARC Annual Council Meeting* (November 23, 2006; Madrid: World Road Association).

Binns, P. (2007), 'Proposal to the Sowing the Seeds of Prosperity: Developing Bioenergy Technology to Alleviate Smallholder Farmer Poverty' (Unpublished: Bill and Melinda Gates Foundation).

BiofuelsDigest (2009), '10 More German Biodiesel Firms in Bankruptcy: Industry to Go from 50 Companies to 10, Says Association', *BiofuelsDigest*, March 15, 2009.

Bionas (2009), 'Bionas Planting Scheme'. www.bionas.com.my/BionasScheme_new. html, accessed December 2014.

Biopact (2008a), 'British MP Committee Calls for Abandonment of EU Liquid Biofuel Targets', *Biopact*, January 21, 2008.

—— (2008b), 'A Sustainable Biofuels Consensus', *Biopact*, January 21, 2008.

Bismarck-Reppert, J. (2009), 'EU Biodiesel Producers Eye Strike against Argentine Rivals', *European Biodiesel Board News Letter* July 22, 2009.

Biswas, K.P., Pohit, S., and Kumar, R. (2010), 'Biodiesel from *Jatropha*: Can India Meet the 20% Blending Target?' *Energy Policy*, 38 (3), 1477–84.

Bloor, M., and Wood, F. (2006), *Keywords in Qualitative Methods* (London: Sage Publications).

BP (2010), *Statistical Review of World Energy 2010* (BP p.l.c.).

Brazil Institute (2007), *The Global Dynamics of Biofuels: Potential Supply and Demand for Ethanol and Biodiesel in the Coming Decade* (Washington DC, USA: The Brazil Institute of the Woodrow Wilson Center).

Brittaine, R. and Lutaladio, N. (2010), *Jatropha: A Smallholder Bioenergy Crop: The Potential for Pro-Poor Development* (Rome, Italy: FAO).

Britton, D. (2010), 'Barriers Commercialization Still Exists for Hybrid Truck Industry', *Truckinginfo,* 19 January 2010.

Brock, K. and McGee, R. (2002), *Knowing Poverty: Critical Reflections on Participatory Research and Policy* (London: Earthscan).

Browne, P. (2009), 'Tanzania Suspends Biofuels Investment', *The New York Times,* October 14, 2009.

Bryceson, D.F. (1993), *Liberalizing Tanzania's Food Trade: Public and Private Faces of Urban Marketing Policy, 1939–1988* (Geneva: United Nations Research Institute for Social Development).

Bulan, R. (2007), 'Native Title in Malaysia: A Complementary Sui Generis Proprietary Right Under the Federal Constitution', *Australian Indigenous Law Review,* 11 (1), 54–78.

CARB (2009), 'Proposed Regulation for Implementing Low Carbon', *Staff Report: Initial Statement of Reasons* (California, US: California Air Resources Board).

Carruthers, B.G. (2002), 'Review of the Book: Individuals, Institutions, and Markets, by C. Mantzavinos', *The American Journal of Sociology,* 108 (3), 730–2.

Chambers, R. (1998), 'Paradigm Shifts and the Practice of Participatory Research and Development', in I. Guijt and M.K. Shah (eds), *The Myth of Community: Gender Issues in Participatory Development* (London: Intermediate Technology Publications).

Chang, H.J. (2002), *Kicking Away the Ladder-Development Strategy in Historical Perspective* (London: Anthem Press).

Chee, S.S., Ismail, M.N., Ng, K.K., and Zawiah, H. (1997), 'Food Intake Assessment of Adults in Rural and Urban Areas from Four Selected Regions in Malaysia', *Malaysia Journal of Nutrition,* 3, 91–102.

Chong, Y.H., Tee, E.S., and Ng, T.K.W. (1984), 'Status of Community Nutrition in Poverty Kampongs', *Bulletin No. 22* (Kuala Lumpur: Institute for Medical Research).

Chopra, S. and Sodhi, M. (2004), 'Avoiding Supply Chain Breakdown', *MIT Sloan Management Review,* 46 (1), 53–62.

CIA (2010), *CIA World Factbook 2010* (Washington, DC: US Central Intelligence Agency).

Clancy, J. (2013), *Biofuels and Rural Poverty* (London: Routledge).

Coase, R.H. (1937), 'The Nature of the Firm', *Economica,* 4, 386–405.

Conceicao, P. and Mendoza, R.U. (2009), 'Anatomy of the Food Crisis', *Third World Quarterly,* 30, 1159–82. http://dx.doi.org/10.1080/01436590903037473

Cooke, F.M. (ed.) (2006), *State, Communities and Forests in Contemporary Borneo* (Asia-Pecific Environment Monograph 1; Australia: ANU E Press).

Cornelissen, S. and Dehue, B. (2009), 'Summary of Approaches to Accounting for Indirect Impacts of Biofuel Production' (Utrecht, The Netherlands: Ecofys).

Cotula, L., Vermeulen, S., Leonard, R., and Keeley, J. (2010), *Land Grab or Development Opportunity? Agricultural Investment and International Land Deals in Africa* (IIED, FAO, IFAD).

Craig, L., Palmquist, R.B. and Weiss, T. (1998), 'Transportation Improvements and Land Values in the Antebellum United States: A Hedonic Approach', *Journal of Real Estate Finance and Economics*, 16 (2), 173–89.

Cramb, R.A. (2009), 'Land and Longhouse: Agrarian Transformation in the Uplands of Sarawak', *Human Ecology*, 37 (3), 389–90.

Cramb, R.A. and Wills, I.R. (1990), 'The Role of Traditional Institutions in Rural Development: Community-Based Land Tenure and Government Land Policy in Sarawak, Malaysia', *World Development*, 18 (3), 347–60.

Cramer, C. (1999), 'Can Africa Industrialize by Processing Primary Commodities? The Case of Mozambican Cashew Nuts', *World Development*, 27 (7), 1247–66.

Creswell, J.W. (1994), *Research Design: Qualitative and Quantitative Approaches* (Thousand Oaks, CA, US: Sage Publications).

Cunha da Costa, R. (2004), 'Potential for Producing Bio-Fuel in the Amazon Deforested Areas', *Biomass and Bioenergy*, 26 (5), 405.

de Almeida, E.F., Bomtempo, J.V., and de Souza e Silva, C.M. (2007), 'The Performance of Brazilian Biofuels: An Economic, Environmental and Social Analysis', *Joint Transport Research Centre Discussion Paper* (2007-5: International Transport Forum).

de Oliveira, J.A.P. (2002), 'The Policymaking Process for Creating Competitive Assets for the Use of Biomass Energy: The Brazilian Alcohol Programme', *Renewable and Sustainable Energy Reviews*, 6, 129–40.

de Schutter, O. (2009), 'Crisis into Opportunity: Reinforcing Multilateralism', *Summary of the Report of the Special Rapporteur on the right to food, presented at the 12th session of the Human Rights Council* (United Nations).

de Wit, M., Junginger, M., Lensink, S., Londo, M., and Faaij, A. (2010), 'Competition between Biofuels: Modeling Technological Learning and Cost Reductions Over Time', *Biomass and Bioenergy*, 34 (2), 203–17.

Delucchi, M. (2004), 'Some Conceptual and Methodological Issues in the Analysis of the Social Cost of Motor-Vehicle Use', *The Annualized Social Cost of Motor-Vehicle Use in the United States, Based on 1990-1991 Data* (Publication No. UCD-ITS-RR-96-3 (2): UC Davis).

—— (2006), 'Lifecycle Analyses of Biofuels', *ITS Working Paper* (Davis: UC Davis).

Demirbas, A. (2007), 'Importance of Biodiesel as Transportation Fuel', *Energy Policy*, 35 (9), 4661.

—— (2009), 'Political, Economic and Environmental Impacts of Biofuels: A Review', *Applied Energy*, 86 (Supplement 1), S108–17.

Demsetz, H. (1967), 'Toward a Theory of Property Rights', *The American Economic Review*, 57 (2), 347–59.

Denzin, N.K. and Lincoln, Y.S. (2000), 'Introduction: The Discipline and Practice of Qualitative Research', in N.K. Denzin and Y.S. Lincoln (eds), *Handbook of Qualitative Research* (London: Sage).

Diao, X.S., Hazell, P., Resnick, D., and Thurlow, J. (2007), 'The Role of Agriculture in Development: Implications for sub-Saharan Africa' (Washington, DC: International Food Policy Research Institute).

Dicken, P. (2003), *Global Shift: Reshaping the Global Economic Map in the 21st Century*. (London: Sage Publishers).

Dicken, P. (2007), *Global Shift: Mapping the Changing Contours of the World Economy* (5th edn; New York: The Guilford Press).

DID (2010a), *Water Management Guidelines for Agricultural Development in Coastal Peat Swamps of Sarawak* (Kuching, Sarawak: Malaysia Department of Irrigation and Drainage Sarawak).

—— (2010b), *Proposed Granary Area for Large Scale Rice Production* (Kuching, Malaysia: Malaysia Department of Irrigation and Drainage, Sarawak).

Dietz, T., Ostrom, E., and Stern, P.C. (2008), 'The Struggle to Govern the Commons', *Urban Ecology*, 611–22.

DOE (2009), *Summary of Expansions and Revisions of the GREET 1.8c Version* (Argonne, IL, US: Argonne National Laboratory: United States Department of Energy). www.transportation.anl.gov/modeling_simulation/GREET/index.html, accessed December 2014.

Dolan, C., Humphrey, J., and Harris-Pascal, C. (1999), *Horticulture Commodity Chain: The Impact of the UK Market on the African Fresh Vegetable Industry* (Brighton, UK: Institute of Development Studies, University of Sussex).

Dorward, A., Kydd, J., and Poulton, C. (eds.) (1998), *Smallholder Cash Crop Production under Market Liberalization: A New Institutional Economics Perspective* (New York: Oxford University Press).

DOS (2000), *Population and Housing Census Malaysia 2000* (Kuala Lumpur: Malaysia Department of Statistics).

—— (2008), *Yearbook of Statistics, Sarawak 2008* (Kuala Lumpur: Malaysia Department of Statistics).

—— (2009), *Population, Household and Living Quarters, Malaysia 2009* (Kuala Lumpur: Malaysia Department of Statistics).

Durham, C., Davies, G., and Bhattacharyya, T. (2012), *Can Biofuels Policy Work for Food Security? An Analytical Paper for Discussion* (UK: UK Department of Environment, Food and Rural Affairs, Report PB13786).

E-EnergyMarket (2010), 'US Biodiesel Companies Folding Left and Right, after Gov't Cuts Tax Credit', 06 January 2010.

EBB (2009), 'Restoring a Level-Playing Field with Argentine Biodiesel Producers', *European Biodiesel Board* (Press Release, 18 December 2009).

Edwards, R., Szekeres, S., Neuwahl, F., and Mahieu, V. (2008), *Biofuels in the European Context: Facts and Uncertainties* (European Commission, Joint Research Centre, European Communities).

Edwin, W. (2007), 'UK Firm Invests $20m in Tanzania Biofuel Farm', *The East African*, 6 August 2007.

Eggertson, T. (1990), *Economic Behaviour and Institutions* (Cambridge, UK: Cambridge University Press).

EIA (2007), *International Energy Outlook 2007* (Washington, DC: US Energy Information Administration).

EIB (2005), *Energy Info Highlights* (Kuala Lumpur: Malaysia Energy Information Bureau).

Eicher, T. and Leukert, A. (2009), 'Institutions and Economic Performance: Endogeneity and Parameter Heterogeneity', *Journal of Money, Credit and Banking*, 41 (1), 197–219.

Eisentraut, A. (2010). *Sustainable Production of Second Generation Biofuels Potential and Perspectives in Major Economies and Developing Countries* (IEA Information Paper, Paris: International Energy Agency).

Elbehri, A. and Macdonald, S. (2004), 'Estimating the Impact of Transgenic Bt Cotton on West and Central Africa: A General Equilibrium Approach', *World Development*, 21 (12), 2049–64.

Ellis, F. and Mdoe, N. (2003), 'Livelihoods and Rural Poverty Reduction in Tanzania', *World Development*, 31 (8), 1367–84.

Ellis, F. and Freeman, H.A. (2004), 'Rural Livelihoods and Poverty Reduction Strategies in Four African Countries', *Journal of Development Studies*, 40 (4), 1–30.

Engerman, S. and Sokoloff, K.L. (2002), 'Factor Endowments, Inequality, and Paths of Development among New World Economics', *Economica*, 3 (1), 41–109.

Erb, K.-H., Mayer, A., Krausmann, F., Lauk, C., Plut, C., Steinberger, J., and Haberl, H. (2012), 'The Interrelations of Future Global Bioenergy Potentials, Food Demand and Agricultural Technology', in A. Gasparatos, P. Stromberg (Eds.), *Socioeconomic and Environmental Impacts of Biofuels: Evidence from Developing Nations* (Cambridge, UK: Cambridge University Press).

Ericsson, K., Rosenqvist, H., Ganko, E., Pisarek, M., and Nilsson, L. (2006), 'An Agro-Economic Analysis of Willow Cultivation in Poland', *Biomass and Bioenergy*, 30 (1), 16–27.

Erixon, F. (2009), *Green Protectionism in the European Union: How Europe's Biofuels Policy and the Renewable Energy Directive Violate WTO Commitments* (Brussels: European Centre for International Political Economy).

EU (2003), *Directive 2003/28/EC of the European Parliament and of the Council* (L 123/4: Official Journal of the European Union).

—— (2009), *Directive 2009/28/EC of the European Parliament and of the Council* (L 140/1; Official Journal of the European Union).

EUActiv (2009), 'EU Biofuel Sustainability Criteria "Inconsistent"', *Climate and Environment* (11 December 2009: EUActiv.com). www.euractiv.com/en/climate-environment/eu-biofuel-sustainability-criteria-inconsistent/article-188224, accessed 4 January 2010.

Europa (2006), *Green Paper: A European Strategy for Sustainable, Competitive and Secure Energy* (8.3.2006; Brussels Commission of the European Communities).

European Commission (2013), 'Assessing the impact of Biofuels Production on Developing Countries from the Point of View of Policy Coherence for Development – Final Report', *The European Union's Framework Contract Commission 2011*, Lot 1 – Contract N° 2012/299193.

Falck-Zepeda, J. (2009), 'Socio-Economic Considerations, Article 26.1 of the Cartagena Protocol on Biosafety: What Are the Issues and What Is at Stake?' *AgBioForum*, 12 (1), 90–107. www.agbioforum.org, accessed December 2014.

FAO (2001), *Forestry Out-Grower Schemes: A Global View* (Rome: Food and Agriculture Organization of the United Nations).

—— (2002), *The State of Food Insecurity in the World 2002* (Rome: Food and Agriculture Organization of the United Nations).

—— (2008), *The State of Food and Agriculture 2008; Biofuels: Prospects, Risks and Opportunities* (Rome: Food and Agriculture Organization of the United Nations).

—— (2009a), *Crop Prospects and Food Situation* (No. 1, February 2009; Rome: Food and Agriculture Organization of the United Nations).

—— (2009b), *The State of the Food Insecurity in the World 2009: Economic Crises, Impacts and Lessons Learned* (No. 1, February 2009; Rome: Food and Agriculture Organization of the United Nations).

—— (2013), *Biofuels and Sustainability Challenge: A Global Assessment of Sustainability Issues, Trends, and Policies for Biofuels and Related Feedstocks* (Rome: Food and Agriculture Organization of the United Nations).

FAPRI (2009), *FAPRI US and World Agricultural Outlook: International Oilseeds Model* (Iowa State, USA: Food and Agricultural Policy Research and Institute).

Fargione, J., Hill, J., Tilman, D., Polasky, S., and Hawthorne, P. (2008), 'Land Clearing and the Biofuel Carbon Debt', *Science*, 319 (1235), 1235–8.

Farrell, A., Plevin, R., Turner, B., Jones, A., O'Hare, M., and Kammen, D. (2006), 'Ethanol Can Contribute to Energy and Environmental Goals', *Science*, 311 (5760), 506–8.

FDA (2008), 'FDA Poisonous Plant Database', *Toxicology References* (Washington, DC: US Food and Drug Administration). www.accessdata.fda.gov/scripts/plantox/index.cfm, accessed December 2014.

Feagin, J.R., Orum, A.M., and Sjoberg, G. (eds.) (1991), *A Case for the Case Study* (Chapel Hill, NC, US: University of North Carolina Press).

Field, C.B., Campbell, J.E., and Lobell, D.B. (2008), 'Biomass Energy: The Scale of the Potential Resource', *Trends in Ecology and Evolution*, 23 (2), 65.

Fischer, G., Tubiello, F.N., van Velthuizen, H., and Wiberg, D. (2007), 'Climate Change Impacts on Irrigation Water Requirements: Effects of Mitigation, 1990–2080', *Technological Forecasting and Social Change*, 74 (7), 1083–107.

Fischer, K., Ekener-Petersen, E., Rydhmer, L. and Björnberg, K.E. (2015), 'Social Impacts of GM Crops in Agriculture: A Systematic Literature Review', *Sustainability*, 7, 8598–8620.

Fitter, R. and Kaplinsky, R. (2001), 'Who Gains from Product Rents as the Coffee Market Becomes More Differentiated? A Value Chain Analysis', *IDS Bulletin*, 32, 69–82.

Fogel, R.W. (1964), *Railroads and American Economic Growth* (Baltimore, US: Johns Hopkins University Press).

Fold, N. (2000), 'Oiling the Palms: Restructuring of Settlement Schemes in Malaysia and the New International Trade Regulations', *World Development*, 28 (3), 473–86.

—— (2001), 'Restructuring of the European Chocolate Industry and its Impact on Cocoa Production in West Africa', *Journal of Economic Geography*, 1 (3), 405–20.

Fontaras, G., Karavalakis, G., Kousoulidou, M., Tzamkiozis, Th., Ntziachristos, L., Bakeas, E., Stournas, S., Samaras, Z. (2009), 'Effects of Biodiesel on Passenger Car Fuel Consumption, Regulated and Non-Regulated Pollutant Emissions over Legislated and Real-World Driving Cycles', *Fuel*, 88 (9), 1608–17.

Freire, P. (1974), *Education for Critical Consciousness* (London: Sheed and Ward).

—— (1985), *Pedagogy of the Oppressed* (Harmondsworth, UK: Pelican Books; Penguin).

Freire, P. and Faundez, A. (1989), *Learning to Question: A Pedagogy of Liberation* (Geneva: Wcc).

Friss-Gensen, E. (2000), *Agricultural Policy in Africa after Adjustment* (Copenhagen: Center for Development Research).

Fritsche, U.R. (2008), 'Beyond the German BSO: Scope of Future Work on Land-Use Related GHG', *Workshop on Sustainable Biofuels* (Brussels).

Fritz, S., See, L.M., Van der Velde, M., Nalepa, R., Perger, C., Schill, C. (2013), 'Downgrading Recent Estimates of Land Available for Biofuel Production', *Environmental Science and Technology*.

FuelsEurope. (2014). Road Fuel Demand in the EU by Country in 2014. https://www.fuelseurope.eu/uploads/Modules/Dataroom/fuelseurope_graph_2015-10.pdf, accessed December 2014.

G-20 (2009), *G20 Leaders' Statement: The Pittsburgh Summit* (24–25 September 2009; Pittsburgh, US: The Group of Twenty).

Galdwin, C.H. (1989), *Ethnographic Decision Tree Modeling* (Newbury Park, CA, US: Sage).

Gasparatos, A. and Stromberg, P. (eds) (2012). *Socioeconomic and Environmental Impacts of Biofuels: Evidence from Developing Nations* (Cambridge, UK: Cambridge University Press).

Gereffi, G. (1994), 'The Organization of Buyer-Driven Global Commodity Chains: How US Retailers Shape Overseas Production Networks', in G. Gereffi and M. Korzeniwicz (eds.), *Commodity Chains and Global Capitalism* (Westport. Conn., US: Greenwood Press).

—— (1999), 'International Trade and Industrial Up-Grading in the Apparel Commodity Chain', *Journal of International Economics*, 48 (1), 37–70.

Gereffi, G. and Korzeniewicz, M. (eds) (1994), *Commodity Chains and Global Capitalism* (Westport, CT, US: Greenwood Press).

Gereffi, G. and Fernandez-Stark, K. (2011), *Global Value Chain Analysis: A Primer* (Durham, NC: Center on Globalization, Governance and Competitiveness [CGGC], Duke University).

Gereffi, G., Humphrey, J., and Sturgeon, T.J. (2005), 'The Governance of Global Value Chains', *Review of International Political Economy*, 12 (1), 78–104.

Gereffi, G., Fernandez-Stark, K. and Psilos, P. (2011), *Skills for Upgrading: Workforce Development and Global Value Chains in Developing Countries* (Durham, NC, US: Duke Center on Globalization, Governance and Competitiveness and the Research Triangle Institute).

GEXSI (2008), *Global Market Study on Jatropha* (London: The Global Exchange for Social Investment).

Ghoshal, S. and Moran, P. (1996), 'Bad for Practice: A Critique of the Transaction Cost Theory', *Academy of Management Review*, 21 (1), 13–47.

Gibbon, P. (2001), 'Upgrading Primary Production: A Global Commodity Chain Approach', *World Development*, 29 (2), 345–63.

Giddens, A. (1984), *The Constitution of Society. Outline of the Theory of Structuration* (Cambridge, UK: Polity).

—— (1990), *The Consequences of Modernity* (Stanford, US: Stanford University Press).

Gifford, A.J. (2003), 'Book Review: Individuals, Institution, and Markets by C. Mantzavinos', *Public Choice*, 115 (1/2), 248–52.

Gillham, B. (2000), *Real World Research: Case Study Research Method* (London: MPG Books Ltd).

Gnansounou, E., Dauriat, A., and Wyman, C. (2005), 'Refining Sweet Sorghum to Ethanol and Sugar: Economic Trade-Offs in the Context of North China', *Biosource Technology*, 96 (6), 985–1002.

Godfray, H.C.J., Beddington, J.R., Crute, I.R., Haddad, L., Lawrence, D., Muir, J.F., Pretty, J., Robinson, S., Thomas, S.M., and Toulmin, C. (2010), 'Food Security: The Challenge of Feeding 9 Billion People', *Science*, 327 (5967), 812–18.

Goldemberg, J. and Johansson, T.B. (2004), *World Energy Assessment Overview: 2004* (New York: United Nations Development Programme).

Goldstein, N. (2007), *Globalization and Free Trade* (New York: Infobase Publishing).

Granovetter, M. (1985), 'Economic Action and Social Structure: The Problem of Embeddedness', *The American Journal of Sociology*, 91 (3), 481–510.

GTZ (2005), *Liquid Biofuels for Transportation in Tanzania: Potential and Implications for Sustainable Agriculture and Energy in the 21st Century* (German Technical Cooperation).

Gubitz, G.M., Mittelbach, M., and Trabi, M. (1999), 'Exploitation of the Tropical Oil Seed Plan *Jatropha curcas* L', *Bioresource Technology*, 67 (1999), 73–82.

Gulbrand, L. (2006), *Memorandum M2006/2879/E* (30 June 2006; Stockholm: Sweden Ministry of Sustainable Development).

Gwilliam, K., Robert, B., Masami, K., and Kseniya, L. (2001), 'Transport Fuel Taxes and Urban Air Quality, Pollution Management', *Focus Discussion*, World Bank (11).

Gwynne, R.N. (1999), 'Globalisation, Commodity Chains and Fruit Exporting Regions in Chile', *Tijdschrift Voor Economische en Sociale Geografie*, 90 (2), 211–25.

Habib-Mintz, N. (2009a), 'To What Extent Can the Informal Economy Concept Adequately Explain the Dynamism of the Non-Formal Sector in Developing Countries', *Journal of International Business Economics*, 10 (1), 1–19.

—— (2009b), *To What Extent Can Primary Sector Producers in LDCs Move up the Global Commodity Chain? A Case Study on the Bangladesh Shrimp Industry* (Contemporary Economic and Financial Issues in Bangladesh; Dhaka, Bangladesh: University Press).

—— (2010), 'Biofuels Investment in Tanzania: Omissions in Implementations', *Energy Policy*, 38 (8), 3985–97.

Hahn-Hagerdal, B., Galbe, M., Gorwa-Grauslund, M.F. Lidén, G., and Zacchi, G. (2006), 'Bio-ethanol – The Fuel of Tomorrow from the Residues of Today', *Trends in Biotechnology*, 24 (12), 549.

Hall, J., Matos, S., Severino, L., and Beltrago, N. (2009), 'Brazilian Biofuels and Social Exclusion: Established and Concentrated Ethanol versus Emerging and Dispersed Biodiesel', *Journal of Cleaner Production*, 17, Supplement 1, S77–85.

Hall, R.E. and Jones, C.I. (1999), 'Why Do Some Countries Produce So Much More Output Per Worker Than Others?' *The Quarterly Journal of Economics*, 114 (1), 83–116.

Harriss, B. (1989), 'Organised Power of Grain Merchants in Dhaka Region of Bangladesh: Comparisons with Indian Cases', *Economic and Political Weekly,* 24 (12), 39–44.

Harriss-White, B. (2003), 'On Understanding Markets as Social and Political Institutions in Developing Economies', in H.-J. Chang (ed.), *Rethinking Development Economics* (London: Anthem), 481–97.

Hart, T. (1993), 'Transportation Investment and Disadvantaged Region: UK and European Policies Since 1950s', *Urban Studies*, 30 (2), 417–35.

Harvey, F. (2010), 'Inputs that Place Huge Pressure on the Land', *Financial Times* sec. Business and Food Sustainability.

Hawke, G.R. (1970), *Railways and Economic Growth in England and Wales, 1840–1870* (Oxford, UK: Clarendon Press).

Hazell, P. and Pachauri, R.K. (2006), *The Promises and Challenges of Biofuels in Developing Countries* (IFPRI, CIGER).

Headey, Derek and Fan, Shenggen (2010), *Reflections on the Global Food Crisis: How Has it Hurt? How Did it Happen? And How can we Prevent the Next One?* Research Monograph, 165. (Washington, US: International Food Policy Research Institute [IFPRI]).

Held, D. (1995), *Democracy and the Global Order: From the Modern State to Cosmopolitan Governance* (Stanford, US: Stanford University Press).

Hendricks, K.B. and Singhal, V.R. (2005), 'Association Between Supply Chain Glitches and Operating Performance', *Management Science*, 51 (5), 695–711.

Henry, A. and Henry, J. (2012), 'The Rise and Imminent Fall of Biodiesel', *Forbes Magazine*, June 27, 2012.

Hepple, L. (1986), 'The Revival of Geopolitics', *Political Geography Quarterly*, Supplement 5 (4).

Hertel, T.W., Tyner, W.E., and Birur, D.K. (2010), 'Global impacts of Biofuels', *Energy Journal*, 31 (1), 75–100.

Hess, M. (2004), '"Spatial" relationships? Towards a Reconceptualization of Embeddedness', *Progress in Human Geography*, 28 (2), 165–86.

Hester, R.E. and Harrison, R.M. (Eds) (2012), *Issues in Environmental Science and Technology*, 34 (Cambridge, UK: Royal Society of Chemistry).

Heston, A., Summers, R., and Aten, B. (2009), *Penn World Table 6.3.* http://pwt.econ.upenn.edu/php_site/pwt63/pwt63_form.php.

Hodgson, G. (1995), 'The Political Economy of Utopia', *Review of Social Economy*, LI1I/2, 195–214.

—— (1997), 'Economics, Environmental Policy and the Transcendence of Utilitarianism', in J. Foster (ed.), *Valuing Nature? Economics, Ethics and Environment* (London: Routledge).

Hoh, R. (2009), 'Malaysia: Biofuels Annual', *GAIN Report MY9026* (Washington, DC, US: USDA Foreign Agricultural Service).

Hooijer, A., Silvius, M., Wösten, H., and Page, S.E. (2006), 'PEAT-CO2, Assessment of CO2 emissions from drained peatlands in SE Asia.' *Delft Hydraulics* report Q3943.

Howarth, R. and Bringezu, S. (eds) (2009), Biofuels: Environmental Consequences and Interactions with Changing Land Use (*Proceedings of the Scientific Committee on Problems of the Environment [SCOPE] International Biofuels Project Rapid Assessment*, Gummersbach, Germany).

Howden, S.M., Soussana, J.F., Tubiello, F.N., Chhetri, N., Dunlop, M., and Meinke, H. (2007), 'Climate Change and Food Security Special Feature: Adapting Agriculture to Climate Change', *Proceedings of the National Academy of Sciences*, 104 (50), 19691–96.

Hoyos, R. and Medvedev, D. (2009), 'Poverty Effects of Higher Food Prices: A Global Perspective', *World Bank Policy Research Working Paper* (1 March 2009).

Hubbert, M.K. (1956), 'Nuclear Energy and the Fossil Fuels', *Spring Meeting of the Southern District. Division of Production. American Petroleum Institute* (San Antonio, Texas, US: Shell Development Company).

Humphrey, J. (2003), 'Globalization and Supply Chain Networks: The Auto Industry in Brazil and India', *Global Networks*, 3 (2), 121–42.

Hurst, P. (2007), *Agricultural Workers and their Contribution to Sustainable Agriculture and Rural Development* (London, UK: International Labour Organization).

Hyden, G. (2008), 'Institutions, Power and Policy Outcomes in Africa', *Africa Power and Politics Programme* (Discussion Paper No. 2; June 2008; London: Overseas Development Institute).

ICRISAT (2007), *Pro-Poor Biofuels Outlook for Asia and Africa*. Working Paper (4 March: International Crops Research Institute for the Semi-Arid Tropics).

Idris, F. (2004), 'Vehicle Emissions Regulations and Future Fuel Quality For Cleaner Environment In Malaysia', *2nd Asian Petroleum Technology Symposium Programme* (Malaysia).

IEA (2004), *Biofuels for Transport: An International Perspective* (Paris: International Energy Agency).

—— (2006), 'IEA Bioenergy – Update 23', *Biomass and Bioenergy*, 30 (6), I.

—— (2007), *World Energy Outlook 2007* (Paris International Energy Agency).

—— (2009), *World Energy Outlook 2009* (Paris International Energy Agency).

—— (2010), *World Energy Outlook 2010* (Paris International Energy Agency).

IEA/WBCSD (2004), *Global Transport Spreadsheet Model* (Paris: International Energy Agency/World Business Council for Sustainable Development).

IFAD (2001), *Rural Poverty Report 2001: The Challenge of Ending Rural Poverty* (Rome: The International Fund for Agricultural Development).

—— (2008), *International Consultation on Pro-Poor Jatropha Development* (Rome: The International Fund for Agricultural Development).

ILO (2009), *Global Employment Trends Report: January 2009* (Geneva: International Labour Organization).

IPCC (2007), 'Climate Change 2007: Mitigation', *The Fourth Assessment Report of the Intergovernmental Panel on Climate Change* (Cambridge, UK: Cambridge University Press).

—— (2011), *Renewable Energy Sources and Climate Change Mitigation*. Ottmar Edenhofer, Ramón Pichs-Madruga, Youba Sokona, Kristin Seyboth, Patrick Matschoss, Susanne Kadner, Timm Zwickel, Patrick Eickemeier, Gerrit Hansen, Steffen Schloemer, Christoph von Stechow (Eds) (Cambridge, UK: Cambridge University Press).

—— (2012), *Managing the Risks of Extreme Events and Disasters to Advance Climate Change Adaptation*. C.B. Field, V. Barros, T.F. Stocker, D. Qin, D.J. Dokken, K.L. Ebi, M.D. Mastrandrea, K.J. Mach, G.-K. Plattner, S.K. Allen, M. Tignor, and P.M. Midgley (Eds) (Cambridge, UK: Cambridge University Press).

IRGC (2008), *Risk Governance Guidelines for Bioenergy Policies* (Geneva: International Risk Governance Council).

IRIN (2004), *Tanzania: Food Insecurity Persists in Dodoma, Singida* Integrated Regional Information Network.

ISA (2001), *Code of Ethics* (Madrid: International Sociological Association). www. isa-sociology.org/about/isa_code_of_ethics.htm, accessed 19 September 2008.

Isa, F.M. (2007), 'Malaysian Fuel Quality and Bio-Fuel Initiative', *5th Asian Petroleum Technology Symposium* (23–25 January 2007; Jakarta, Indonesia: Petronas).

ISAAA (2011), *Global Status of Commercialized Biotech/GM Crops: 2010–2011.* The International Service for the Acquisition of Agri-biotech Applications (ISAAA). www.isaaa.org, accessed December 2014.

Isinika, A., Ashimogo, G.C., and Mlangwa, E.D. (2005), 'From Ujamaa to Structural Adjustment: Agricultural Intensification in Tanzania', in G. Djurfeldt (ed.), *African Food Crisis: Lessons from the Asian Green Revolution* (Cambridge, US: CABI Publisher).

Ivanic, M. and Martin, W. (2008), *Implications of Higher Global Food Prices for Poverty in Low Income Countries*, World Bank Policy Research Working Paper (Washington DC: World Bank).

Jacobsen, D.I. (1999), 'Trust in Political-Administrative Relations: The Case of Local Authorities in Norway and Tanzania', *World Development*, 27 (5), 839–53.

Jansson, C., Westerbergh, A., Zhang, J.M., Hu, X.W. and Sun, C.X. (2009), 'Cassava, a Potential Biofuel Crop in China', *Applied Energy*, 86 (Supplement 1), S95–99.

Jin, K.K. (2006), 'Meeting Targets ... and missing people?' *UNDP Meeting in Sarawak* (Kuching, Malaysia).

John, E. and Damis, A. (2008), 'Good Mechanism to Stabilize Prices', *The New Straits Times*, 27 January 2008.

Johnston, M. and Holloway, T. (2007), 'A Global Comparison of National Biodiesel Production Potentials', *Environmental Science and Technology*, 41 (23), 7967–73.

Jongschaap, R.E.E., Corre, W.J., Bindraban, P.S., and Brandenburg, W.A. (2007), *Claims and Facts on Jatropha curcas L.* (Wageningen, The Netherlands: Plant Research International).

Jungbluth, N., Sybille Büsser, S., Frischknecht, R., and Tuchschmid, M. (2008), *Life Cycle Assessment of Biomass-to-Liquid Fuels* (ESU-services GmbH, Uster: The Federal Office for Energy (BFE), the Federal Office for the Environment (BAFU) and the Federal Office for Agriculture (BLW)).

Kabeer, N. (2000), *Discussing Women's Empowerment: Theory and Practice* (Stockholm: Swedish International Development Cooperation Agency).

Kadigi, R.M.J., Mdoe, N.S.Y., and Ashimogo, G.C. (2007), 'Collective Arrangements and Social Networks: Coping Strategies for the Poor Households in the Great Ruaha Catchment in Tanzania', *Physics and Chemistry of the Earth* – Parts A/B/C, 32 (15–18), 1315–21.

Kamil, N. (2005), *Agricultural Policy and Sustainable Development* (Terengganu, Malaysia: Kolej Universiti Sains dan Teknologi Malaysia).

Kammen, D., Farrel, A.E., Plevin, R.J., Jones, A.D., Nemet, G.F. and Delucchi, M.A. (2007), *Energy and Greenhouse Impacts of Biofuels: A Framework for Analysis*, Discussion Paper No 2007–2 (Organization for Economic Co-operation and Development and International Transport Forum).

Kaplinsky, R., Terheggen, A., and Tijaja, J. (2010), *What Happens when the Market Shifts to China? The Gabon Timber and Thai Cassava Value Chains*, World Bank Policy Research Working Paper, 5206.

Kelly, G.A. (1955), *The Psychology of Personal Constructs* (New York: Norton).

Keohane, Robert O. and Nye Jr., Joseph S. (2000), 'Globalization: What's New? What's Not? (And So What?)', *Foreign Policy*; Spring 2000, Issue 118, 104.

Keynes, J.M. (1939), 'Professor Tinbergen's Method', *Economic Journal*, 49 (195), 558–77.

Khan, M.H. (2005), 'Markets, States and Democracy: Patron-Client Relations and the Case for Democracy in Developing Countries', *Democratization*, 12 (5), 704–24.

Khanna, M., Dhungana, B., and Clifton-Brown, J. (2007), *Costs of Perennial Grasses for Bioenergy in Illinois*, Working paper, Department of Agriculture and Consumer Economics (Urban-Champaign, Illinois, US: University of Illinois).

King, V. (1992), *The People of Borneo* (Oxford, UK: Oxford Press).

Kirilenko, A.P. and Sedjo, R.A. (2007), 'Climate Change and Food Security Special Feature: Climate Change Impacts on Forestry', *Proceedings of the National Academy of Sciences*, 104 (50), 19697–702.

Kisarawe (2008), *District Profile 2007/08* (Kisarawe, Tanzania: District Commissioner).

Klümper, W. and Qaim, M. (2014), 'A Meta-Analysis of the Impacts of Genetically Modified Crops', *PLoS ONE* 2014, 9, e111629.

Knaup, H. (2008), 'Africa Becoming a Biofuel Battleground: Western Companies are Pushing to Acquire Vast Stretches of African Land to Meet the World's Biofuel Needs', *Business Week*, 8 September 2008.

Knothe, G. (2001), 'Historical Perspective on Vegetable Oil-Based Diesel Fuels', *AOCS Inform* (12), 1103–07.

Koerbitz, W. (2007), 'New and Specific Oils for Biodiesel Production – Non-Food Oilseed Crops for Semi-Arid Regions', *Proceedings, COMPETE Bioenergy and Land Use Workshop* (Mauritius Sugar Industry Research Institute, www.compete-bioenergy.net).

Kogut, B. and Zander, U. (1992), 'Knowledge of the Firm, Combinative Capabilities, and the Replication of Technology', *Organization Science*, 3 (3), 383–97.

Koh, L.P. and Ghazoul, J. (2008), 'Biofuels, Biodiversity, and People: Understanding the Conflicts and Finding Opportunities', *Biological Conservation*, 141 (10), 2450–60.

Kojima, M. and Johnson, T. (2006), 'Biofuels for Transport in Developing Countries: Socioeconomic Considerations', *Energy for Sustainable Development*, 10 (2), 59–66.

Kretschmer, B. and Peterson, S. (2010), 'Integrating Bioenergy into Computable General Equilibrium Models – A Survey', *Energy Economics*, 32 (3), 673–86.

Kretschmer, B., Narita, D., and Peterson, S. (2009), 'The Economic Effects of the EU Biofuel Target', *Energy Economics*, 31 (Supplement 2), S285–94.

Krugman, P. (1995), 'Growing World Trade: Causes and Consequences', *Brookings Papers on Economic Activity*, 1, 327–77.

Lall, S. (2013), 'Reinventing Industrial Strategy: The Role of Government Policy in Building Industrial Competitiveness', *Annals of Economics and Finance, Society for AEF*, vol. 14 (2), 785–829, November.

Lam, M.K., Tan, K.T., and Lee, K.T. (2009), 'Malaysian Palm Oil: Surviving the Food versus Fuel Dispute for a Sustainable Future', *Renewable and Sustainable Energy Reviews*, In Press, Uncorrected Proof.

Lamers, P., McCormick, K., and Hilbert, J.A. (2008), 'The Emerging Liquid Biofuel Market in Argentina: Implications for Domestic Demand and International Trade', *Energy Policy*, 36 (4), 1479–90.

Landis, D.A., Gardiner, M.M., van der Werf, W., and Swinton, S. (2008), 'Increasing Corn for Biofuel Production Reduces Biocontrol Services in Agricultural Landscapes', *National Academy of Science* (105), 20552–7.

Lane, J. (2008), 'Malaysia Proposes $103 billion Sarawak Corridor Renewables Development Plan', *BiofuelsDigest*, 14 February 2008.

—— (2009), '10 More German Biodiesel Firms in Bankruptcy: Industry to Go from 50 Companies to 10, Says Association', *BiofuelsDigest*, 15 March 2009.

Lee, H.L. (2004), 'The Triple-A Supply Chain', *Harvard Business Review*, 82 (10), 102–12.

Lewis, A. (1954), 'Economic Development with Unlimited Supplies of Labour', *The Manchester School*, 22 (2), 139–91.

Leys, C. (1996), *The Rise and Fall of Development Theory* (Indiana, US: Indiana University Press).

Link, P.M., Ramos, C.I., Schneider, U.A., Schmid, E., Balkovič, J., and Skalský R. (2009), *The Interdependencies Between Food and Biofuel Production in European Agriculture – An Application of EUFASOM*, Working Paper FNU-165 (Hamburg: Research Unit Sustainability and Global Change, Center for Marine and Atmospheric Sciences, Hamburg University, Germany).

Lipsky, J. (2008), 'Commodity Prices and Global Inflation', Speech given to the Council on Foreign Relations (8 May 2008; New York).

Lopez, G.P. (2007), *Paddy Sub-Sector: Economic Reforms Necessary* (25 June 2007; Kuala Lumpur: Malaysian Institute of Economic Research).

Lund, C. (2008), *Local Politics and Dynamics of Property in Africa* (Cambridge, UK: Cambridge University Press).

Macedo, I.d.C., Leal, M.R.L.V., and Silva, J.E.A.R.d. (2003), 'Greenhouse Gas (GHG) Emissions in the Production and Use of Ethanol in Brazil: Present Situation (2002)' (Sao Paulo: Brazil Secretariat of the Environment).

MacIntyre, B. (2007), 'Poison Plant Could Help to Cure the Planet', *The Times*, 28 July 2007.

Madhok, A. (2002), 'Reassessing the Fundamentals and Beyond: Ronald Coase, the Transaction Cost and Resource-based Theories of the Firm and the Institutional Structure of Production', *Strategic Management Journal*, 23 (6), 535.

Madubansi, M. and Shackleton, C.M. (2006), 'Changing Energy Profiles and Consumption Patterns Following Electrification in Five Rural Villages, South Africa', *Energy Policy*, 34 (18), 4081.

MAFC (2006), *Follow-Up of the Implementation of the World Food Summit Plan of Action* (Dar es Salaam: Tanzania Ministry of Agriculture, Food and Cooperatives).

—— (2008), 'Volume I: Crop Monitoring and Early Warning', *Agstats for Food Security* (Dar es Salaam: Tanzania Ministry of Agriculture, Food and Cooperatives).

—— (2009), 'Tanzania Government Perspective on Biofuels', Presented to The Roundtable on Sustainable Biofuels (Nairobi, Kenya: Tanzania Ministry of Agriculture, Food and Cooperatives).

—— (various years), *Agstats for Food Security* (Dar es Salaam: Ministry of Agriculture, Food and Cooperatives).

Malaysia (2006), *Ninth Malaysia Plan* (Kuala Lumpur: Government of Malaysia).

—— (2008), *Economic Report 2008/2009: Economic Performance and Prospects*, Malaysia Economic Planning Unit (Kuala Lumpur: Government of Malaysia).

Manski, C. (2000), 'Economic Analysis of Social Interactions', *The Journal of Economic Perspectives*, 14 (3), 115–36.

Mantzavinos, C. (2001), *Individuals, Institutions and Markets* (Cambridge, UK: Cambridge University Press).

Mantzavinos, C., North, D., and Shariq, S. (2004), 'Learning, Institutions and Economic Performance', *Perspectives on Politics*, 2 (1), 75–84.

MARDI (2002), *Sarawak: Peat Agricultural Use* (Kuala Lumpur, Malaysia: Malaysian Agricultural Research and Development Institute).

Markusen, A. (1999), 'Fuzzy Concepts, Scanty Evidence, Policy Distance: The Case for Rigour and Policy Relevance in Critical Regional Studies' *Regional Studies*, 33, 869–84.

Martha, J. and Subbakrishna, S. (2002), 'Targeting a Just-In-Case Supply Chain for the Inevitable Next Disaster', *Supply Chain Management Review*, 5 (4), 18–23.

Masangi, S. and Ewing, M. (2009), 'Biofuels Production in Developing Countries: Assessing Tradeoffs in Welfare and Food Security', *Journal of Environmental Science and Policy*, 12, 520–28.

Mathews, J.A. (2007), 'Biofuels: What a Biopact between North and South could achieve', *Energy Policy*, 35 (7), 3550–70.

Matthey, H. (2008), 'OECD-FAO Biofuel Modeling and Applications', *Modeling Workshop on Biofuels and Food Security* (21 October 2008; Stanford University, US).

Mays, N., Roberts, E. and Popay, J. (2001), 'Synthesising Research Evidence', in N. Fulop, P. Allen, A. Clarke, and N. Black (Eds), *Methods for Studying the Delivery and Organisation of Health Services* (London: Routledge).

MEM (2008), 'Biofuels Policy Guideline (Draft)' (Dar es Salaam: Tanzania Ministry of Energy and Minerals).

Mingorance, F. (2007), *The Flow of Palm Oil: Colombia–Belgium/Europe; A Study from a Human Rights Perspective* (Brussels: Belgian Coordinating Group for Colombia).

Mintz-Habib, N. (2013), 'Malaysian Biofuels Experience: A Socio-political Analysis of the Commercial Environment', *Energy Policy*, 64 (February) 2013.

Mitchell, D. (2008), A Note on Rising Food Prices', *World Bank Policy Research Working Paper Series 4682*, The World Bank.

Mookherjee, D. (2005), 'Is There Too Little Theory in Development Economics Today?' in R. Kanbur (ed.), *New Directions in Development Economics: Theory or Empirics?* (A Symposium in *Economic and Political Weekly*).

Morgan, D.L. (1988), *Focus Groups as Qualitative Research* (Newbury Park, CA, US: Sage).

Morton, J.F. (2007), 'Climate Change and Food Security Special Feature: The Impact of Climate Change on Smallholder and Subsistence Agriculture', *Proceedings of the National Academy of Sciences*, 104 (50), 19680–85.

MPIC (2006), *The National Biofuel Policy* (Kuala Lumpur: Malaysia Ministry of Plantation Industries and Commodities).

MPOC (2007a), *MPOC Annual Report 2007* (Kelana Jaya, Malaysia: Malaysian Palm Oil Council).

—— (2007b), *Fact Sheets on Malaysian Palm Oil* (Kelana Jaya, Malaysia: Malaysian Palm Oil Counsel).

Msangi, S. and Ewing, M. (2009), 'Biofuels Production in Developing Countries: Assessing Tradeoffs in Welfare and Food Security', *Journal of Environmental Science and Policy* 12, 520-28.

Mulakala, A. (2008), 'The Kingmakers: Sabah, Sarawak and the 12th Malaysia General Elections', *Weekly Insights and Features from the Asia Foundation* (Malaysia: The Asia Foundation). http://asiafoundation.org/in-asia/2008/03/26/the-kingmakers-sabah-sarawak-and-the-12th-malaysia-general-elections/, accessed 1 December 2015.

Mulugetta, Y. (2009), 'Evaluating Economics of Biodiesel in Africa', *Journal of Renewable and Sustainable Energy Reviews*, 13, 1592–98.

Mundlak, Yair, Butzer, Rita, and Larson, Donald F. (2012), 'Heterogeneous Technology and Panel Data: The Case of the Agricultural Production Function', *Journal of Development Economics*, Volume 99, Issue 1, September 2012, 139–49, ISSN 0304-3878, http://dx.doi.org/10.1016/j.jdeveco.2011.11.003.

Murphy, J.T. (2002), 'Networks, Trust, and Innovation in Tanzania's Manufacturing Sector', *World Development*, 30 (4), 591–619.

Murphy, S. (2010), 'Bad Year for Biofuel Ends on a Sour Note', *Washington Post*, 1 January 2010.

Murugesan, A., Umarani, C., Subramanian, R., and Nedunchezhian, N. (2009), 'Bio-Diesel as an Alternative Fuel for Diesel Engines: A Review', *Renewable and Sustainable Energy Reviews*, 13 (3), 653–62.

Myers, N., Mittermeier, R.A., Mittermeier, C.G., Da Fonseca, G.A.B., and Kent. J. (2000), 'Biodiversity Hotspots for Conservation Priorities', *Nature*, 403, 853–58.

Naik, S.N., Goud, V.V., Rout, P.K., and Dalai, A.K. (2010), 'Production of First and Second Generation Biofuels: A Comprehensive Review', *Renewable and Sustainable Energy Reviews*, 14 (2), 578–97.

National Academy of Science (2012), *A Sustainability Challenge: Food Security for All: Report of Two Workshops*. Committee on Food Security for All as a Sustainability Challenge, Science and Technology for Sustainability Program, Policy and Global Affairs (Washington, DC: National Academy Press).

Natural Earth Data (2015) *Free Vector and Raster Map Data at 1:10m, 1:50m, and 1:110m scale*. www.naturalearthdata.com/, accessed December 2014.

Nature Chemical Biology (2010), 'A Practical Philosophy', *Nature Chemical Biology*, 6 (August 2010), 559.

Naylor, R.L., Adam, J., Liska, J.A., Burke, B.M., Falcon, P.W., Gaskell, C.J., Rozelle, D.J., and Cassman, G.K. (2007), 'The Ripple Effect: Biofuels, Food Security, and the Environment', *Environment*, 49 (9), 30–43.

NBS (2006), *Tanzania in Figures 2005*, National Bureau of Statistics (Dar es Salaam: Tanzania Ministry of Planning, Economy and Empowerment).

—— (2007), *Tanzania in Figures 2006*, National Bureau of Statistics (Dar es Salaam: Tanzania Ministry of Planning, Economy and Empowerment).

NDMC (1997), *Reported Effects of the 1997–98 El Niño* (Lincoln, NE, USA: National Drought Mitigation Center).

NEF (2008), 'Food Price Increases: Is it Fair to Blame Biofuels?' *Research Note Insight Services: Biofuels* (27 May 2008; London: New Energy Finance).

Neuhoff, K. (2008), 'Tackling Carbon: How to Price Carbon for Climate Policy', *Climate Strategies* (29 September 2008: Economics Department, University of Cambridge, UK).

Ngidang, D. (2007), *Rural Livelihood: Employment, Household Income and Poverty Among the Rural Iban* (Kuching, Malaysia: University of Malaysia in Sarawak).

NIT (2003), *Study on Tanzania Road Network* (Dar es Salaam: National Institute of Transportation).

Nolan, P. (2008), *Capitalism and Freedom: The Contradictory Character of Globalization* (London: Anthem Press).

—— (2009), *Crossroads: The End of Wild Capitalism and the Future of Humanity* (London: Marshall Cavendish Press).

Nolan, P., Zhang, J., and Chunhang, L. (2007), *Global Business Revolution and the Cascade Effect: Systems Integrations in the Aerospace, Beverage and Retail Industry* (Basingstoke, UK: Palgrave Macmillan).

North, D. (1990), *Institutions, Institutional Change, and Economic Performance* (Cambridge, UK: Cambridge University Press).

North, D. and Thomas, R. (1973), *The Rise of the Western World* (Cambridge, UK: Cambridge University Press).

Nunn, N. (2009), 'The Importance of History for Economic Development', *Annual Review of Economics*, Annual Reviews, vol. 1 (1), 65–92, 05.

OECD (2000), *Environmental Effects of Liberalising Fossil Fuels Trade: Results from the OECD Green Model* (Paris: Organization for Economic Co-Operation and Development).

—— (2006), 'Agricultural Market Impacts of Future Growth in the Production of Biofuels.' *OECD Papers*, 6 (1), 1–57 (Organization for Economic Co-Operation and Development).

—— (2007), *A Review of Policy Measures Supporting Production and Use of Bioenergy*, Trade and Agriculture Directorate: Committee for Agriculture (Paris: Organization for Economic Co-Operation and Development).

—— (2008), *Economic Assessment of Biofuels Support Policies* (Paris: Organization for Economic Co-Operation and Development).

OECD/FAO (2008), *OECD-FAO Agricultural Outlook 2008–2017* (Paris, Rome: Organization for Economic Co-Operation and Development, Food and Agriculture Organization of the United Nations).

—— (2009), *OECD-FAO Agricultural Outlook 2008–2019* (Paris, Rome: Organization for Economic Co-Operation and Development, Food and Agriculture Organization of the United Nations).

OECD/IEA (2008), *Energy Technology Perspective 2008: Scenarios and Strategies to 2050* (Paris: Organization for Economic Co-Operation and Development, International Energy Agency).

Olson, M. (1965), *The Logic of Collective Action* (Cambridge, UK: Cambridge University Press).

—— (1982), *The Rise and Decline of Nations* (New Haven, CT, US: Yale University Press).

Ostrom, E. (1990), *Governing the Commons: The Evolution of Institutions for Collective Action* (Cambridge, UK: Cambridge University Press).

—— (ed.) (2003), *Drama of the Commons* (Washington, DC, US: National Research Council).

—— (2011), 'Background on the Institutional Analysis and Development Framework. *Policy Studies Journal*, 39, 7–27. http://dx.doi.org/10.1111/j.1541-0072.2010.00394.x

Patel, R. and Gimenez-Holt, E. (2010), *Food Rebellions: Crisis and the Hunger for Justice* (Oakland, CA, US: Food First Publisher).

Paul, H. and Ernsting, A. (2007), *Second Generation Biofuels: An Unproven Future Technology with Unknown Risks*. www.wrm.org.uy/subjects/agrofuels/Secon_Generation_Biofuels.pdf, accessed December 2014.

Pearce, D. and Warford, J. (1993), *World without End: Economics, Environment, and Sustainable Development – A Summary* (Washington, DC, US: World Bank).

Pelkmans, L. and Papageorgiou, A. (2005), 'Biofuels in India', *PREMIA WP2: International Activities on Alternative Motor Fuels* (PREMIA).

Pimbert, M. and Wakeford, T. (2001), 'Overview – Deliberative Democracy and Citizen Empowerment', *Participatory Learning and Action*, 40 (February 2001).

Pimentel, David. (Ed.) (2012), *Global Economic and Environmental Aspects of Biofuels* (Boca Raton, US: CRC Press, Taylor & Francis Group).

Pimentel, D. and Patzek, T.W. (2005), 'Ethanol Production Using Corn, Switchgrass, and Wood; Biodiesel Production Using Soybean and Sunflower', *Natural Resources Research*, 14 (1), 65–76.

Pimentel, D., Herz, M., Glickstein, M., Zimmerman, M., Allen, R., Becker, K., Evans, J., Hussain, B., Sarsfield, R., Grosfeld, A., and Seidel, T. (2002), 'Renewable Energy: Current and Potential Issues', *Bioscience*, 52 (12), 1111–19.

Polanyi, K. (1944), *The Great Transformation* (New York: Holt, Rinehart).

—— (1947), 'Our Obsolete Market Mentality', *Commentary*, 3 (February), 109–17.

Ponte, S. (2002), 'The "Late Revolution"? Regulation, Markets and Consumption in the Global Coffee Chain', *World Development*, 30 (7), 1099–122.

Popp, D. (2006), 'R&D Subsidies and Climate Policy: Is There a Free Lunch?' *Climatic Change*, 77 (3), 311–41.

Poulton, C., Gibbon, P., Hanyani-MLambo, P., Kydd, B., Maro, J., Larsen, N.W., Osorio, M., Tschirley, D., and Zulu, B. (2004), 'Competition and Coordination in Liberalized African Cotton Market Systems', *World Development*, 32 (3), 519–36.

Prathaban, V. (2006), 'The Biodiesel Promise', *Malaysian Business*, 16 April 2006.

Punch, K.F. (2001), *Introduction to Social Research: Quantitative and Qualitative Approaches* (London: Sage).

Putterman, L. (1995), 'Economic Reform and Smallholder Agriculture in Tanzania: A Discussion of Recent Market Liberalization, Road Rehabilitation, and Technology Dissemination Efforts', *World Development*, 23 (2), 311–26.

QFinance (2009), *QFinance: The Ultimate Resource* (London: Bloomsbury Information Ltd).

Rahman, M.A. (1984), *Grass-Roots Participation and Self-Reliance: Experiences in South and South East Asia* (New Delhi: Oxford and IBH in collaboration with the Society for Participatory Research in Asia).

—— (1993), *People's Self-Development: Perspectives on Participatory Action Research: A Journey through Experience* (London: Zed Books).

Raikes, P., Jensen, M.F., and Ponte, S. (2000), 'Global Commodity Chain Analysis and the French Filière Approach: Comparison and Critique', *Economy and Society*, 29 (3), 390–417.

Rainer, J. (2006), 'Opportunities for Biofuels in Tanzania', *Global Forum on Sustainable Energy – 6th Meeting 'Africa is energizing itself'* (29 November – 1 December 2006; Vienna, Austria).

Rajagopal, D. and Zilberman, D. (2007), *Review of Environmental, Economic and Policy Aspects of Biofuels* (Washington, DC, US: World Bank).

Rapaczynski, A. (1987), *Nature and Politics: Liberalism in the Philosophies of Hobbs, Locke and Rousseau* (Ithaca, NY, US: Cornell University Press).

Rashid, S., Gulati, A., and Cummings, R., Jr. (eds) (2008), *From Parastatals to Private Trade: Lessons from Asian Agriculture* (Baltimore, MD, US: Johns Hopkins University Press for the International Food Policy Research Institute).

Rasul, G. and Thapa, B. (2003), 'Shifting Cultivation in the Mountains of South and Southeast Asia: Regional Patterns and Factors Influencing the Change', *Land Degradation and Development*, 14 (5), 495–508.

Raswant, V. (2009), 'Water for Bioenergy and Food?' *5th World Water Forum* (Istanbul, Turkey: IFED).

Raufflet, E., Berranger, A., and Platas-Aguilar, A. (2008), 'Innovative Business Approaches and Poverty: Toward a First Evaluation', in C. Wanke (ed.), *Alleviating Poverty Through Business Strategy* (New York: Palgrave Macmillan).

Ravallion, M. (1990), 'Reaching the Poor Through Rural Public Employment; A Survey of Theory and Evidence', *World Bank – Discussion Papers* 94, World Bank.

—— (1991), 'The Challenging Arithmetic of Poverty in Bangladesh', *Policy Research Working Paper Series 586*, The World Bank.

Reijnders, L. (2010), 'Transport Biofuel Yields from Food and Lignocellulosic C4 Crops', *Biomass and Bioenergy*, 34 (1), 152–55.

Reilly, J. and Paltsev, S. (2007), 'Biomass Energy and Competition for Land', *MIT Report No. 145: Joint Program on the Science and Policy of Global Change* (Cambridge, US: Massachusetts Institute of Technology).

REN21 (2007), *Renewables 2007: Global Status Report* (Washington, DC, US: Renewable Energy Policy Network for the 21st Century).

—— (2009), *Renewables Global Status Report 2009 Update* (Renewable Energy Policy Network for the 21st Century [REN 21]).

Rieley, J.O., Wüst, R.A., Jauhiainen, J., Page, S.E., Wösten, H., Hooijer, A., Siegert, F., Limin, S.H., Vasander, H., and Stahlhut, M. (2008), 'Tropical Peatlands: Carbon Stores, Carbon Gas Emissions and Contribution to Climate Change Processes', in M. Strack (ed.), *Peatlands and Climate Change* (Jyväskylä, Finland: International Peat Society), 148–81.

Rodrik, D. (2004), *How to Make the Trade Regime Work for Development* (Cambridge, MA, US: Harvard University).

Rodrik, D., Subramanian, A., and Trebbi, F. (2004), 'Institutions Rule: The Primacy of Institutions Over Geography and Integration in Economic Development', *Journal of Economic Growth*, 9 (2), 135–65.

Rogers, E.M. (1995), *Diffusion of Innovation* (New York: The Free Press).

Romer, P. (1994), 'The Origins of Endogenous Growth', *The Journal of Economic Perspectives*, 8(1), 3–22.

Rose, A. (2005), *Foreign Service and Foreign Trade: Embassies as Export Promotion* (Boston, Mass., US: National Bureau of Economic Research).

Rosegrant, M.W., Zhu, T., Msangi, S., and Sulser, T. (2008), 'Global Scenarios for Biofuels: Impacts and Implications for Food Security', *Review of Agricultural Economics* 30 (3), 495–505.

Rosenau, J.N. (2000), 'Governance in a Globalizing World', in D. Held and A.G. McGrew (eds), *The Global Transformations Reader: An Introduction to the Globalization Debate* (Cambridge, UK: Polity).

Rosenthal, E. (2009), 'Europe, Cutting Biofuel Subsidies, Redirects Aid to Stress Greenest Options', *The New York Times*, 22 January 2009.

Royal Society (2009), *Reaping the Benefits: Science and the Sustainable Intensification of Global Agriculture* (October 2009; London: The Royal Society).

RSB (2008), *Direct and Indirect Land Use*, Expert Advisory Group and Working Group on GHGs (Background Paper – Teleconference June 3rd, 2008: Roundtable on Sustainable Biofuels).

—— (2009), *Proceeding of the East African Regional Stakeholder Meeting* (Nairobi, Kenya: The Roundtable on Sustainable Biofuels).

Sai, L.J. (2002), *National Report for the UNCCD Implementation: Combating Land Degradation and Promoting Sustainable Land Management in Malaysia* (Kuala Lumpur: Malaysia Department of Agriculture).

Saith, R. (2001), 'Capabilities: The Concept and its Operationalisation', *QEH Working Paper Series* (No. 66; Oxford: Queen Elizabeth House, University of Oxford).

Sala, O., Sax, D., and Leslie, L. (2009), 'Biodiversity Consequences of Increased Biofuel Production', in R.W. Howarth and S. Bringezu (eds), *Biofuels: Environmental Consequences and Interactions with Changing Land Use* (Gummersbach, Germany: Scientific Committee on Problems of the Environment, International Biofuels Project Rapid Assessment).

Sala-i-Martin, X. (1997), 'I Just Ran Four Million Regressions', *Economics Working Papers 201*, Department of Economics and Business, Barcelona, Spain: Universitat Pompeu Fabra.

Sawe, E.N. (2008), 'Bioenergy Policies in Tanzania', *COMPETE International Workshop on Bioenergy Policies for Sustainable Development in Africa* (Bamako, Mali: COMPETE-Bioenergy.net).

Schenk, P.M., Thomas-Hall, S.R., Stephens, E., Marx, U.C., Mussgnug, J.H., Posten, C., Kruse, O., and Hankamer, B. (2008), 'Second Generation Biofuels: High-Efficiency Microalgae for Biodiesel Production', *BioEnergy Research*, 1 (1), 20–43.

Schmidhuber, J. and Tubiello, F.N. (2007), 'Climate Change and Food Security Special Feature: Global Food Security under Climate Change', *Proceedings of the National Academy of Sciences*, 104 (50), 19703–08.

Schmitz, H. (1999), 'Global Competition and Local Cooperation: Success and Failures in the Sions Valley, Brazil', *World Development*, 27 (9), 1627–50.

Schneider, H. (1999), 'Participatory Governance for Poverty Reduction', *Journal of International Development*, 11, 521–34.

Scholte, J.A. (2000), *Globalization: A Critical Introduction* (Basingstoke, UK: Palgrave).

Scholte, J.A. (2002), 'Civil Society and Democracy in Global Governance', *Global Governance*, 8, 281–304.

Schubert, R. and Blasch, J. (2010), 'Sustainability Standards for Bioenergy: A Means to Reduce Climate Change Risks?' *Energy Policy*, 38 (6), 2797–805.

Schumpeter, J.A. (1954), *History of Economic Analysis* (New York, NY: Oxford University Press).

Searchinger, T. (2009), 'Government Policies and Drivers of World Biofuels, Sustainability Criteria, Certification Proposals and Their Limitations', in R.W. Howarth and S. Bringezu (eds), *Biofuels: Environmental Consequences and Interactions with Changing Land Use* (Gummersbach, Germany: Scientific

Committee on Problems of the Environment, International Biofuels Project Rapid Assessment).

Searchinger, T., Heimlich, R., Houghton, R.A., Dong, F., Elobeid, A., Fabiosa, J., Tokgoz, S., Hayes, D., and Yu, T.-H. (2008), 'Use of US Croplands for Biofuels Increases Greenhouse Gases Through Emissions from Land-Use Change', *Science*, 319 (5867), 1238–40.

SEKAB (2009), 'SEKAB Sells Subsidiaries in Tanzania and Moçambique to EcoDevelopment in Europe AB' (Press Release: 29 October 2009; Örnsköldsvik, Sweden: SEKAB).

Sen, A.K. (1977), 'Rational Fools: A Critique of the Behavioural Foundations of Economic Theory', *Philosophy and Public Affairs*, 6 (4), 317–44.

—— (1979), 'Personal Utilities and Public Judgements: Or What's Wrong with Welfare Economics?' *Economic Journal*, 89, 537–558.

—— (1993), 'Markets and Freedoms: Achievements and Limitations of the Market Mechanism in Promoting Individual Freedoms', *Oxford Economic Papers*, 45 (4), 519–41.

—— (1997), 'From Income Inequality to Economic Inequality', *Southern Economic Journal*, 64 (2), 384–401.

—— (1999a), *Development as Freedom* (Oxford, UK: Oxford University Press).

—— (1999b), *Commodities and Capabilities* (Oxford, UK: Oxford University Press).

—— (2005), *Reflections on Theory in the Social Sciences: Conversation with Amartya Sen*, Institute of International Studies, UC Berkeley. http://globetrotter. berkeley.edu/people5/Sen/sen-con0.html.

Sen, A.K. and Dreze, J. (1989), *Hunger and Public Action* (Oxford, UK: Clarendon Press).

Shay, G. (1993), 'Diesel Fuel from Vegetable Oils: Status and Opportunities', *Biomass and Bioenergy*, 4 (4), 227–42.

Siamwallah, A. (1996), 'Thai Agriculture: From Engine of Growth to Sunset Status', *TDRI Quarterly Review*.11 (3), 3–10.

Simeh, A. and Ahmad, T. (2001), *The Case Study on the Malaysian Palm Oil* (Bangkok: United Nations Conference on Trade and Development).

Simon, H.A. and Newell, A. (1972), *Human Problem Solving* (Princeton, NJ, US: Princeton Hall).

Simpson, T.W., Martinelli, L.A., Sharpley, A.N., and Howarth, R.W. (2009), 'Impact of Ethanol Production on Nutrient Cycles and Water Quality: The United States and Brazil as Case Studies', in R. Howarth and R.W. Bringezu (eds), *Biofuels: Environmental Consequences and Implications of Changing Land Use* (Gummersbach, Germany: Scientific Committee on Problems of the Environment, International Biofuels Project Rapid Assessment).

Sims, R.E.H., Mabee, W., Saddler, J.N., and Taylor, M. (2010), 'An Overview of Second Generation Biofuel Technologies', *Bioresource Technology*, 101 (6), 1570–80.

Sivalingam, G. (1993), *Malaysia Agricultural Transformation* (Selangor Darul Ehsan, Malaysia: Pelanduk Publisher).

Sivapragasam, A. (2008), '*Jatropha curcas*: R&D Perspectives for Rural Development in Malaysia Context', *Jatropha Summit 2008* (Kuala Lumpur, Malaysia).

Smeets, E.M.W., Faaij, A.P.C., Lewandowski, I.M., and Turkenburg, W.C. (2007), 'A Bottom-Up Assessment and Review of Global Bio-Energy Potentials to 2050', *Progress in Energy and Combustion Science*, 33 (1), 56.

Smolker, R., Tokar, B., Petermann, A., and Hernandez, A. (2009), 'Devastated Lands, Displaced Peoples: Agrofuel Costs in Indonesia, Malaysia, Papua New Guinea', *Agroenergy and Alternatives*, Summer 2009.

Smouts, M.-C. (1998), 'The Proper Use of Governance in International Relations', *International Social Science Journal*, 50 (155), 81–89.

Sobey, R. and Watson, H.K. (2008), 'An Investigation into the Biofuel Potential of Two Trees Indigenous to Southern Africa', *COMPETE Newsletter*, 2.

Soda, R. (2007), *People on the Move: Rural–Urban Interactions in Sarawak* (Kyoto, Japan: Kyoto University Press).

Soetaert, Wim and Vandamme, Erik (2009), *Biofuels* (US: Wiley).

Songstad, D.D., Lakshmanan, P., Chen, J., Gibbons, W., Hughes, S., and Nelson, R. (2009), 'Historical Perspective of Biofuels: Learning from the Past to Rediscover the Future', *The Society for In Vitro Biology*, 45, 189–92.

Steenblik, R. (2007), *Biofuels at What Cost? Government Support for Ethanol and Biodiesel in Selected OECD Countries* (Geneva, Switzerland: The Global Subsidies Initiative of the International Institute for Sustainable Development).

Stephanie, P. and Soraya, P. (2008), 'Malaysia Plans to Spend 5.6 Billion Ringgit on Food Security', *Bloomberg News*, 29 August 2008.

Stern, N. (2006), *The Stern Review of the Economics of Climate Change, 2006* (London: UK Treasury).

Stiglitz, J.E. (2002), 'Participation and Development: Perspectives from the Comprehensive Development Paradigm', *Review of Development Economics*, 6 (2), 163–82.

Stiglitz, J.E. and Charlton, A. (2005), *Fair Trade For All: How Trade Can Promote Development* (Oxford, UK: Oxford University Press).

Stiglitz, J., Sen, A. and Fitoussi, J.P. (2009), *Rapport de la Commission sur la mesure des performances économiques et du progrès social* (Paris: Éditions Odile Jacob).

Stoker, G. (1998), 'Governance as Theory: Five Propositions', *International Social Science Journal*, 155, 17–27.

Sumathi, S., Chai, S.P., and Mohamed, A.R. (2007), 'Utilization of Oil Palm as a Source of Renewable Energy in Malaysia', *Renewable and Sustainable Energy Reviews*, 12 (9), 2404–21.

Sun Biofuels (2009), *Sun Biofuels Tanzania ltd Acquires Lease to 8,000Ha of Land in Tanzania* (4 August 2009; London: Sun Biofuels Ltd).

Taheripour, F., Hertel, T., and Tyner, W.E. (2010), 'Biofuels and their By-Products: Global Economic and Environmental Implications', *Biomass and Bioenergy*, 34 (3), 278–89.

Tamura, R. (2006), 'Human Capital and Economic Development', *Journal of Development Economics*, 79 (1), 26–72, February.

Tanzania, The Government of (1982), *Local Government Act* (Dar es Salaam: The Government of Tanzania).

—— (1999), *The Village Land Act* (Dar es Salaam: The Government of Tanzania).

—— (2004), *The Third National Report on the Implementation of the UN Convention to Combat Desertification (UNCCD)* (Dar es Salaam: Tanzania Division of Environment).

—— (2006), *National Sample Census of Agriculture 2002/2003: Dodoma Regional Report* (Dar es Salaam: Government of Tanzania).

—— (2007), *National Sample Census of Agriculture 2002/2003: Pwani Regional Report* (Dar es Salaam: Government of Tanzania).

—— (2008a), *The Tanzania Development Vision 2025*, Planning Commission (Dar es Salaam: The Government of Tanzania). www.tanzania.go.tz/vision.htm, accessed December 2014.

—— (2008b), *Agricultural Sector Development Programme (ASDP): Support Through Basket Fund* (Dar es Salaam: Government of Tanzania).

Tey, Y.S. (2010), 'Malaysia's Strategic Food Security Approach', *International Food Research Journal*, 17, 501–07.

Thum, C. (2004), 'United Republic of Tanzania: Transport Sector Snapshot', *Findings from a World Bank Transport Sector Mission to Tanzania, May 3rd–14th, 2004* (World Bank).

Thurmond, W. (2008), *Biodiesel 2020: A Global Market Survey, Feedstock Trends and Forecasts* (2nd edn; Houston, US: Emerging Markets Online).

Tickell, J. (2000), *From the Fryer to the Fuel Tank: The Complete Guide to Using Vegetable Oil as an Alternative Fuel* (Ashland, OH, US: BookMasters).

Tiffany, D.G. and Eidman, V.R. (2003), 'Factors Associated with Success of Fuel Ethanol Producers', *Staff Paper Series P03–07* (University of Minnesota, Department of Applied Economics).

Tokgoz, S., Elobeid, A., Fabiosa, J., Hayes, D., Babcok, B., Yu, T-H., Dong, F., Hart, C., and Behin, J. (2007), 'Emerging Biofuels: Outlook of Effects on US Grain, Oilseed, and Livestock Markets', *Staff Report 07-SR 101* (Iowa State University, US: Center for Agricultural and Rural Development).

Tomomatsu, Y. and Swallow, B. (2007), *Jatropha curcas Biodiesel Production in Kenya: Economics and Potential Value Chain Development for Smallholder Farmers* (Nairobi, Kenya: World Agroforestry Center).

Tschirley, D., Poulton, C. and Labaste, P. (eds) (2009), *Organization and Performance of Cotton Sectors in Africa: Learning from Reform Experience*. Agriculture and Rural Development series (Washington DC: World Bank).

Tubiello, F.N., Soussana, J.-F., and Howden, S.M. (2007), 'Climate Change and Food Security Special Feature: Crop and Pasture Response to Climate Change', *Proceedings of the National Academy of Sciences*, 104 (50), 19686–90.

Tversky, A. (1972), 'Elimination by Aspects: A Theory of Choice', *Psychological Review*, 79, 281–99.

Tyner, W.E. and Taheripour, F. (2007), 'Ethanol Subsidies, Who Gets the Benefits?' *Biofuels, Food and Feed Tradeoffs Conference* (St. Louis, Missouri, US: Farm Foundation and USDA).

UNCTAD (2008), *Making Certification Work for Sustainable Development: The Case of Biofuels* (New York: United Nations Conference on Trade and Development).

—— (2009), *The Biofuels Market: Current Situation and Alternative Scenarios* (New York: United Nations Conference on Trade and Development).

UNDP (2009), 'Human Development Report 2009: Country Fact Sheets – Tanzania', *Human Development Report 2009: Overcoming Barriers – Human Mobility and Development* (New York: United Nations Development Programme).

UNEP (2007), *Last Stand of the Orangutan – State of Emergency: Illegal Logging, Fire and Palm Oil in Indonesia's National Parks* (Nairobi, Kenya: United Nations Environment Programme).

—— (2008), *Reforming Energy Subsidies: Opportunities to contribute to the Climate Change Agenda* (Nairobi, Kenya: United Nations Environment Programme).

—— (2009a), *Towards Sustainable Production and Use of Resources: Assessing Biofuels* (Nairobi, Kenya: United Nations Environment Programme).

—— (2009b), 'Biofuels – New Report Brings Greater Clarity to Burning Issue' (Press Release, 26 October 2009; Nairobi, Kenya: United Nations Environment Programme).

—— (2009c), *Global Trend in Sustainable Energy Investment 2009: Analysis of Trends and Issues in the Financing of Renewable Energy and Energy Efficiency* (United Nations Environment Programme in collaboration with New Energy Finance).

UNICA (2009), 'Flex-Fuel Cars Selling at Record Pace in Brazil' (Press Release: 7 July 2009; Brasilia, Brazil: Brazilian Sugarcane Industry Association).

UNPP (2008), *World Population Prospects: The 2008 Revision Population Database*. www.un.org/esa/population/publications/wpp2014/wpp2014_highlights.pdf, accessed December 2014.

USDA (2008), 'USDA Officials Briefing with Reporters on the Case for Food and Fuel' (Press Briefing: 19 May 2008; Washington DC: United States Department of Agriculture).

van Dam, M., Junginger, M., Faaij, A., Jurgens, I., Best, G., and Fritsche, U. (2008), 'Overview of Recent Developments in Sustainable Biomass Certification', *Biomass and Bioenergy*, 32 (8), 749–80.

Van den Akker, J.J.H., Branch, R., Gustafson, K., Nieveen, N.M. and Plomp, T. (eds) (1999), *Design Approaches and Tools in Education and Training* (Dordrecht, Netherlands: Kluwer Academic Publishers).

van Eijck, J. and Romijn, H. (2008), 'Prospects for *Jatropha* Biofuels in Tanzania: An Analysis with Strategic Niche Management', *Energy Policy*, 36 (1), 311.

Veblen, T. (2008), *The Theory of the Leisure Class* (BiblioBazzar, LLC).

VeneKlasen, L. and Miller, V. (2002), *New Weave of Power, People and Politics: The Action Guide for Advocacy and Citizen Participation* (Oklahoma City, US: World Neighbors).

Victor, D. (2009), *The Politics of Fossil-Fuel Subsidies* (Manitoba, Canada: IISD).

von Braun, J. (2008), 'Biofuels, International Food Price and the Poor' (Testimony to the United States Senate Committee on Energy and Natural Resources Full Committee's hearing on Thursday, 12 June 2008 at 2:15 p.m. in Room 366 of the Dirksen Senate Office Building in Washington, DC, on the relationship between the United States' renewable fuels policy and food prices).

Wadhams, N. (2009), 'How a "Miracle" Biofuel Plant Ruined Kenyan Farmers', *Time*, 4 October 2009.

Wallerstein, I. (1974), *The Modern World System* (New York: Academic Press).

Wang, M., Huo, H., and Arora, S. (2011), 'Methods of Dealing with Co-Products of Biofuels in Life-Cycle Analysis and Consequent Results within the US Context', *Energy Policy*, 39 (10), 5726–36.

WCED (1987), *Our Common Future* (New York: World Commission on Environment and Development).

Weitzman, H. (2010), 'Slow Burn for US Crop Ambitions', *Financial Times*, 19 January 2010.

Werner, A. (2004), *A Guide to Implementation Research* (New York, US: The Urban Institute Press).

Westergaard, K. (1994), 'People's Empowerment in Bangladesh – NGO Strategies', *Centre for Development Research Working Paper*, 94.10.

WFP (2007), *Tanzania Comprehensive Food Security and Vulnerability Analysis* (Rome: World Food Programme of the United Nations).

Wiemer, H.-J. (1996), 'Financial and Economic Analysis of the *Jatropha*: An Integrated Approach of Combating Desertification by Producing Fuel Oil from *Jatropha* Plants' (Paper 92.2202.5-01.100: German Society for Technical Cooperation).

Wiesenthal, T., Leduc, G., Christidis, P., Schade, B., Pelkmans, L., Govaerts, L., and Georgopoulos, P. (2009), 'Biofuel Support Policies in Europe: Lessons Learnt for the Long Way Ahead', *Renewable and Sustainable Energy Reviews*, 13 (4), 789–800.

Williamson, O.E. (2000), 'The New Institutional Economics: Taking Stock, Looking Ahead', *Journal of Economic Literature*, 38 (3), 595–613.

Windle, J. (2008), 'Land and Longhouse: Agrarian Transformation in the Uplands of Sarawak', *Australian Journal of Agricultural and Resource Economics*, 52 (3), 363–64.

Windle, J. and Cramb, R.A. (1997), 'Remoteness, Roads and Rural Development: Economic Impacts of Rural Roads in Sarawak, Malaysia', *Asia Pacific Viewpoint*, 38, 37–53.

Wirl, F. (2008), 'Why Do Oil Prices Jump (or Fall)?' *Energy Policy*, 36 (3), 1029–43.

Wong, J. (2010a), 'Sarawak Disputes Poverty Rate of 2%', *The Star*, 20 January 2010.

—— (2010b), 'Sarawak to Double Oil Palm Plantation Area', *The Star*, 30 November 2010.

Woods, J. (2006), 'Science and Technology Options for Harnessing Bioenergy's Potential', in P. Hazell and P.K. Pachuri (eds), *Bioenergy and Agriculture: Promises and Challenges* (Washington, DC, US: International Food Policy Research Institute).

World Bank (1994), *World Economic Prospects and the Developing Countries* (Washington, DC, US: World Bank).

—— (2008a), *World Development Report 2008: Agriculture for Development* (Washington, DC, US: World Bank).

—— (2008b), 'Global Purchasing Power Parities and Real Expenditures', *International Comparison Program* (Washington, DC, US: World Bank).

—— (2009a), *World Development Indicators* (Washington, DC, US: World Bank). http://data.worldbank.org/indicator/.

—— (2009b), 'Governance Matters 2009', *Worldwide Governance Indicators, 1996–2008* (Washington, DC, US: World Bank).

—— (2010a), 'Doing Business: Economy Rankings', *Doing Business: Measuring Business Regulations* (Washington, DC, US: World Bank). www.doingbusiness.org/economyrankings/, accessed December 2014.

—— (2010b), *Food Price Watch* (Washington, DC, US: World Bank).

—— (2010c), 'Data Visualizer', *Development Data* (Washington, DC, US: World Bank). http://devdata.worldbank.org/DataVisualizer/.

WTO (2010), 'Activities of the WTO and the Challenge of Climate Change', *Trade Topics* (World Trade Organization). www.wto.org/english/tratop_e/envir_e/climate_challenge_e.htm, accessed 22 December 2010.

Yee, K.F., Tat, T.K., Zuhairi, A.A., and Teong, K.L. (2009), 'Life Cycle Assessment of Palm Biodiesel: Revealing Facts and Benefits for Sustainability', *Applied Energy*, 86 (Supplement 1), S189–96.

Yeung, H.W.C. (2003), 'Practicing New Economic Geographies: A Methodological Examination', *Annals of the Association of American Geographers*, 93 (2), 442–62.

Yin, R. (1994), *Case Study Research: Design and Methods* (2nd edn; Beverly Hills, CA, US: Sage Publisher).

—— (2003), *Application of Case Study Research* (2nd edn; Beverly Hills, CA, US: Sage Publisher).

Young, O. (2010), 'Institutional Dynamics: Resilience, Vulnerability and Adaptation in Environmental and Resource Regimes', *Global Environmental Change* 20, 378–85.

Zah, R., Hischier, R., Gauch, M., Lehmann, M., Böni, H., and Wäger, P. (2007), *Life Cycle Assessment of Energy Products: Environmental Impact Assessment of Biofuels* (St. Gallen, Switzerland: EMPA, Swiss Technology and Society Lab).

Zhou, A. and Thomson, E. (2009), 'The Development of Biofuels in Asia', *Applied Energy*, 86 (Supplement 1), S11–20.

Index

For Product Safety Concerns and Information please contact our EU
representative GPSR@taylorandfrancis.com
Taylor & Francis Verlag GmbH, Kaufingerstraße 24, 80331 München, Germany

www.ingramcontent.com/pod-product-compliance
Ingram Content Group UK Ltd.
Pitfield, Milton Keynes, MK11 3LW, UK
UKHW021614240425
457818UK00018B/549